BLACK REBELLION

EYEWITNESS ACCOUNTS OF MAJOR SLAVE REVOLTS

EDITED BY DR. SUJAN DASS

TWO HORIZONS PRESS

ATLANTA • NEW YORK • LONDON

PO Box 10887
Atlanta, GA 30310
(404) 759-8799

WWW.TWOHORIZONSPRESS.COM

Published by Two Horizons Press, a division of Supreme Design, LLC.

Copyright ©2010 Supreme Design, LLC. All rights reserved.

Two Horizons Press books are printed on long-lasting acid-free paper. When it is available, we choose paper that has been manufactured by environmentally responsible practices. These may include using trees grown in sustainable forests, incorporating recycled paper, minimizing chlorine in bleaching, or recycling the energy produced at the paper mill.

Two Horizons Press is also a member of the Tree Neutral™ initiative, which works to offset paper consumption through tree planting.

TreeNeutral

Publisher's Cataloging-in-Publication Data

Black rebellion : eyewitness accounts of major slave revolts / [edited by] Sujan Dass.

p. cm.

ISBN: 978-0-9816170-4-6

1. Slave insurrections—United States. 2. Slave insurrections—Jamaica. 3. Slave insurrections—Suriname. 4. Haiti—History—Revolution, 1791-1804. 5. Maroons—Jamaica. 6. Maroons—Suriname. I. Dass, Sujan Kumar. II. Higginson, Thomas Wentworth, 1823-1911. III. Coffin, Joshua, 1792-1864. IV. Title.

E447 .B53 2010

306.3—dc22

2010922183

Second Printing

Quantity Sales. Special discounts are available on quantity purchases by nonprofit organizations, corporations, governmental agencies, retailers, and educational institutions interested in course adoption. For details, contact us by mail at the address above, Attention: Wholesale Orders. You can also contact us via email, at orders@twohorizonspress.com

Individual Sales. Two Horizons Press publications are available through most bookstores. They can also be ordered directly from the Two Horizons Press website, at www.TwoHorizonsPress.com

CONTENTS

INTRODUCTION

Acursory glance of our traditional history curriculum suggests that slave revolts, like the one led by Nat Turner, were few and far in between. Further, the uprisings themselves are typically thought of as disorganized clashes between angry slaves and local whites in the South. Instead, the historical record reveals that uprisings, and revolt plots were common and widespread, that it was often free Blacks and those enslaved under the least repressive conditions that led insurrections, that these insurrections were often highly-organized and required months of planning and thousands of committed participants, and that enslaved Africans and their descendants rebelled against captivity from its very onset.

The history of European slave trading in Africa begins in 1441, when Portuguese captains Antão Gonçalves and Nuno Tristão captured twelve Africans in Cabo Branco (in present-day Mauritania) and brought them to Portugal as slaves. The Africans worked as servants, but were also used to supply strategic information to the Portuguese about Africa. The following year, church authorities framed the edict *Illius qui*, which promised all those who joined slave-raiding parties spiritual reward and eternal salvation. Soon thereafter, Lançarote de Freitas, a Portuguese tax-collector, formed a company to trade with Africa. In 1444, he ships 235 kidnapped and enslaved Africans to Portugal, the first large group of African slaves brought to Europe. Seeing immense potential for profit in the African slave trade, the Portuguese sought confirmation from the Church that they could also enslave "infidels" seized in the Crusades. In 1452, the Pope responded with *Dum Diversus*, which allowed them to conquer and reduce to "perpetual slavery" all "Saracens and pagans and other infidels and enemies of Christ." Two years later, the Pope issued *Romanus Pontifex*, a Papal bull granting the Portuguese a perpetual monopoly in trade with Africa.

Despite Papal opposition, Spanish merchants also began to trade in large numbers of African slaves, and in 1476, Spaniard Carlos de Valera brought a shipment of 400 slaves to Spain. In 1509, Christopher Columbus's son, Diego Cólon, is appointed governor of the new Spanish empire in the Caribbean, ruling from Santo Domingo in Hispaniola (present-day Haiti and the Dominican Republic). He soon complained about the Native American slaves escaping and not working hard enough. King Ferdinand of Spain responded by authorizing a shipment of fifty African slaves to be sent to Santo Domingo. By 1522, the first large-scale slave uprising in the Western Hemisphere took place on the plantation of Diego Cólon.

The first African slaves used by Europeans in the present-day United States were among Lucas Vásquez de Ayllón's colonization attempt of present-day South Carolina in 1526. However, this attempt is a failure, because the slaves almost immediately revolted and fled into the wilderness to live among the indigenous Cofitachiqui people. This is the first documented occurrence of a slave rebellion followed by the rebels fleeing into an indigenous Native American community, a pattern that is repeated numerous times in the historical records.

Often, such flights would occur on such a massive scale that the rebel communities would need to set up strongholds to maintain their freedom. In 1552, an African of the Mandinka people named Bayano led possibly the largest slave revolt of the 16th century in Spanish Panama. After the revolt, the rebel slaves, called Cimarrones (meaning "wild" or "runaway"), set up strongholds known as palenques, many of which successfully fended off Spanish control for centuries using guerrilla warfare and alliances with indigenous nations who were in similar circumstances. The development of such communities was typically rapid and impressive. Sir Francis Drake, encountering the Cimarrones of Panama in 1572, described them as "a black people which about eighty years past fled from the Spaniards their masters, by reason of their cruelty, and are since grown to a nation, under two kings of their own." Such palenques became a common phenomenon in Latin American colonies. In 1570, Gaspar Yanga, an African of the Bran people of Gabon, led a revolt near the Mexican city of Veracruz that similarly culminated in an escape to the highlands and the development of a free colony, which successfully defended itself for over 30 years. In 1609, Spain ordered a group consisting of Indians, Creoles (Spaniards born in Mexico), Mestizos (people of mixed European and Indian parentage), and a handful of Africans to attack the palenque and regain control of the area. This would be one of the first of many times that such a confederation be assembled to destroy a slave uprising or Maroon colony.

Although Sir Francis Drake quickly allied with the Cimarrones of Panama for English attacks on the Spanish, such alliances were short-lived. By the mid-1500s, Sir John Hawkins, the first Englishman we know about to have taken part in the slave trade, was making enormous profits obtaining hundreds of African slaves and selling them in the West Indies.

In 1619, Africans brought to Jamestown became the first slaves imported into Britain's North American colonies. First called indentured servants, many were probably freed after a fixed period of service. However, it is clear that the word "servant" was used practically synonymously with "slave," and brutal violence was employed on these servants who were typically paid in food and often died before their term of service ended. By 1640, one Virginian slave, convicted of trying to escape, was sentenced to thirty lashes, with the letter "R" for "runaway" branded on his cheek and "work in a shackle one year or more as his master shall see cause." In 1663, a massive slave revolt conspiracy was discovered in Virginia when the conspirators were betrayed by a fellow slave. This too becomes a recurrent pattern in the history of American slave revolts.

A few years later, a Virginia law is enacted providing for a bounty on the heads of fugitive slaves, known as "Maroons" (from Cimarrones). These Maroons, like their Latin American counterparts, formed communities in the mountains, swamps, and forests of southern colonies. In addition to the fact that these Maroon communities regularly attacked plantations and liberated slaves, their existence provided much needed motivation to many would-be rebels and runaways, who saw in the communities the potential of their freedom on American soil.

This ideal of freedom by any means has served as a constant thread in the story of American slavery. This story, if told in its entirety, would arguably have to begin with the fierce battles fought by African people like the Hausa and Mende against slave raiders in their native villages and towns. This story would address the resistance of kidnapped Africans who led at least 400 documented mutinies on slave ships like the Amistad and the Creole, as well as the early revolts and developments of hundreds of Maroon communities throughout the Americas. It goes without question that this story would tell about notable rebels like Turner, Prosser, Vesey, and L'Ouverture, but they were not alone. Not only are countless revolt leaders and plotters mostly unknown, but it is misguided to think that the history of Black rebellion is only a history of significant events and their leaders. Instead, a complete story would incorporate the day-to-day resistance of slaves who fought back by poisoning their masters, running away, sabotaging productivity, feigning sickness and incompetence to avoid work, or stealing incrementally to eventually buy their own freedom. A complete story would go beyond the historical events, and explore the cultural aspects of rebellion, like the songs found in the appendix of this title, or the use of the drum to communicate revolt plots, as occurred in the Stono Rebellion. It would explore the psychological aspects of rebellion, such as the ideology of David Walker's *Appeal* or the reasons why most revolts were betrayed by fellow slaves.

A comprehensive study would also address white perceptions of Black rebellion. This text provides the accounts of several white writers, most of whom wrote in a period not far removed from the time when the actual events occurred. In some instances, the accounts are written by eyewitnesses, or compiled from firsthand accounts. However, in many cases, these accounts were written by relatively sympathetic authors, like Higginson, who served as colonel of the first federally authorized Black Union regiment, and – following the war – devoted much of the rest of his life to fighting for the rights of freed slaves, women and other disenfranchised peoples. It is important to note that many whites viewed slave rebellions very differently. While Frederick Douglass and others argued on behalf of Black resistance to slavery, calling on the example of the American Revolution, most of the country failed to see the connection. Few whites shared the sentiments of John Brown and believed that Blacks had as much right to a violent revolution as the American colonists. In fact, whites were rarely vocal about condemning slavery outright, and even groups like the Quakers originally supported slavery, though they later went on become the first abolitionist, yet only after significant dispute about how to oppose the institution. For many others, slavery was either supported or passively tolerated until growing incidents of revolt encouraged some to reconsider. Following the discovery of a local insurrection plot, Abigail Adams confided to her husband in 1774, "I wish most sincerely there was not a slave in the province, it always appeared a most iniquitous scheme to me to fight ourselves for what we are daily robbing and plundering from those who have as good a right to freedom as we have."

Presumably, many of the whites living in slave-dominated communities shared the sentiments of Fanny Kemble, who reported:

> A most ominous tolling of bells and beating of drums...of the first evening of my arrival in Charleston, made me almost fancy myself in one of the old fortified frontier towns of the Continent, where the tocsin is sounded, and the evening drum beaten, and the guard set as regularly every night as if an invasion were expected. In Charleston, however, it is not the dread of foreign invasion, but of domestic insurrection, which occasions these nightly precautions...Of course, it is very necessary where a large class of persons exists in the very bosom of a community whose interests are known to be at variance and incompatible with those of its other members. And no doubt these daily and nightly precautions are but trifling drawbacks upon the manifold blessings of slavery...Still, I should prefer going to sleep without the apprehension of my servants' cutting my throat in the my bed, even to having a guard provided to prevent their doing so.

As revealing as such accounts are, equally revealing is the amount of legislation that typically followed a slave rebellion or the discovery of a revolt plot. From restrictive "Black codes" to bans on further importation of African slaves, officials enacted measure after measure to reduce the likelihood of widespread rebellion. After a rash of revolt plots are discovered in Virginia, lawmakers allowed owners to bequeath their slaves. The same law allowed masters to "kill and destroy" rebels and runaways. After Nat Turner led a revolt based on his interpretation of a Biblical prophecy, lawmakers made it illegal to teach slaves to read and write. After several Maroon communities proved difficult to eliminate entirely, local governments agreed to ending their military campaigns against the communities in exchange for their cooperation in capturing future runaways and rebels. And yet, even with all these measures, rebellion against slavery persisted. Even after abolition, Black resistance and rebellion has persisted, albeit in muted forms. More recent events like the Watts Riots of 1965 and the Newark Riots of 1967 suggest that violent uprising is not an artifact of a distant past. Instead, rebellion is a historical constant wherever you find oppression. The following texts provide insight to the factors behind several of the Black rebellions of the past, yet – for the enlightened reader – they also provide profound insight to more modern affairs. Understanding the human response to historical oppression – even in centuries past – is key to understanding the conflicts our future may hold.

FIVE BLACK SLAVE REVOLTS

Thomas Wentworth Higginson

T. W. Higginson (December 22, 1823 – May 9, 1911) was active in the American Abolitionism movement during the 1840s and 1850s, identifying himself with disunion and militant abolitionism. He was indicted with Wendell Phillips and Theodore Parker for participation in the attempt to release the fugitive slave, Anthony Burns, in Boston in 1853, and was engaged in the effort to make Kansas a free state after the passage of the Kansas-Nebraska Bill of 1854. During the Civil War, he served as colonel of the 1st South Carolina Volunteers, the first federally authorized Black regiment, from 1862-1864. After the War, he spent a great deal of time writing about his ideas and experiences, describing his experiences with Black troops in *Army Life in a Black Regiment* in 1870. The following text contains five chapters of Higginson's *Travellers and Outlaws: Episodes in American History*, originally published in 1889. This collection is commonly referred to as "Black Rebellion: Five Negro Slave Revolts."

THE MAROONS OF JAMAICA

The Maroons! It was a word of peril once. Terror spread along the skirts of the blue mountains of Jamaica when some fresh foray of those unconquered guerrillas swept down from the outlying plantations. Startled were the Assembly from its order, Gen. Williamson from his billiards, and Lord Balcarres from his diplomatic ease,--endangering, according to the official statement, "public credit," "civil rights," and "the prosperity, if not the very existence, of the country," until they were "persuaded to make peace" at last. They were the Circassians of the New World, but they were black, instead of white; and as the Circassians refused to be transferred from the Sultan to the Czar, so the Maroons refused to be transferred from Spanish dominion to English, and thus their revolt began. The difference is, that while the white mountaineers numbered four hundred thousand, and only defied Nicholas, the black mountaineers numbered less than two thousand, and defied Cromwell; and while the Circassians, after years of revolt, were at last subdued, the Maroons, on the other hand, who rebelled in 1655, were never conquered, but only made a compromise of allegiance, and exist as a separate race to-day.

When Admirals Penn and Venables landed in Jamaica, in

1655, there was not a remnant left of the sixty thousand natives whom the Spaniards had found there a century and a half before. Their pitiful tale is told only by those caves, still known among the mountains, where thousands of human skeletons strew the ground. In their place dwelt two foreign races,--an effeminate, ignorant, lazy white community of fifteen hundred, with a black slave population quite as large and infinitely more hardy and energetic. The Spaniards were readily subdued by the English: the negroes remained resilient. The slaveholders were banished from the island: the slaves only exiled themselves to the mountains; thence the English could not dislodge them, nor the buccaneers whom the English employed. And when Jamaica subsided into a British colony, and peace was made with Spain, and the children of Cromwell's Puritan soldiers were beginning to grow rich by importing slaves for Roman-Catholic Spaniards, the Maroons still held their own wild empire in the mountains, and, being sturdy heathens every one, practiced Obeah rites in approved pagan fashion.

The word Maroon is derived, according to one etymology, from the Spanish word *Marrano*, a wild boar,--these fugitives being all boar-hunters; according to another, from *Marony*, a river separating French and Dutch Guiana, where a colony of them dwelt and still dwells; and by another still, from *Cimarron*, a word meaning untamable, and used alike for apes and runaway slaves. But whether these rebel marauders were regarded as monkeys or men, they made themselves equally formidable. As early as 1663, the Governor and Council of Jamaica offered to each Maroon, who should surrender, his freedom and twenty acres of land; but not one accepted the terms. During forty years, forty-four Acts of Assembly were passed in respect to them, and at least a quarter of a million pounds sterling were expended in the warfare against them. In 1733, the force employed in this service consisted of two regiments of regular troops, and the whole militia of the island; but the Assembly said that "the Maroons had within a few years greatly increased, notwithstanding all the measures that had been concerted for their suppression," "to the great terror of his Majesty's subjects," and "to the manifest weakening and preventing the further increase of strength and inhabitants of the island."

The special affair in progress, at the time of these statements, was called Cudjoe's War. Cudjoe was a gentleman of extreme brevity and blackness, whose full-length portrait can hardly be said to adorn Dallas's History of the Maroons; but he was as formidable a guerrilla as Marion. Under his leadership, the various bodies of fugitives were consolidated into one force, and thoroughly organized. Cudjoe, like Schamyl, was religious as well as military head of his people; by Obeah influence he established a thorough freemasonry among both slaves and insurgents; no party could be sent forth, by the government, but he knew it in time to lay an ambush, or descend with fire and sword on the region left unprotected. He was thus always supplied with arms and ammunition; and as his men were perfect marksmen, never wasted a shot, and never risked a battle, his forces naturally increased, while those of his opponents were decimated. His men were never captured, and never took a prisoner; it was impossible to tell when they were defeated; in dealing with them, as Pelissier said of the Arabs, "peace was not purchased by victory;" and the only men who could obtain the slightest advantage against them were the imported Mosquito Indians, or the "Black Shot," a company of Government negroes. For nine full years this particular war continued unchecked, Gen. Williamson ruling Jamaica by day and Cudjoe by night.

The rebels had every topographical advantage, for they held possession of the "Cockpits." Those highlands are furrowed through and through, as by an earthquake, with a series of gaps or ravines, resembling the California canyons, or those similar fissures in various parts of the Atlantic States, known to local fame either poetically as ice-glens, or symbolically as purgatories. These Jamaica chasms vary from two hundred yards to a mile in length; the rocky walls are fifty or a hundred feet high, and often absolutely inaccessible, while the passes at each end admit but one man at a time. They are thickly wooded, wherever trees can grow; water flows within them; and they often communicate with one another, forming a series of traps for an invading force. Tired and thirsty with climbing, the weary soldiers toil on, in single file, without seeing or hearing an enemy, up the steep and winding path they traverse one "cockpit," then enter another. Suddenly a shot is fired from the dense and sloping forest on the right, then another and another, each dropping its man; the startled troops face hastily in that direction, when a more murderous volley is poured from the other side; the heights above flash with musketry, while the precipitous path by which they came seems to close in fire behind them. By the time the troops have formed in some attempt at military order, the woods around them are empty, and their agile and noiseless foes have settled themselves into ambush again, farther up the narrow pass, ready for a second attack, if needed. But one is usually sufficient; disordered, exhausted, bearing their wounded with them, the soldiers retreat in panic, if permitted to escape at all, and carry fresh dismay to the barracks, the plantations, and the Government House.

It is not strange, then, that high military authorities, at that period, should have pronounced the subjugation of the Maroons a thing more difficult than to obtain a victory over any army in Europe. Moreover, these people were fighting for their liberty, with which aim no form of warfare seemed to them unjustifiable; and the description given by Lafayette of the American Revolution was true of this one,--"the grandest of causes, won by contests of sentinels and outposts." The utmost hope of a British officer, ordered against the Maroons, was to lay waste a provision-ground, or cut them off from water. But there was little satisfaction in this: the wild-pine leaves and the grapevine-withes supplied the rebels with water; and their plantation-grounds were the wild pineapple and the plantain-groves, and the forests, where the wild boars harbored, and the ringdoves were as easily shot as if they were militiamen. Nothing but sheer weariness of fighting seems to have brought about a truce at last, and then a treaty, between those high contracting parties, Cudjoe and Gen. Williamson.

But how to execute a treaty between these wild Children of the Mist and respectable diplomatic Englishmen? To establish any official relations without the medium of a preliminary bullet required some ingenuity of maneuvering. Cudjoe was willing, but inconveniently cautious for he would not come halfway to meet any one; nothing would content him but an interview in his own chosen cockpit. So he selected one of the most difficult passes, posting in the forests a series of outlying parties, to signal with their horns, one by one, the approach of the plenipotentiaries, and then to retire on the main body. Through this line of dangerous sentinels, therefore, Col. Guthrie and his handful of men bravely advanced; horn after horn they heard sounded, but there was no other human noise in the woods, and they had advanced till they saw the smoke of the Maroon huts before they caught a glimpse of a human form.

A conversation was at last opened with the invisible rebels. On their promise of safety, Dr. Russell advanced alone to treat with them; then several Maroons appeared, and finally Cudjoe himself. The formidable chief was not highly military in appearance, being short, fat, humpbacked, dressed in a tattered blue coat without skirts or sleeves, and an old felt hat without a rim. But if he had blazed with regimental scarlet, he could not have been treated with more distinguished consideration; indeed, in that case, "the exchange of hats" with which Dr. Russell finally volunteered, in Maroon fashion, to ratify negotiations, might have been a less severe test of good fellowship. This fine stroke of diplomacy had its effect, however; the rebel captains agreed to a formal interview with Col. Guthrie and Capt. Sadler, and a treaty was at last executed with all due solemnity, under a large cotton-tree at the entrance of Guthrie's Defile. This treaty recognized the military rank of "Capt. Cudjoe," "Capt. Accompong," and the rest; gave assurance that the Maroons should be "forever hereafter in a perfect state of freedom and liberty;" ceded to them fifteen hundred acres of land; and stipulated only that they should keep the peace, should harbor no fugitive from justice or from slavery, and should allow two white commissioners to remain among them, simply to represent the British Government.

During the following year a separate treaty was

made with another large body of insurgents, called the Windward Maroons. This was not effected, however, until after an unsuccessful military attempt, in which the mountaineers gained a single triumph. By artful devices,--a few fires left burning with old women to watch them,--a few provision-grounds exposed by clearing away the bushes,--they lured the troops far up among the mountains, and then surprised them by an ambush. The militia all fled, and the regulars took refuge under a large cliff in a stream, where they remained four hours up to their waists in water, until finally they forded the river, under full fire, with terrible loss. Three months after this, however, the Maroons consented to an amicable interview, exchanging hostages first. The position of the white hostage, at least, was not the most agreeable; he complained that he was beset by the women and children with indignant cries of "Buckra, Buckra," while the little boys pointed their fingers at him as if stabbing him, and that with evident relish. However, Capt. Quao, like Capt. Cudjoe, made a treaty at last; and hats were interchanged, instead of hostages.

Independence being thus won and acknowledged, there was a suspension of hostilities for some years. Among the wild mountains of Jamaica, the Maroons dwelt in a savage freedom. So healthful and beautiful was the situation of their chief town, that the English Government has erected barracks there of late years, as being the most healthy situation on the island. They breathed an air ten degrees cooler than that inhaled by the white population below; and they lived on a daintier diet, so that the English epicures used to go up among them for good living. The mountaineers caught the strange land-crabs, plodding in companies of millions their sidelong path from mountain to ocean, and from ocean to mountain again. They hunted the wild boars, and prepared the flesh by salting and smoking it in layers of aromatic leaves, the delicious "jerked hog" of buccaneer annals. They reared cattle and poultry, cultivated corn and yams, plantains and cocoas, guavas, and papayas and mameys, and avocados, and all luxurious West-Indian fruits; the very weeds of their orchards had tropical luxuriance in their fragrance and in their names; and from the doors of their little thatched huts they looked across these gardens of delight to the magnificent lowland forests, and over those again to the faint line of far-off beach, the fainter ocean-horizon, and the illimitable sky.

They had senses like those of American Indians; tracked each other by the smell of the smoke of fires in the air, and called to each other by horns, using a special note to designate each of their comrades, and distinguishing it beyond the range of ordinary hearing. They spoke English diluted with Spanish and African words, and practiced Obeah rites quite undiluted with Christianity. Of course they associated largely with the slaves, without any very precise regard to treaty stipulations; sometimes brought in fugitives, and sometimes concealed them; left their towns and settled on the planters' lands when they preferred them: but were quite orderly and luxuriously happy. During the formidable insurrection of the Koromantyn slaves, in 1760, they played a dubious part. When left to go on their own way, they did something towards suppressing it; but when placed under the guns of the troops, and ordered to fire on those of their own color, they threw themselves on the ground without discharging a shot. Nevertheless, they gradually came up into reputable standing; they grew more and more industrious and steady; and after they had joined very heartily in resisting D'Estaing's threatened invasion of the island in 1779, it became the fashion to speak of "our faithful and affectionate Maroons."

In 1795, their position was as follows: Their numbers had not materially increased, for many had strayed off and settled on the outskirts of plantations; nor materially diminished, for many runaway slaves had joined them; while there were also separate settlements of fugitives, who had maintained their freedom for twenty years. The white superintendents had lived with the Maroons in perfect harmony, without the slightest official authority, but with a great deal of actual influence. But there was an "irrepressible conflict" behind all this apparent peace, and the slightest occasion might, at any moment, revive all the old terror. That occasion was close at hand.

Capt. Cudjoe and Capt. Accompong, and the other founders of Maroon independence, had passed away; and "Old Montagu" reigned in their stead, in Trelawney Town. Old Montagu had all the ceremonial circumstance of Maroon majesty: he wore a laced red coat, and a hat superb with gold lace and plumes; none but captains could sit in his presence; he was helped first at meals, and no woman could eat beside him; he presided at councils as magnificently as at table, though with less appetite; and possessed, meanwhile, not an atom of the love or reverence of any human being. The real power lay entirely with Major James, the white superintendent, who had been brought up among the Maroons by his father (and predecessor), and who was the idol of this wild race. In an evil hour, the Government removed him, and put a certain unpopular Capt. Craskell in his place; and as there happened to be, about the same time, a great excitement concerning a hopeful pair of young Maroons, who had been seized and publicly whipped on a charge of hog-stealing, their kindred refused to allow the new superintendent to remain in the town. A few attempts at negotiation only brought them to a higher pitch of wrath, which ended in their dispatching the following peculiar diplomatic note to the Earl of Balcarres:

> "The Maroons wishes nothing else from the country but battle, and they desires not to see Mr. Craskell up here at all. So they are waiting every moment for the above on Monday. Mr. David Schaw will see you on Sunday morning for an answer. They will wait till Monday, nine o'clock, and if they don't come up, they will come down themselves." Signed, "Col. Montagu and all the rest."

It turned out, at last, that only two or three of the Maroons were concerned in this remarkable defiance; but meanwhile it had its effect. Several ambassadors were sent among the insurgents, and were so favorably impressed by their reception as to make up a subscription of money for their hosts, on departing; only the "gallant Col. Gallimore," a Jamaica Camillus, gave iron instead of gold, by throwing some bullets into the contribution-box. And it was probably in accordance with his view of the subject, that, when the Maroons sent ambassadors in return, they were at once imprisoned, most injudiciously and unjustly; and when Old Montagu himself and thirty-seven others, following, were seized and imprisoned also, it is not strange that the Maroons, joined by many slaves, were soon in open insurrection.

Martial law was instantly proclaimed throughout the island.

The fighting men among the insurgents were not, perhaps, more than five hundred; against whom the Government could bring nearly fifteen hundred regular troops and several thousand militiamen. Lord Balcarres himself took the command, and, eager to crush the affair, promptly marched a large force up to Trelawney Town, and was glad to march back again as expeditiously as possible. In his very first attack, he was miserably defeated, and had to flee for his life, amid a perfect panic of the troops, in which some forty or fifty were killed,--including Col. Sandford, commanding the regulars, and the bullet-loving Col. Gallimore, in command of the militia,-- while not a single Maroon was even wounded, so far as could be ascertained.

After this a good deal of bush-fighting took place. The troops gradually got possession of several Maroon villages, but not till every hut had been burnt by its owner. It was in the height of

the rainy season; and, between fire and water, the discomfort of the soldiers was enormous. Meanwhile the Maroons hovered close around them in the woods, heard all their orders, picked off their sentinels, and, penetrating through their lines at night, burned houses and destroyed plantations far below. The only man who could cope with their peculiar tactics was Major James, the superintendent just removed by Government; and his services were not employed, as he was not trusted. On one occasion, however, he led a volunteer party farther into the mountains than any of the assailants had yet penetrated, guided by tracks known to himself only, and by the smell of the smoke of Maroon fires. After a very exhausting march, including a climb of a hundred and fifty feet up the face of a precipice, he brought them just within the entrance of Guthrie's Defile. "So far," said he, pointing to the entrance, "you may pursue, but no farther; no force can enter here; no white man except myself, or some soldier of the Maroon establishment, has ever gone beyond this. With the greatest difficulty I have penetrated four miles farther, and not ten Maroons have gone so far as that. There are two other ways of getting into the defile, practicable for the Maroons, but not for any one of you. In neither of them can I ascend or descend with my arms, which must be handed to me, step by step, as practiced by the Maroons themselves. One of the ways lies to the eastward, and the other to the westward; and they will take care to have both guarded, if they suspect that I am with you; which, from the route you have come to-day, they will. They now see you, and if you advance fifty paces more, they will convince you of it." At this moment a Maroon horn sounded the notes indicating his name; and, as he made no answer, a voice was heard, inquiring if he were among them. "If he is," said the voice, "let him go back, we do not wish to hurt him, but as for the rest of you, come on and try battle if you choose." But the gentlemen did not choose.

In September the House of Assembly met. Things were looking worse and worse. For five months a handful of negroes and mulattoes had defied the whole force of the island, and they were defending their liberty by precisely the same tactics through which their ancestors had won it. Half a million pounds sterling had been spent within this time, besides the enormous loss incurred by the withdrawal of so many able-bodied men from their regular employments. "Cultivation was suspended," says an eye-witness; "the courts of law had long been shut up; and the island at large seemed more like a garrison under the power of law-martial, than a country of agriculture and commerce, of civil judicature, industry, and prosperity." Hundreds of the militia had died of fatigue, large numbers had been shot down, the most daring of the British officers had fallen; while the insurgents had been invariably successful, and not one of them was known to have been killed. Capt. Craskell, the banished superintendent, gave it to the Assembly as his opinion that the whole slave population of the island was in sympathy with the Maroons, and would soon be beyond control. More alarming still, there were rumors of French emissaries behind the scenes; and though these were explained away, the vague terror remained. Indeed, the lieutenant-governor announced in his message that he had satisfactory evidence that the French Convention was concerned in the revolt. A French prisoner, named Murenson, had testified that the French agent at Philadelphia (Fauchet) had secretly sent a hundred and fifty emissaries to the island, and threatened to land fifteen hundred negroes. And though Murenson took it all back at last, yet the Assembly was moved to make a new offer of three hundred dollars for killing or taking a Trelawney Maroon, and a hundred and fifty dollars for killing or taking any fugitive slave who had joined them. They also voted five hundred pounds as a gratuity to the Accompong tribe of Maroons, who had thus far kept out of the insurrection; and various prizes and gratuities were also offered by the different parishes, with the same object of self-protection.

The commander-in-chief being among the killed, Col. Walpole was promoted in his stead, and brevetted as general, by way of incentive. He found a people in despair, a soldiery thoroughly intimidated, and a treasury not empty, but useless. But the new general had not served against the Maroons for nothing, and was not ashamed to go to school to his opponents. First, he waited for the dry season; then he directed all his efforts towards cutting off his opponents from water, and, most effectual move of all, he attacked each successive cockpit by dragging up a howitzer, with immense labor, and throwing in shells. Shells were a visitation not dreamed of in Maroon philosophy, and their quaint compliments to their new opponent remain on record. "Damn dat little buckra!" they said, "he cunning more dan dem toder. Dis here da new fashion for fight: him fire big ball arter you, and when big ball 'top, de damn sunting [something] fire arter you again." With which Parthian arrows of rhetoric the mountaineers retreated.

But this did not last long. The Maroons soon learned to keep out of the way of the shells, and the island relapsed into terror again. It was deliberately resolved at last, by a special council gathering for the purpose, "to persuade the rebels to make peace." But as they had not as yet shown themselves very accessible to softer influences, it was thought best to combine as many arguments as possible, and a certain Col. Quarrell had hit upon a wholly new one. His plan simply was, since men, however well disciplined, had proved powerless against Maroons, to try a Spanish fashion against them, and use dogs. The proposition was met, in some quarters, with the strongest hostility. England, it was said, had always denounced the Spaniards as brutal and dastardly for hunting down the natives of that very soil with hounds; and should England now follow the humiliating example? On the other side, there were plenty who eagerly quoted all known instances of zoological warfare: all Oriental nations, for instance, used elephants in war, and, no doubt, would gladly use lions and tigers also, but for their extreme carnivorousness, and their painful indifference to the distinction between friend and foe; why not, then, use these dogs, comparatively innocent and gentle creatures? At any rate, "something must be done;" the final argument always used, when a bad or desperate project is to be made palatable. So it was voted at last to send to Havana for an invoice of Spanish dogs, with their accompanying chasseurs; and the efforts at persuading the Maroons were postponed till the arrival of these additional persuasives. And when Col. Quarrell finally set sail as commissioner to obtain the new allies, all scruples of conscience vanished in the renewal of public courage and the chorus of popular gratitude; a thing so desirable must be right; thrice they were armed who knew their Quarrell just.

But after the parting notes of gratitude died away in the distance, the commissioner began to discover that he was to have a hard time of it. He sailed for Havana in a schooner manned with Spanish renegadoes, who insisted on fighting every thing that came in their way,--first a Spanish schooner, then a French one. He landed at Batabano, struck across the mountains towards Havana, stopped at Besucal to call on the wealthy Marquesa de San Felipe y San Jorge, grand patroness of dogs and chasseurs, and finally was welcomed to Havana by Don Luis de las Casas, who overlooked, for this occasion only, an injunction of his court against admitting foreigners within his government; "the only accustomed exception being," as Don Luis courteously assured him, "in favor of foreign traders who came with new negroes." To be sure, the commissioner had not brought any of these commodities; but then he had come to obtain the means of capturing some, and so might pass for an irregular practitioner of the privileged profession.

Accordingly, Don Guillermo Dawes Quarrell (so ran his passport) found no difficulty in obtaining permission from the governor to buy as many dogs as he desired. When, however, he carelessly hinted at the necessity of taking, also, a few men who should have care of the dogs,--this being, after all, the essential part of his expedition,--Don Luis de las Casas put on instantly a double force of courtesy, and assured him of the entire impossibility of recruiting a single Spaniard for English service. Finally, however, he gave permission and passports for six chasseurs. Under cover of this, the commissioner lost no time in enlisting forty; he got them safe to Batabano; but at the last moment, learning the state of affairs, they refused to embark on such very irregular authority. When he had persuaded them, at length, the officer of the fort interposed objections. This was not to be borne, so Don Guillermo bribed him and silenced him; a dragoon was, however, sent to report to the governor; Don Guillermo sent a messenger after him, and bribed him too; and thus at length, after myriad rebuffs, and after being obliged to spend the last evening at a puppet-show in which the principal figure was a burlesque on his own personal peculiarities, the weary Don Guillermo, with his crew of renegadoes, and his forty chasseurs and their one hundred and four muzzled dogs, set sail for Jamaica.

These new allies were certainly something formidable, if we may trust the pictures and descriptions in Dallas's History. The chasseur was a tall, meager, swarthy Spaniard or mulatto, lightly clad in cotton shirt and drawers, with broad straw hat, and moccasins of raw-hide; his belt sustaining his long, straight, flat sword or *machete*, like an iron bar sharpened at one end; and he wore by the same belt three cotton leashes for his three dogs, sometimes held also by chains. The dogs were a fierce breed, crossed between hound and mastiff, never umuzzled except for attack, and accompanied by smaller dogs called *finders*. It is no wonder, when these wild and powerful creatures were landed at Montego Bay, that terror ran through the town, doors were everywhere closed, and windows crowded; not a negro dared to stir; and the muzzled dogs, infuriated by confinement on shipboard, filled the silent streets with their noisy barking and the rattling of their chains.

How much would have come of all this in actual conflict, does not appear. The Maroons had already been persuaded to make peace upon certain conditions and guaranties,--a decision probably accelerated by the terrible rumors of the bloodhounds, though they never saw them. It was the declared opinion of the Assembly, confirmed by that of Gen. Walpole, that "nothing could be clearer than that, if they had been off the island, the rebels could not have been induced to surrender." Nevertheless, a treaty was at last made, without the direct intervention of the hounds. Again commissioners went up among the mountains to treat with negotiators at first invisible; again were hats and jackets interchanged, not without coy reluctance on the part of the well-dressed Englishmen; and a solemn agreement was effected. The most essential part of the bargain was a guaranty of continued independence, demanded by the suspicious Maroons. Gen. Walpole, however, promptly pledged himself that no such unfair advantage should be taken of them as had occurred with the hostages previously surrendered, who were placed in irons; nor should any attempt be made to remove them from the island. It is painful to add, that this promise was outrageously violated by the Colonial Government, to the lasting grief of Gen. Walpole, on the ground that the Maroons had violated the treaty by a slight want of punctuality in complying with its terms, and by remissness in restoring the fugitive slaves who had taken refuge among them. As many of the tribe as surrendered, therefore, were at once placed in confinement, and ultimately shipped from Port Royal to Halifax, to the number of six hundred, on the 6th of June, 1796. For the credit of English honor, we rejoice to know that Gen. Walpole not merely protested against this utter breach of faith, but indignantly declined the sword of honor which the Assembly had voted him, in its gratitude, and then retired from military service forever.

The remaining career of this portion of the Maroons is easily told. They were first dreaded by the inhabitants of Halifax, then welcomed when seen, and promptly set to work on the citadel, then in process of reconstruction, where the "Maroon Bastion" still remains,--their only visible memorial. Two commissioners had charge of them, one being the redoubtable Col. Quarrell; and twenty-five thousand pounds were appropriated for their temporary support. Of course they did not prosper; pensioned colonists never do, for they are not compelled into habits of industry. After their delicious life in the mountains of Jamaica, it seemed rather monotonous to dwell upon that barren soil,--for theirs was such that two previous colonies had deserted it,--and in a climate where winter lasts seven months in the year. They had a schoolmaster, and he was also a preacher; but they did not seem to appreciate that luxury of civilization, utterly refusing, on grounds of conscience, to forsake polygamy, and, on grounds of personal comfort, to listen to the doctrinal discourses of their pastor, who was an ardent Sandemanian. They smoked their pipes during service time, and left Old Montagu, who still survived, to lend a vicarious attention to the sermon. One discourse he briefly reported as follows, very much to the point: "Massa parson say no mus tief, no mus meddle wid somebody wife, no mus quarrel, mus set down softly." So they sat down very softly, and showed an extreme unwillingness to get up again. But, not being naturally an idle race,--at least, in Jamaica the objection lay rather on the other side,--they soon grew tired of this inaction. Distrustful of those about them, suspicious of all attempts to scatter them among the community at large, frozen by the climate, and constantly petitioning for removal to a milder one, they finally wearied out all patience. A long dispute ensued between the authorities of Nova Scotia and Jamaica, as to which was properly responsible for their support; and thus the heroic race, that for a century and a half had sustained themselves in freedom in Jamaica, were reduced to the position of troublesome and impracticable paupers, shuttlecocks between two selfish parishes. So passed their unfortunate lives, until, in 1800, their reduced population was transported to Sierra Leone, at a cost of six thousand pounds; since which they disappear from history.

It was judged best not to interfere with those bodies of Maroons which had kept aloof from the late outbreak, at the Accompong settlement, and elsewhere. They continued to preserve a qualified independence, and retain it even now. In 1835, two years after the abolition of slavery in Jamaica, there were reported sixty families of Maroons as residing at Accompong Town, eighty families at Moore Town, one hundred and ten families at Charles Town, and twenty families at Scott Hall, making two hundred and seventy families in all,-- each station being, as of old, under the charge of a superintendent. But there can be little doubt, that, under the influences of freedom, they are rapidly intermingling with the mass of colored population in Jamaica.

The story of the exiled Maroons attracted attention in high quarters, in its time: the wrongs done to them were denounced in Parliament by Sheridan, and mourned by Wilberforce; while the employment of bloodhounds against them was vindicated by Dundas, and the whole conduct of the Colonial Government defended, through thick and thin, by Bryan Edwards. This thorough partisan even had the assurance to tell Mr. Wilberforce, in Parliament, that he knew the Maroons, from personal knowledge, to be cannibals, and that, if a missionary were sent among them in Nova Scotia, they would immediately eat him; a charge so absurd that he did not venture to repeat it in his History of the West Indies, though his injustice to the Maroons is even there so glaring as to provoke the indignation of the more moderate Dallas. But, in spite of Mr. Edwards, the public indignation ran quite high in England, against the bloodhounds and their employers, so that the home ministry found it necessary to send a severe reproof to the Colonial Government. For a few years the tales of the Maroons thus emerged from mere colonial annals, and found their way into annual registers and parliamentary debates; but they have long since vanished from popular memory. Their record still retains its interest, however, as that of one of the heroic races of the world; and all the more, because it is with their kindred that the American nation has to deal, in solving one of the most momentous problems of its future career.

THE MAROONS OF SURINAM

When that eccentric individual, Capt. John Gabriel Stedman, resigned his commission in the English Navy, took the oath of abjuration, and was appointed ensign in the Scots brigade employed for two centuries by Holland, he little knew that "their High Mightinesses the States of the United Provinces" would send him out, within a year, to the forests of Guiana, to subdue rebel negroes. He never imagined that the year 1773 would behold him beneath the rainy season in a tropical country, wading through marshes and splashing through lakes, exploring with his feet for submerged paths, commanding impracticable troops, and commanded by an insufferable colonel, feeding on greegree worms and fed upon by mosquitoes, howled at by jaguars, hissed at by serpents, and shot at by those exceedingly unattainable gentlemen, "still longed for, never seen," the Maroons of Surinam.

Yet, as our young ensign sailed up the Surinam River, the world of tropic beauty came upon him with enchantment. Dark, moist verdure was close around him, rippling waters below; the tall trees of the jungle and the low mangroves beneath were all hung with long vines and lianas, a maze of cordage, like a fleet at anchor; lithe monkeys travelled ceaselessly up and down these airy paths, in armies, bearing their young, like knapsacks, on their backs; macaws and humming-birds, winged jewels, flew from tree to tree. As they neared Paramaribo, the river became a smooth canal among luxuriant plantations; the air was perfumed music, redolent of orange-blossoms and echoing with the songs of birds and the sweet plash of oars; gay barges came forth to meet them; "while groups of naked boys and girls were promiscuously playing and flouncing, like so many tritons and mermaids, in the water." And when the troops disembarked,-- five hundred fine young men, the oldest not thirty, all arrayed in new uniforms and bearing orange-flowers in their caps, a bridal wreath for beautiful Guiana,--it is no wonder that the Creole ladies were in ecstasy; and the boyish recruits little foresaw the day, when, reduced to a few dozens, barefooted and ragged as filibusters, their last survivors would gladly re-embark from a country beside which even Holland looked dry and even Scotland comfortable.

For over all that earthly paradise there brooded not alone its terrible malaria, its days of fever and its nights of deadly chill, but the worse shadows of oppression and of sin, which neither day nor night could banish. The first object which met Stedman's eye, as he stepped on shore, was the figure of a young girl stripped to receive two hundred lashes, and chained to a hundred-pound weight. And the few first days gave a glimpse into a state of society worthy of this exhibition,--men without mercy, women without modesty, the black man a slave to the white man's passions, and the white man a slave to his own. The later West-Indian society in its worst forms is probably a mere dilution of the utter profligacy of those early days. Greek or Roman decline produced nothing more debilitating or destructive than the ordinary life of a Surinam planter, and his one virtue of hospitality only led to more unbridled excesses and completed the work of vice. No wonder that Stedman himself, who, with all his peculiarities, was essentially simple and manly, soon became disgusted, and made haste to get into the woods and cultivate the society of the Maroons.

The rebels against whom this expedition was sent were not the original Maroons of Surinam, but a later generation. The originals had long since established their independence, and their leaders were flourishing their honorary silver-mounted canes in the streets of Paramaribo. Fugitive negroes had begun to establish themselves in the woods from the time when the colony was finally ceded by the English to the Dutch, in 1674. The first open outbreak occurred in 1726, when the plantations on the Seramica River revolted; it was found impossible to subdue them, and the government very imprudently resolved to make an example of eleven captives, and thus terrify the rest of the rebels. They were tortured to death, eight of the eleven being women: this drove the others to madness, and plantation after plantation was visited with fire and sword. After a long

conflict, their chief, Adoe, was induced to make a treaty, in 1749. The rebels promised to keep the peace, and in turn were promised freedom, money, tools, clothes, and, finally, arms and ammunition.

But no permanent peace was ever made upon a barrel of gunpowder as a basis; and, of course, an explosion followed this one. The colonists naturally evaded the last item of the bargain; and the rebels, receiving the gifts, and remarking the omission of the part of Hamlet, asked contemptuously if the Europeans expected negroes to subsist on combs and looking-glasses? New hostilities at once began; a new body of slaves on the Ouca River revolted; the colonial government was changed in consequence, and fresh troops shipped from Holland; and after four different embassies had been sent into the woods, the rebels began to listen to reason. The black generals, Capt. Araby and Capt. Boston, agreed upon a truce for a year, during which the colonial government might decide for peace or war, the Maroons declaring themselves indifferent. Finally the government chose peace, delivered ammunition, and made a treaty, in 1761; the white and black plenipotentiaries exchanged English oaths and then negro oaths, each tasting a drop of the other's blood during the latter ceremony, amid a volley of remarkable incantations from the black *gadoman* or priest. After some final skirmishes, in which the rebels almost always triumphed, the treaty was at length accepted by all the various villages of Maroons. Had they known that at this very time five thousand slaves in Berbice were just rising against their masters, and were looking to them for assistance, the result might have been different; but this fact had not reached them, nor had the rumors of insurrection in Brazil among negro and Indian slaves. They consented, therefore, to the peace. "They write from Surinam," says the "Annual Register" for Jan. 23, 1761, "that the Dutch governor, finding himself unable to subdue the rebel negroes of that country by force, hath wisely followed the example of Gov. Trelawney at Jamaica, and concluded an amicable treaty with them; in consequence of which, all the negroes of the woods are acknowledged to be free, and all that is passed is buried in oblivion." So ended a war of thirty-six years; and in Stedman's day the original three thousand Ouca and Seramica Maroons had multiplied, almost incredibly, to fifteen thousand.

But for those slaves not sharing in this revolt it was not so easy to "bury the whole past in oblivion." The Maroons had told some very plain truths to the white ambassadors, and had frankly advised them, if they wished for peace, to mend their own manners and treat their chattels humanely. But the planters learned nothing by experience,--and, indeed, the terrible narrations of Stedman were confirmed by those of Alexander, so lately as 1831. Of course, therefore, in a colony comprising eighty thousand blacks to four thousand whites, other revolts were stimulated by the success of this one. They reached their highest point in 1772, when an insurrection on the Cottica River, led by a negro named Baron, almost gave the finishing blow to the colony; the only adequate protection being found in a body of slaves liberated expressly for that purpose,--a dangerous and humiliating precedent. "We have been obliged to set three or four hundred of our stoutest negroes free to defend us," says an honest letter from Surinam, in the "Annual Register" for Sept. 5, 1772. Fortunately for the safety of the planters, Baron presumed too much upon his numbers, and injudiciously built a camp too near the seacoast, in a marshy fastness, from which he was finally ejected by twelve hundred Dutch troops, though the chief work was done, Stedman thinks, by the "black rangers" or liberated slaves. Checked by this defeat, he again drew back into the forests, resuming his guerrilla warfare against the plantations. Nothing could dislodge him; blood-hounds were proposed, but the moisture of the country made them useless: and thus matters stood when Stedman came sailing, amid orange-blossoms and music, up the winding Surinam.

Our young officer went into the woods in the condition of Falstaff, "heinously unprovided." Coming from the unbounded luxury of the plantations, he found himself entering "the most horrid and impenetrable forests, where no kind of refreshment was to be had,"--he being provisioned only with salt pork and pease. After a wail of sorrow for this inhuman neglect, he bursts into a gush of gratitude for the private generosity which relieved his wants at the last moment by the following list of supplies: "24 bottles best claret, 12 ditto Madeira, 12 ditto porter, 12 ditto cider, 12 ditto rum, 2 large loaves white sugar, 2 gallons brandy, 6 bottles muscadel, 2 gallons lemon-juice, 2 gallons ground coffee, 2 large Westphalia hams, 2 salted bullocks' tongues, 1 bottle Durham mustard, 6 dozen spermaceti candles." The hams and tongues seem, indeed, rather a poor halfpennyworth to this intolerable deal of sack; but this instance of Surinam privation in those days may open some glimpse at the colonial standards of comfort. "From this specimen," moralizes our hero, "the reader will easily perceive, that, if some of the inhabitants of Surinam show themselves the disgrace of the creation by their cruelties and brutality, others, by their social feelings, approve themselves an ornament to the human species. With this instance of virtue and generosity I therefore conclude this chapter."

But the troops soon had to undergo worse troubles than those of the commissariat. The rainy season had just set in. "As for the negroes," said Mr. Klynhaus, the last planter with whom they parted, "you may depend on never seeing a soul of them, unless they attack you off guard; but the climate, the climate, will murder you all." Bringing with them constitutions already impaired by the fevers and dissipation of Paramaribo, the poor boys began to perish long before they began to fight. Wading in water all day, hanging their hammocks over water at night, it seemed a moist existence, even compared with the climate of England and the soil of Holland. It was a case of "Invent a shovel, and be a magistrate," even more than Andrew Marvell found it in the United Provinces. In fact, Raynal evidently thinks that nothing but Dutch experience in hydraulics could ever have cultivated Surinam.

The two gunboats which held one division of the expedition were merely old sugar-barges, roofed over with boards, and looking like coffins. They were pleasantly named the "Charon" and the "Cerberus," but Stedman thought that the "Sudden Death" and the "Wilful Murder" would have been titles more appropriate. The chief duty of the troops consisted in lying at anchor at the intersections of wooded streams, waiting for rebels who never came. It was dismal work, and the raw recruits were full of the same imaginary terrors which have haunted other heroes less severely tested: the monkeys never rattled the cocoa-nuts against the trees, but they all heard the axes of Maroon wood-choppers; and when a sentinel declared, one night, that he had seen a negro go down the river in a canoe, with his pipe lighted, the whole force was called to arms--against a firefly. In fact, the insect race brought by far the most substantial dangers. The rebels eluded the military, but the chigres, locusts, scorpions, and bush-spiders were ever ready to come half-way to meet them; likewise serpents and alligators proffered them the freedom of the forests, and exhibited a hospitality almost excessive. Snakes twenty feet long hung their seductive length from the trees; jaguars volunteered their society through almost impenetrable marshes; vampire bats perched by night with lulling endearments upon the toes of the soldiers. When Stedman describes himself as killing thirty-eight mosquitoes at one stroke, we must perhaps pardon something to the spirit of martyrdom. But when we add to these the other woes of his catalogue,--prickly-heat, ringworm, putrid-fever, "the growling of Col. Fougeaud, dry sandy savannas, unfordable marshes, burning hot days, cold and damp nights, heavy rains, and short allowance,"--we can hardly wonder that three captains died in a month, and that in two months his detachment of forty-two was reduced to a miserable seven.

Yet, through all this, Stedman himself kept his health. His theory of the matter almost recalls the time-honored prescription of "A light heart and a thin pair of breeches," for he attributes his good condition to his keeping up his spirits and kicking off his shoes. Daily bathing in the river had also something to do with it; and, indeed, hydropathy was first learned of the West-India Maroons,--who did their "packing" in wet clay,--and was carried by Dr. Wright to England. But his extraordinary personal qualities must have contributed most to his preservation. Never did a "meagre, starved, black, burnt, and ragged tatterdemalion," as he calls himself, carry about him such a fund of sentiment, philosophy, poetry, and art. He had a great faculty for sketching, as the engravings in his volumes, with all their odd peculiarities, show; his deepest woes he coined always into couplets, and fortified himself against hopeless despair with Ovid and Valerius Flaccus, Pope's Homer and Thomson's "Seasons." Above all reigned his passion for natural history, a ready balm for every ill. Here he was never wanting to the occasion; and, to do justice to Dutch Guiana, the occasion never was wanting to him. Were his men sickening, the peccaries were always healthy without the camp, and the cockroaches within; just escaping from a she-jaguar, he satisfies himself, ere he flees, that the print of her claws on the sand is precisely the size of a pewter dinner-plate; bitten by a scorpion, he makes sure of a scientific description in case he should expire of the bite; is the water undrinkable, there is at least some rational interest in the number of legs possessed by the centipedes which pre-occupy it. This is the highest triumph of man over his accidents, when he thus turns his pains to gains, and becomes an entomologist in the tropics.

Meanwhile the rebels kept their own course in the forests, and occasionally descended upon plantations beside the very river on whose upper waters the useless troops were sickening and dying. Stedman himself made several campaigns, with long intervals of illness, before he came any nearer to the enemy than to burn a deserted village or destroy a rice-field. Sometimes they left the "Charon" and the "Cerberus" moored by grape-vines to the pine-trees, and made expeditions into the woods, single file. Our ensign, true to himself, gives the minutest schedule of the order of march, and the oddest little diagram of manikins with cocked hats, and blacker manikins bearing burdens. First, negroes with bill-hooks to clear the way;

then the van-guard; then the main body, interspersed with negroes bearing boxes of ball-cartridges; then the rear-guard, with many more negroes, bearing camp-equipage, provisions, and new rum, surnamed "kill-devil," and appropriately followed by a sort of palanquin for the disabled. Thus arrayed, they marched valorously forth into the woods, to some given point; then they turned, marched back to the boats, then rowed back to camp, and straightway went into the hospital. Immediately upon this, the coast being clear, Baron and his rebels marched out again, and proceeded to business.

In the course of years, these Maroons had acquired their own peculiar tactics. They built stockaded fortresses on marshy islands, accessible by fords which they alone could traverse. These they defended further by sharp wooden pins, or crows'-feet, concealed beneath the surface of the miry ground,--and, latterly, by the more substantial protection of cannon, which they dragged into the woods, and learned to use. Their bush-fighting was unique. Having always more men than weapons, they arranged their warriors in threes,--one to use the musket, another to take his place if wounded or slain, and a third to drag away the body. They had Indian stealthiness and swiftness, with more than Indian discipline; discharged their fire with some approach to regularity, in three successive lines, the signals being given by the captain's horn. They were full of ingenuity: marked their movements for each other by scattered leaves and blazed trees; ran zigzag, to dodge bullets; gave wooden guns to their unarmed men, to frighten the plantation negroes on their guerrilla expeditions; and borrowed the red caps of the black rangers whom they slew, to bewilder the aim of the others. One of them, finding himself close to the muzzle of a ranger's gun, threw up his hand hastily. "What!" he exclaimed, "will you fire on one of your own party?" "God forbid!" cried the ranger, dropping his piece, and was instantly shot through the body by the Maroon, who the next instant had disappeared in the woods.

These rebels were no saints: their worship was obi-worship; the women had not far outgrown the plantation standard of chastity, and the men drank "kill-devil" like their betters. Stedman was struck with the difference between the meaning of the word "good" in rebellious circles and in reputable. "It must, however, be observed, that what we Europeans call a good character was by the Africans looked upon as detestable, especially by those born in the woods, whose only crime consisted in avenging the wrongs done to their forefathers." But if martial virtues be virtues, such were theirs. Not a rebel ever turned traitor or informer, ever flinched in battle or under torture, ever violated a treaty or even a private promise. But it was their power of endurance which was especially astounding; Stedman is never weary of paying tribute to this, or of illustrating it in sickening detail; indeed, the records of the world show nothing to surpass it; "the lifted axe, the agonizing wheel," proved powerless to subdue it; with every limb lopped, every bone broken, the victims yet defied their tormentors, laughed, sang, and died triumphant.

Of course they repaid these atrocities in kind. If they had not, it would have demonstrated the absurd paradox, that slavery educates higher virtues than freedom. It bewilders all the relations of human responsibility, if we expect the insurrectionary slave to commit no outrages; if slavery has not depraved him, it has done him little harm. If it be the normal tendency of bondage to produce saints like Uncle Tom, let us all offer ourselves at auction immediately. It is Cassy and Dred who are the normal protest of human nature against systems which degrade it. Accordingly, these poor, ignorant Maroons, who had seen their brothers and sisters flogged, burned, mutilated, hanged on iron hooks, broken on the wheel, and had been all the while solemnly assured that this was paternal government, could only repay the paternalism in the same fashion, when they had the power. Stedman saw a negro chained to a red-hot distillery-furnace; he saw disobedient slaves, in repeated instances, punished by the amputation of a leg, and sent to boat-service for the rest of their lives; and of course the rebels borrowed these suggestions. They could bear to watch their captives expire under the lash, for they had previously watched their parents. If the government rangers received twenty-five florins for every rebel right-hand which they brought in, of course they risked their own right hands in the pursuit. The difference was that the one brutality was that of a mighty state, and the other was only the retaliation of the victims. And after all, Stedman never ventures to assert that the imitation equalled the original, or that the Maroons had inflicted nearly so much as they had suffered.

The leaders of the rebels, especially, were men who had each his own story of wrongs to tell. Baron, the most formidable, had been the slave of a Swedish gentleman, who had taught him to read and write, taken him to Europe, promised to free him on his return--and then, breaking his word, sold him to a Jew.

Baron refused to work for his new master, was publicly flogged under the gallows, fled to the woods next day, and became the terror of the colony. Joli Coeur, his first captain, was avenging the cruel wrongs of his mother. Bonny, another leader, was born in the woods, his mother having taken refuge there just previously, to escape from his father, who was also his master. Cojo, another, had defended his master against the insurgents until he was obliged by ill usage to take refuge among them; and he still bore upon his wrist, when Stedman saw him, a silver band, with the inscription,--"True to the Europeans." In dealing with wrongs like these, Mr. Carlyle would have found the despised negroes quite as ready as himself to take the total-abstinence pledge against rose-water.

In his first two-months' campaign, Stedman never saw the trace of a Maroon; in the second, he once came upon their trail; in the third, one captive was brought in, two surrendered themselves voluntarily, and a large party was found to have crossed a river within a mile of the camp, ferrying themselves on palm-trunks, according to their fashion. Deep swamps and scorching sands, toiling through briers all day, and sleeping at night in hammocks suspended over stagnant water, with weapons supported on sticks crossed beneath,--all this was endured for two years and a half, before Stedman personally came in sight of the enemy.

On Aug. 20, 1775, the troops found themselves at last in the midst of the rebel settlements. These villages and forts bore a variety of expressive names, such as "Hide me, O thou surrounding verdure," "I shall be taken," "The woods lament for me," "Disturb me, if you dare," "Take a tasting, if you like it," "Come, try me, if you be men," "God knows me, and none else," "I shall moulder before I shall be taken." Some were only plantation-grounds with a few huts, and were easily laid waste; but all were protected more or less by their mere situations. Quagmires surrounded them, covered by a thin crust of verdure, sometimes broken through by one man's weight, when the victim sank hopelessly into the black and bottomless depths below. In other directions there was a solid bottom, but inconveniently covered by three or four feet of water, through which the troops waded breast-deep, holding their muskets high in the air, unable to reload them when once discharged, and liable to be picked off by rebel scouts, who ingeniously posted themselves in the tops of palm-trees.

Through this delectable region Col. Fougeaud and his followers slowly advanced, drawing near the fatal shore where Capt. Meyland's detachment had just been defeated, and where their mangled remains still polluted the beach. Passing this point of danger without attack, they suddenly met a small party of rebels, each bearing on his back a beautifully woven hamper of snow-white rice: these loads they threw down, and disappeared. Next appeared an armed body from the same direction, which fired upon them once and swiftly retreated; and in a few moments the soldiers came upon a large field of standing rice, beyond which lay, like an amphitheatre, the rebel village. But between the village and the field had been piled successive defenses of logs and branches, behind which simple redoubts the Maroons lay concealed. A fight ensued, lasting forty minutes, during which nearly every soldier and ranger was wounded; but, to their great amazement, not one was killed. This was an enigma to them until after the skirmish, when the surgeon found that most of them had been struck, not by bullets, but by various substitutes, such as pebbles, coat-buttons, and bits of silver coin, which had penetrated only skin deep. "We also observed that several of the poor rebel negroes, who had been shot, had only the shards of Spa-water cans instead of flints, which could seldom do execution; and it was certainly owing to these circumstances that we came off so well."

The rebels at length retreated, first setting fire to their village; a hundred or more lightly built houses, some of them two stories high, were soon in flames; and as this conflagration occupied the only neck of land between two impassable morasses, the troops were unable to follow, and the Maroons had left nothing but rice-fields to be pillaged. That night the military force was encamped in the woods; their ammunition was almost gone, so they were ordered to lie flat on the ground, even in case of attack; they could not so much as build a fire. Before midnight an attack was made on them, partly with bullets, and partly with words. The Maroons were all around them in the forest, but their object was a puzzle; they spent most of the night in bandying compliments with the black rangers, whom they alternately denounced, ridiculed, and challenged to single combat. At last Fougeaud and Stedman joined in the conversation, and endeavored to make this midnight volley of talk the occasion for a treaty. This was received with inextinguishable laughter, which echoed through the woods like a concert of screech-owls, ending in a *charivari* of horns and hallooing. The colonel, persisting, offered them "life, liberty, victuals, drink, and all they wanted;" in return, they ridiculed him unmercifully. He was a half-starved Frenchman, who had run away from his own country, and would soon run away from theirs; they profoundly pitied him and his soldiers; they would scorn to spend powder on such scarecrows; they would rather feed and clothe them, as being poor white slaves, hired to be shot at, and starved for fourpence a day. But as for the planters, overseers, and rangers, they should die, every one of them, and Bonny should be governor of the colony. "After this, they tinkled their bill-hooks, fired a volley, and gave three cheers; which, being answered by the rangers, the clamor ended, and the rebels dispersed with the rising sun."

Very aimless nonsense it certainly appeared. But the next day put a new aspect on it; for it was found, that, under cover of all this noise, the Maroons had been busily occupied all night, men, women, and children, in preparing and filling great hampers of the finest rice, yams, and cassava, from the adjacent provision-grounds, to be used for subsistence during their escape, leaving only chaff and refuse for the hungry soldiers. "This was certainly such a masterly trait of generalship in a savage people, whom we affected to despise, as would have done honor to any European commander."

From this time the Maroons fulfilled their threats. Shooting down without mercy every black ranger who came within their reach,--one of these rangers being, in Stedman's estimate, worth six white soldiers,--they left Col. Fougeaud and his regulars to die of starvation and fatigue. The enraged colonel, "finding himself thus foiled by a naked negro, swore he would pursue Bonny to the world's end." But he never got any nearer than to Bonny's kitchen-gardens. He put the troops on half-allowance, sent back for provisions and ammunition,--and within ten days changed his mind, and retreated to the settlements in despair. Soon after, this very body of rebels, under Bonny's leadership, plundered two plantations in the vicinity, and nearly captured a powder-magazine, which was, however, successfully defended by some armed slaves.

For a year longer these expeditions continued. The troops never gained a victory, and they lost twenty men for every rebel killed; but they gradually checked the plunder of plantations, destroyed villages and planting-grounds, and drove the rebels, for the time at least, into the deeper recesses of the woods, or into the adjacent province of Cayenne. They had the slight satisfaction of burning Bonny's own house, a two-story wooden hut, built in the fashion of our frontier guardhouses. They often took single prisoners,--some child, born and bred in the woods, and frightened equally by the first sight of a white man and of a cow,--or some warrior, who, on being threatened with torture, stretched forth both hands in disdain, and said, with Indian eloquence, "These hands have made tigers tremble." As for Stedman, he still went barefooted, still quarrelled with his colonel, still sketched the scenery and described the reptiles, still reared greegree worms for his private kitchen, still quoted good poetry and wrote execrable, still pitied all the sufferers around him, black, white, and red, until finally he and his comrades were ordered back to Holland in 1776.

Among all that wasted regiment of weary and broken-down men, there was probably no one but Stedman who looked backward with longing as they sailed down the lovely Surinam. True, he bore all his precious collections with him,--parrots and butterflies, drawings on the backs of old letters, and journals kept on bones and cartridges. But he had left behind him a dearer treasure; for there runs through all his eccentric narrative a single thread of pure romance, in his love for his beautiful quadroon wife and his only son.

Within a month after his arrival in the colony, our susceptible ensign first saw Joanna, a slave-girl of fifteen, at the house of an intimate friend. Her extreme beauty and modesty first fascinated him, and then her piteous narrative,--for she was the daughter of a planter, who had just gone mad and died in despair from the discovery that he could not legally emancipate his own children from slavery. Soon after, Stedman was dangerously ill, was neglected and alone; fruits and cordials were anonymously sent to him, which proved at last to have come from Joanna; and she came herself, ere long, and nursed him, grateful for the visible sympathy he had shown to her. This completed the conquest; the passionate young Englishman, once recovered, loaded her with presents which she refused; talked of purchasing her, and educating her in Europe, which she also declined as burdening him too greatly; and finally, amid the ridicule of all good society in Paramaribo, surmounted all legal obstacles, and was united to the beautiful girl in honorable marriage. He provided a cottage for her, where he spent his furloughs, in perfect happiness, for four years.

The simple short poem of their loves was unbroken by any stain or disappointment, and yet always shadowed with the deepest anxiety for the future. Though treated with the utmost indulgence, she was legally a slave, and so was the boy of whom she became the mother. Cojo, her uncle, was a captain among the rebels against whom her husband fought. And up to the time when Stedman was ordered back to Holland, he was unable to purchase her freedom; nor could he, until the very last moment, procure the emancipation of his boy. His perfect delight at this last triumph, when obtained, elicited some satire from his white friends. "While the well-thinking few highly applauded my sensibility, many not only blamed but publicly derided me for my paternal affection, which was called a weakness, a whim." "Nearly forty beautiful boys and girls were left to perpetual slavery by their parents of my acquaintance, and many of them without being so much as once inquired after at all."

But Stedman was a true-hearted fellow, if his sentiment did sometimes become boastful; he left his Joanna only in the hope that a year or two in Europe would repair his ruined fortunes, and he could return to treat himself to the purchase of his own wedded wife. He describes, with unaffected pathos, their parting scene,--though, indeed, there were several successive partings,--and closes the description in a characteristic manner:

"My melancholy having surpassed all description, I at last determined to weather one or two painful years in her absence; and in the afternoon went to dissipate my mind at a Mr. Roux' cabinet of Indian curiosities; where, as my eye chanced to fall on a rattlesnake, I will, before I leave the colony, describe this dangerous reptile."

It was impossible to write the history of the Maroons of Surinam except through the biography of our ensign (at last promoted captain), because nearly all we know of them is through his quaint and picturesque narrative, with its profuse illustrations by his own hand. It is not fair, therefore, to end without chronicling his safe arrival in Holland, on June 3, 1777. It is a remarkable fact, that, after his life in the woods, even the Dutch looked slovenly to his eyes. "The inhabitants, who crowded about us, appeared but a disgusting assemblage of ill-formed and ill-dressed rabble,--so much had my prejudices been changed by living among Indians and blacks: their eyes seemed to resemble those of a pig; their complexions were like the color of foul linen; they seemed to have no teeth, and to be covered over with rags and dirt. This prejudice, however, was not against these people only, but against all Europeans in general, when compared to the sparkling eyes, ivory teeth, shining skin, and remarkable cleanliness of those I had left behind me." Yet, in spite of these superior attractions, he never recrossed the Atlantic; for his Joanna died soon after, and his promising son, being sent to the father, was educated in England, became a midshipman in the navy, and was lost at sea. With his elegy, in which the last depths of bathos are sadly sounded by a mourning parent,--who is induced to print them only by "the effect they had on the sympathetic and ingenious Mrs. Cowley,"--the "Narrative of a Five Years' Expedition" closes.

The war, which had cost the government forty thousand pounds a year, was ended, and left both parties essentially as when it began. The Maroons gradually returned to their old abodes, and, being unmolested themselves, left others unmolested thenceforward. Originally three thousand,--in Stedman's time, fifteen thousand,--they were estimated at seventy thousand by Capt. Alexander, who saw Guiana in 1831; and a later American scientific expedition, having visited them in their homes, reported them as still enjoying their wild freedom, and multiplying, while the Indians on the same soil decay. The beautiful forests of Surinam still make the morning gorgeous with their beauty, and the night deadly with their chill; the stately palm still rears, a hundred feet in air, its straight gray shaft and its head of verdure; the mora builds its solid, buttressed trunk, a pedestal for the eagle; the pine of the tropics holds out its myriad hands with water-cups for the rain and dews, where all the birds and the monkeys may drink their fill; the trees are garlanded with epiphytes and convolvuli, and anchored to the earth by a thousand vines. High among their branches, the red and yellow mocking-birds still build their hanging nests, uncouth storks and tree-porcupines cling above, and the spotted deer and the tapir drink from the sluggish stream below. The night is still made noisy with a thousand cries of bird and beast; and the stillness of the sultry noon is broken by the slow tolling of the *campañero*, or bell-bird, far in the deep, dark woods, like the chime of some lost convent. And as Nature is unchanged there, so apparently is man; the Maroons still retain their savage freedom, still shoot their wild game and trap their fish, still raise their rice and cassava, yams and plantains,--still make cups from the gourd-tree and hammocks from the silk-grass plant, wine from the palm-tree's sap, brooms from its leaves, fishing-lines from its fibres, and salt from its ashes. Their life does not yield, indeed, the very highest results of spiritual culture; its mental and moral results may not come up to the level of civilization, but they rise far above the level of slavery. In the changes of time, the Maroons may yet elevate themselves into the one, but they will never relapse into the other.

GABRIEL'S DEFEAT

In exploring among dusty files of newspapers for the true records of Denmark Vesey and Nat Turner, I have caught occasional glimpses of a plot perhaps more wide in its outlines than that of either, which has lain obscure in the darkness of half a century, traceable only in the political events which dated from it, and the utter incorrectness of the scanty traditions which assumed to preserve it. And though researches in public libraries have only proved to me how rapidly the materials for American history are vanishing,--since not one of our great institutions possessed, a few years since, a file of any Southern newspaper of the year 1800,--yet the little which I have gained may have an interest that makes it worth preserving. Three times, at intervals of thirty years, did a wave of unutterable terror sweep across the Old Dominion, bringing thoughts of agony to every Virginian master, and of vague hope to every Virginian slave. Each time did one man's name become a spell of dismay and a symbol of deliverance. Each time did that name eclipse its predecessor, while recalling it for a moment to fresher memory: John Brown revived the story of Nat Turner, as in his day Nat Turner recalled the vaster schemes of Gabriel.

On Sept. 8, 1800, a Virginia correspondent wrote thus to the Philadelphia *United-States Gazette:*--

> "For the week past, we have been under momentary expectation of a rising among the negroes, who have assembled to the number of nine hundred or a thousand, and threatened to massacre all the whites. They are armed with desperate weapons, and secrete themselves in the woods. God only knows our fate: we have strong guards every night under arms."

It was no wonder, if there were foundation for such rumors. Liberty was the creed or the cant of the day. France was being disturbed by revolution, and England by Clarkson. In America, slavery was habitually recognized as a misfortune and an error, only to be palliated by the nearness of its expected end. How freely anti-slavery pamphlets had been circulated in Virginia, we know from the priceless volumes collected and annotated by Washington, and now preserved in the Boston Athenaeum. Jefferson's "Notes on Virginia," itself an anti-slavery tract, had passed through seven editions. Judge St. George Tucker, law-professor in William and Mary College, had recently published his noble work, "A Dissertation on Slavery, with a Proposal for the Gradual Abolition of it in the State of Virginia." From all this agitation, a slave insurrection was a mere corollary. With so much electricity in the air, a single flash of lightning foreboded all the terrors of the tempest. Let but a single armed negro be seen or suspected, and at once, on many a lonely plantation, there were trembling hands at work to bar doors and windows that seldom had been even closed before, and there was shuddering when a gray squirrel scrambled over the roof, or a shower of walnuts came down clattering from the overhanging boughs.

Early in September, 1800, as a certain Mr. Moseley Sheppard, of Henrico County in Virginia, was one day sitting in his counting-room, two negroes knocked at the door, and were let in. They shut the door themselves, and began to unfold an insurrectionary plot, which was subsequently repeated by one of them, named Ben Woodfolk or Woolfolk, in presence of the court, on the 15th of the same month.

He stated, that about the first of the preceding June, he had been asked by a negro named Colonel George whether he would like to be made a Mason. He refused; but George ultimately prevailed on him to have an interview with a certain leading man among the blacks, named Gabriel. Arrived at the place of meeting, he found many persons assembled, to whom a preliminary oath was administered, that they would keep secret all which they might hear. The leaders then began, to the dismay of this witness, to allude to a plan of insurrection, which, as they stated, was already far advanced toward maturity. Presently a man named Martin, Gabriel's brother, proposed religious services, caused the company to be duly seated, and began an impassioned exposition of Scripture, bearing upon the perilous theme. The Israelites were glowingly portrayed as a type of successful resistance to tyranny; and it was argued, that now, as then, God would stretch forth his arm to save, and would strengthen a hundred to overthrow a thousand. Thus passed, the witness stated, this preparatory meeting. At a subsequent gathering the affair was brought to a point; and the only difficult question was, whether to rise in rebellion upon a certain Saturday, or upon the Sunday following. Gabriel said that Saturday was the day already fixed, and that it must not be altered; but George was for changing it to Sunday, as being more convenient for the country negroes, who could travel on that day without suspicion. Gabriel, however, said decisively that they had enough to carry Richmond without them; and Saturday was therefore retained as the momentous day.

This was the confession, so far as it is now accessible; and on the strength of it, Ben Woolfolk was promptly pardoned by the court for all his sins, past, present, or to come, and they proceeded with their investigation. Of Gabriel little appeared to be known, except that he had been the property of Thomas Prosser, a young man who had recently inherited a plantation a few miles from Richmond, and who had the reputation among his neighbors of "behaving with great barbarity to his slaves." Gabriel was, however, reported to be "a fellow of courage and intellect above his rank in life," to be about twenty-five years of age, and to be guiltless of the alphabet.

Further inquiry made it appear that the preparations of the insurgents were hardly adequate to any grand revolutionary design,--at least, if they proposed to begin with open warfare. The commissariat may have been well organized, for black Virginians are apt to have a prudent eye to the larder; but the ordnance department and the treasury were as low as if Secretary Floyd had been in charge of them. A slave called "Prosser's Ben" testified that he went with Gabriel to see Ben Woolfolk, who was going to Caroline County to enlist men, and that "Gabriel gave him three shillings for himself and three other negroes, to be expended in recruiting men." Their arms and ammunition, so far as reported, consisted of a peck of bullets, ten pounds of powder, and twelve scythe-swords, made by Gabriel's brother Solomon, and fitted with handles by Gabriel himself. "These cutlasses," said subsequently a white eye-witness, "are made of scythes cut in two and fixed into well-turned handles. I have never seen arms so murderous. Those who still doubt the importance of the conspiracy which has been so fortunately frustrated would shudder with horror at the sight of these instruments of death." And as it presently appeared that a conspirator named Scott had astonished his master by accidentally pulling ten dollars from a ragged pocket which seemed inadequate to the custody of ten cents, it was agreed that the plot might still be dangerous, even though the resources seemed limited.

And indeed, as was soon discovered, the effective weapon of the insurgents lay in the very audacity of their plan. If the current statements of all the Virginia letter-writers were true, "nothing could have been better contrived." It was to have taken effect on the first day of September. The rendezvous for the blacks was to be a brook six miles from Richmond. Eleven hundred men were to assemble there, and were to be divided into three columns, their officers having been designated in advance. All were to march on Richmond,--then a town of eight thousand inhabitants,--under cover of night. The right wing was instantly to seize upon the penitentiary building, just converted into an arsenal; while the left wing was to take possession of the powder-house. These two columns were to be armed chiefly with clubs, as their undertaking depended for success upon surprise, and was expected to prevail without hard fighting. But it was the central force, armed with muskets, cutlasses, knives, and pikes, upon which the chief responsibility rested; these men were to enter the town at both ends simultaneously, and begin a general carnage, none being excepted save the French inhabitants, who were supposed for some reason to be friendly to the negroes. In a very few hours, it was thought, they would have entire control of the metropolis. And that this hope was not in the least unreasonable, was shown by the subsequent confessions of weakness from the whites. "They could scarcely have failed of success," wrote the Richmond correspondent of the Boston *Chronicle*; "for, after all, we could only muster four or five hundred men, of whom not more than thirty had muskets."

For the insurgents, if successful, the penitentiary held several thousand stand of arms; the powder-house was well stocked; the Capitol contained the State treasury; the mills would give them bread; the control of the bridge across James River would keep off enemies from beyond. Thus secured and provided, they planned to issue proclamations summoning to their standard "their fellow-negroes and the friends of humanity throughout the continent." In a week, it was estimated, they would have fifty thousand men on their side, with which force they could easily possess themselves of other towns; and, indeed, a slave named John Scott--possibly the dangerous possessor of the ten dollars--was already appointed to head the attack on Petersburg. But in case of final failure, the project included a retreat to the mountains, with their new-found property. John Brown was therefore anticipated by Gabriel, sixty years before, in believing the Virginia mountains to have been "created, from the foundation of the world, as a place of refuge for fugitive slaves."

These are the statements of the contemporary witnesses; they are repeated in many newspapers of the year 1800, and are in themselves clear and consistent. Whether they are on the whole exaggerated or under-stated, it is now impossible to say. It is certain that a Richmond paper of Sept. 12 (quoted in the

New-York *Gazette* of Sept. 18) declares that "the plot has been entirely exploded, which was shallow; and, had the attempt been made to carry it into execution, but little resistance would have been required to render the scheme entirely abortive." But it is necessary to remember that this is no more than the Charleston newspapers said at the very crisis of Denmark Vesey's formidable plot. "Last evening," wrote a lady from Charleston in 1822, "twenty-five hundred of our citizens were under arms to guard our property and lives. But it is a subject not to be mentioned [so underscored]; and unless you hear of it elsewhere, say nothing about it." Thus it is always hard to know whether to assume the facts of an insurrection as above or below the estimates. This Virginian excitement also happened at a period of intense political agitation, and was seized upon as a boon by the Federalists. The very article above quoted is ironically headed "Holy Insurrection," and takes its motto from Jefferson, with profuse capital letters: "The Spirit of the Master is abating, that of the Slave rising from the dust, his condition mollifying."

In view of the political aspect thus given to the plot, and of its ingenuity and thoroughness likewise, the Virginians were naturally disposed to attribute to white men some share in it; and speculation presently began to run wild. The newspapers were soon full of theories, no two being alike, and no one credible. The plot originated, some said, in certain handbills written by Jefferson's friend Callender, then in prison at Richmond on a charge of sedition; these were circulated by two French negroes, aided by a "United Irishman" calling himself a Methodist preacher, and it was in consideration of these services that no Frenchman was to be injured by the slaves. When Gabriel was arrested, the editor of the *United-States Gazette* affected much diplomatic surprise that no letters were *yet* found upon his person "from Fries, Gallatin, or Duane, nor was he at the time of his capture accompanied by any United Irishman." "He, however, acknowledges that there are others concerned, and that he is not the principal instigator." All Federalists agreed that the Southern Democratic talk was constructive insurrection,--which it certainly was,---and they painted graphic pictures of noisy "Jacobins" over their wine, and eager dusky listeners behind their chairs. "It is evident that the French principles of liberty and equality have been effused into the minds of the negroes, and that the incautious and intemperate use of the words by some whites among us have inspired them with hopes of success." "While the fiery Hotspurs of the State vociferate their *French babble* of the natural equality of man, the insulted negro will be constantly stimulated to cast away his cords, and to sharpen his pike." "It is, moreover, believed, though not positively known, that a great many of our profligate and abandoned whites (who are distinguished by the burlesque appellation of *Democrats*) are implicated with the blacks, and would have joined them if they had commenced their operations.... The Jacobin printers and their friends are panic-struck. Never was terror more strongly depicted in the countenances of men." These extracts from three different Federalist newspapers show the amiable emotions of that side of the house; while Democratic Duane, in the *Aurora*, could find no better repartee than to attribute the whole trouble to the policy of the administration in renewing commercial intercourse with San Domingo.

I have discovered in the Norfolk *Epitome of the Times*, for Oct. 9, 1800, a remarkable epistle written from Richmond Jail by the unfortunate Callender himself. He indignantly denies the charges against the Democrats, of complicity in dangerous plots, boldly retorting them upon the Federalists. "An insurrection at this critical moment by the negroes of the Southern States would have thrown every thing into confusion, and consequently it was to have prevented the choice of electors in the whole or the greater part of the States to the south of the Potomac. Such a disaster must have tended directly to injure the interests of Mr. Jefferson, and to promote the slender possibility of a second election of Mr. Adams." And, to be sure, the *United-States Gazette* followed up the thing with a good, single-minded party malice which cannot be surpassed in these present days, ending in such altitudes of sublime coolness as the following: "The insurrection of the negroes in the Southern States, which appears to be organized on the true French plan, must be decisive, with every reflecting man in those States, of the election of Mr. Adams and Gen. Pinckney. The military skill and approved bravery of the general must be peculiarly valuable to his countrymen at these trying moments." Let us have a military Vice-President, by all means, to meet this formidable exigency of Gabriel's peck of bullets, and this unexplained three shillings in the pocket of "Prosser's Ben"!

But Gabriel's campaign failed, like that of the Federalists; and the appointed day brought disasters more fatal than even the sword of Gen. Pinckney. The panicked negroes declared that "the stars in their courses fought against Sisera." The most furious tempest ever known in Virginia burst upon the land that day, instead of an insurrection. Roads and plantations were submerged. Bridges were carried away. The fords, which then, as now, were the frequent substitutes for bridges in that region, were rendered wholly impassable. The Brook Swamp, one of the most important strategic points of the insurgents, was entirely inundated, hopelessly dividing Prosser's farm from Richmond; the country negroes could not get in, nor those from the city get out. The thousand men dwindled to a few hundred, and these half paralyzed by superstition; there was nothing to do but to dismiss them, and before they could re-assemble they were betrayed.

That the greatest alarm was instantly created throughout the community, there is no question. All the city of Richmond was in arms, and in all large towns of the State the night-patrol was doubled. It is a little amusing to find it formally announced, that "the Governor, impressed with the magnitude of the danger, has appointed for himself three aides-de-camp." A troop of United-States cavalry was ordered to Richmond. Numerous arrests were made. Men were convicted on one day, and hanged on the next,--five, six, ten, fifteen at a time, almost without evidence. Three hundred dollars were offered by Gov. Monroe for the arrest of Gabriel; as much more for another chief named Jack Bowler, *alias* Ditcher; whereupon Bowler *alias* Ditcher surrendered himself, but it took some weeks to get upon the track of Gabriel. He was finally captured at Norfolk, on board a schooner just arrived from Richmond, in whose hold he had concealed himself for eleven days, having thrown overboard a bayonet and bludgeon, which were his only arms. Crowds of people collected to see him, including many of his own color. He was arrested on Sept. 24, convicted on Oct. 3, and executed on Oct. 7; and it is known of him further, only, that, like almost all leaders of slave insurrections, he showed a courage which his enemies could not gainsay. "When he was apprehended, he manifested the greatest marks of firmness and confidence, showing not the least disposition to equivocate, or screen himself from justice,"--but making no confession that could implicate any one else. "The behavior of Gabriel under his misfortunes," said the Norfolk *Epitome* of Sept. 25, "was such as might be expected from a mind capable of forming the daring project which he had conceived." The *United-States Gazette* for Oct. 9 states, more sarcastically, that "the general is said to have manifested the utmost composure, and with the true spirit of heroism seems ready to resign his high office, and even his life, rather than gratify the officious inquiries of the Governor."

Some of these newspapers suggest that the authorities found it good policy to omit the statement made by Gabriel, whatever it was. At any rate, he assured them that he was by no means the sole instigator of the affair; he could name many, even in Norfolk, who were more deeply concerned. To his brother Solomon he is said to have stated that the real head of the plot was Jack Bowler. Still another leader was "Gen. John Scott," already mentioned, the slave of Mr. Greenhow, hired by Mr. McCrea. He was captured by his employer in Norfolk, just as he was boldly entering a public conveyance to escape; and the Baltimore *Telegraphe* declared that he had a written paper directing him to apply to Alexander Biddenhurst or Weddenhurst in Philadelphia, "corner of Coats Alley and Budd Street, who would supply his needs." What became of this military individual, or of his Philadelphia sympathizers, does not appear. But it was noticed, as usually happens in such cases, that all the insurgents had previously passed for saints. "It consists within my knowledge," says one letter-writer, "that many of these wretches who were or would have been partakers in the plot have been treated with the utmost tenderness by their masters, and were more like children than slaves."

These appear to be all the details now accessible of this once famous plot. They were not very freely published, even at the time. "The minutiae of the conspiracy have not been detailed to the public," said the Salem (Mass.) *Gazette* of Oct. 7, "and perhaps, through a mistaken notion of prudence and policy, will not be detailed in the Richmond papers." The New-York *Commercial Advertiser* of Oct. 13 was still more explicit. "The trials of the negroes concerned in the late insurrection are suspended until the opinions of the Legislature can be had on the subject. This measure is said to be owing to the immense numbers who are interested in the plot, whose death, should they all be found guilty and be executed, will nearly produce the annihilation of the blacks in this part of the country." And in the next issue of the same journal a Richmond correspondent makes a similar statement, with the following addition:

> "A conditional amnesty is perhaps expected. At the next session of the Legislature [of Virginia], they took into consideration the subject referred to them, in secret session, with closed doors. The whole result of their deliberations has never yet been made public, as the injunction of secrecy has never been removed. To satisfy the court, the public, and themselves, they had a task so difficult to perform, that it is not surprising that their deliberations were in secret."

It is a matter of historical interest to know that in these mysterious sessions lay the germs of the American Colonization Society. A correspondence was at once secretly commenced between the Governor of Virginia and the President of the United States, with a view to securing a grant of land whither troublesome slaves might be banished. Nothing came of it then; but in 1801, 1802, and 1804, these attempts were renewed. And finally, on Jan. 22, 1805, the following vote was passed, still in secret session: "*Resolved*, that the Senators of this State in the Congress of the United States be instructed, and the Representatives be requested, to use their best efforts for the obtaining from the General Government a competent portion of territory in the State of Louisiana, to be appropriated to the residence of such people of color as have been or shall be emancipated, or hereafter may become dangerous to the public safety," etc. But of all these efforts nothing was known till their record was accidentally discovered by Charles Fenton Mercer in 1816. He at once brought the matter to light, and moved a similar resolution in the Virginia Legislature; it was almost unanimously adopted, and the first formal meeting of the Colonization Society, in 1817, was called "in aid" of this Virginia movement. But the whole correspondence was never made public until the Nat Turner insurrection of 1831 recalled the previous excitement; and these papers were demanded by Mr. Summers, a member of the Legislature, who described them as "having originated in a convulsion similar to that which had recently, but more terribly, occurred."

But neither these subsequent papers, nor any documents which now appear accessible, can supply any authentic or trustworthy evidence as to the real extent of the earlier plot. It certainly was not confined to the mere environs of Richmond. The Norfolk *Epitome* of Oct. 6 states that on the 6th and 7th of the previous month one hundred and fifty blacks, including twenty from Norfolk, were assembled near Whitlock's Mills in Suffolk County, and remained in the neighborhood till the failure of the Richmond plan became known. Petersburg newspapers also had letters containing similar tales. Then the alarm spread more widely. Near Edenton, N.C., there was undoubtedly a real insurrection, though promptly suppressed; and many families ultimately removed from that vicinity in consequence. In Charleston, S.C., there was still greater excitement, if the contemporary press may be trusted; it was reported that the freeholders had been summoned to appear in arms, on penalty of a fine of fifteen pounds, which many preferred to pay rather than risk taking the fever which then prevailed. These reports were, however, zealously contradicted in letters from Charleston, dated Oct. 8; and the Charleston newspapers up to Sept. 17 had certainly contained no reference to any especial excitement. This alone might not settle the fact, for reasons already given. But the omission of any such affair from the valuable pamphlet published in 1822 by Edwin C. Holland, containing reminiscences of insurrections in South Carolina, is presumptive evidence that no much extended agitation occurred.

But wherever there was a black population, slave or emancipated, men's startled consciences made cowards of them all, and recognized the negro as a dangerous man, because an injured one. In Philadelphia it was seriously proposed to prohibit the use of sky-rockets for a time, because they had been employed as signals in San Domingo. "Even in Boston," said the New-York *Daily Advertiser* of Sept. 20, "fears are expressed, and measures of prevention adopted." This probably refers to a singular advertisement which appeared in some of the Boston newspapers on Sept. 16, and runs as follows:--

"NOTICE TO BLACKS.

"The officers of the police having made returns to the subscriber of the names of the following persons who are Africans or negroes, not subjects of the Emperor of Morocco nor citizens of any of the United States, the same are hereby warned and directed to depart out of this Commonwealth before the tenth day of October next, as they would avoid the pains and penalties of the law in that case provided, which was passed by the Legislature March 26, 1788.

"CHARLES BULFINCH, Superintendent.

"By order and direction of the Selectmen."

The names annexed are about three hundred, with the places of their supposed origin, and they occupy a column of the paper. So at least asserts the *United-States Gazette* of Sept. 23. "It seems probable," adds the editor, "from the nature of the notice, that some suspicion of the design of the negroes is entertained; and we regret to say there is too much cause." The law of 1788 above mentioned was "An Act for suppressing rogues, vagabonds, and the like," which forbade all persons of African descent, unless citizens of some one of the United States or subjects of the Emperor of Morocco, from remaining more than two months within the Commonwealth, on penalty of imprisonment and hard labor. This singular statute remained unrepealed until 1834.

Amid the general harmony in the contemporary narratives of Gabriel's insurrection, it would be improper to pass by one exceptional legend, which by some singular fatality has obtained more circulation than all the true accounts put together. I can trace it no farther back than Nat Turner's time, when it was published in the Albany *Evening Journal*; thence transferred to the *Liberator* of Sept. 17, 1831, and many other newspapers; then refuted in detail by the *Richmond Enquirer* of Oct. 21; then resuscitated in the John-Brown epoch by the Philadelphia *Press*, and extensively copied. It is fresh, spirited, and full of graphic and interesting details, nearly every one of which is altogether false.

Gabriel in this narrative becomes a rather mythical being, of vast abilities and life-long preparations. He bought his freedom, it is stated, at the age of twenty-one, and then travelled all over the Southern States, enlisting confederates and forming stores of arms. At length his plot was discovered, in consequence of three negroes having been seen riding out of a stable-yard together; and the Governor offered a reward of ten thousand dollars for further information, to which a Richmond gentleman added as much more. Gabriel concealed himself on board the "Sally Ann," a vessel just sailing for San Domingo, and was revealed by his little nephew, whom he had sent for a jug of rum. Finally, the narrative puts an eloquent dying speech into Gabriel's mouth, and, to give a properly tragic consummation, causes him to be torn to death by four wild horses. The last item is, however, omitted in the more recent reprints of the story.

Every one of these statements appears to be absolutely erroneous. Gabriel lived and died a slave, and was probably never out of Virginia. His plot was voluntarily revealed by accomplices. The rewards offered for his arrest amounted to three hundred dollars only. He concealed himself on board the schooner "Mary," bound to Norfolk, and was discovered by the police. He died on the gallows, with ten associates, having made no address to the court or the people. All the errors of the statement were contradicted when it was first made public, but they have proved very hard to kill.

Some of these events were embodied in a song bearing the same title with this essay, "Gabriel's Defeat," and set to a tune of the same name, both being composed by a colored man. Several witnesses have assured me of having heard this sung in Virginia, as a favorite air at the dances of the white people, as well as in the huts of the slaves. It is surely one of history's strange parallelisms, that this fatal enterprise, like that of John Brown afterwards, should thus have embalmed itself in music. And twenty-two years after these events, their impression still remained vivid enough for Benjamin Lundy, in Tennessee, to write: "So well had they matured their plot, and so completely had they organized their system of operations, that nothing but a seemingly miraculous intervention of the arm of Providence was supposed to have been capable of saving the city from pillage and flames, and the inhabitants thereof from butchery. So dreadful was the alarm and so great the consternation produced on this occasion, that a member of Congress from that State was some time after heard to express himself in his place as follows: 'The night-bell is never heard to toll in the city of Richmond, but the anxious mother presses her infant more closely to her bosom.'" The Congressman was John Randolph of Roanoke, and it was Gabriel who had taught him the lesson.

And longer than the melancholy life of that wayward statesman,--down even to the beginning of the American civil war,--there lingered in Richmond a memorial of those days, most peculiar and most instructive. Before the days of secession, when the Northern traveller in Virginia, after traversing for weary leagues its miry ways, its desolate fields, and its flowery forests, rode at last into its metropolis, he was sure to be guided ere long to visit its stately Capitol, modelled by Jefferson, when French minister, from the Maison Carrée. Standing before it, he might admire undisturbed the Grecian outline of its exterior; but he found himself forbidden to enter, save by passing an armed and uniformed sentinel at the doorway. No other State of the Union then found it necessary to protect its State House by a permanent cordon of bayonets. Yet there for half a century stood sentinel the "Public Guard" of Virginia; and when the traveler asked the origin of the precaution, he was told that it was the lasting memorial of Gabriel's Defeat.

DENMARK VESEY

On Saturday afternoon, May 25, 1822, a slave named Devany, belonging to Col. Prioleau of Charleston, S.C., was sent to market by his mistress,--the colonel being absent in the country. After doing his errands, he strolled down upon the wharves in the enjoyment of that magnificent wealth of leisure which usually characterized the former "house-servant" of the South, when beyond hail of the street-door. He presently noticed a small vessel lying in the stream, with a peculiar flag flying; and while looking at it, he was accosted by a slave named William, belonging to Mr. John Paul, who remarked to him, "I have often seen a flag with the number 76, but never one with the number 96 upon it before." After some further conversation on this trifling point, William suddenly inquired, "Do you know that something serious is about to take place?" Devany disclaiming the knowledge of any graver impending crisis than the family dinner, the other went on to inform him that many of the slaves were "determined to right themselves." "We are determined," he added, "to shake off our bondage, and for that purpose we stand on a good foundation; many have joined, and if you will go with me, I will show you the man who has the list of names, and who will take yours down."

This startling disclosure was quite too much for Devany: he was made of the wrong material for so daring a project; his genius was culinary, not revolutionary. Giving some excuse for breaking off the conversation, he went forthwith to consult a free colored man, named Pensil or Pencell, who advised him to warn his master instantly. So he lost no time in telling the secret to his mistress and her young son; and on the return of Col. Prioleau from the country, five days afterward, it was at once revealed to him. Within an hour or two he stated the facts to Mr. Hamilton, the intendant, or, as he would now be called, mayor; Mr. Hamilton at once summoned the corporation, and by five o'clock Devany and William were under examination.

This was the first warning of a plot which ultimately filled Charleston with terror. And yet so thorough and so secret was the organization of the negroes, that a fortnight passed without yielding the slightest information beyond the very little which was obtained from these two. William Paul was, indeed, put in confinement, and soon gave evidence inculpating two slaves as his employers,--Mingo Harth and Peter Poyas. But these men, when arrested, behaved with such perfect coolness, and treated the charge with such entire levity;--their trunks and premises, when searched, were so innocent of all alarming contents;--that they were soon discharged by the wardens. William Paul at length became alarmed for his own safety, and began to let out further facts piecemeal, and to inculpate other men. But some of those very men came voluntarily to the intendant, on hearing that they were suspected, and indignantly offered themselves for examination. Puzzled and bewildered, the municipal government kept the thing as secret as possible, placed the city guard in an efficient condition, provided sixteen hundred rounds of ball cartridges, and ordered the sentinels and patrols to be armed with loaded muskets. "Such had been our fancied security, which the guard had previously gone on duty without muskets, and with only sheathed bayonets and bludgeons."

It has since been asserted, though perhaps on questionable authority, that the Secretary of War was informed of the plot, even including some details of the plan and the leader's name, before it was known in Charleston. If so, he utterly disregarded it; and, indeed, so well did the negroes play their part, that the whole report was eventually disbelieved, while--as was afterwards proved--they went on to complete their secret organization, and hastened by a fortnight the appointed day of attack. Unfortunately for their plans, however, another betrayal took place at the very last moment, from a different direction. A class-leader in a Methodist church had been persuaded or bribed by his master to procure further disclosures. He at length came and stated, that, about three months before, a man named Rolla, slave of Gov. Bennett, had communicated to a friend of his the fact of an intended insurrection, and had said that the time fixed for the outbreak was the following Sunday night, June 16. As this conversation took place on Friday, it gave but a very short time for the city authorities to act, especially as they wished neither to endanger the city nor to alarm it.

Yet so cautiously was the game played on both sides that the whole thing was still kept a secret from the Charleston public; and some members of the city government did not fully appreciate their danger till they had passed it. "The whole was concealed," wrote the governor afterwards, "until the time came; but secret preparations were made. Saturday night and Sunday morning passed without demonstrations; doubts were excited, and counter orders issued for diminishing the guard." It afterwards proved that these preparations showed to the slaves that their plot was betrayed, and so saved the city without public alarm. Newspaper correspondence soon was full of the story, each informant of course hinting plainly that he had been behind the scenes all along, and had withheld it only to gratify the authorities in their policy of silence. It was "now no longer a secret," they wrote; adding, that, for five or six weeks, but little attention had been paid by the community to these rumors, the city council having kept it carefully to themselves until a number of suspicious slaves had been arrested. This refers to ten prisoners who were seized on June 18, an arrest which killed the plot, and left only the terrors of what might have been. The investigation, thus publicly commenced, soon revealed a free colored man named Denmark Vesey as the leader of the enterprise,--among his chief coadjutors being that innocent Peter and that unsuspecting Mingo who had been examined and discharged nearly three weeks before.

It is matter of demonstration, that, but for the military preparations on the appointed Sunday night, the attempt would have been made. The ringleaders had actually met for their final arrangements, when, by comparing notes, they found themselves foiled; and within another week they were prisoners on trial. Nevertheless, the plot which they had laid was the most elaborate insurrectionary project ever formed by American slaves, and came the nearest to a terrible success. In boldness of conception and thoroughness of organization there has been nothing to compare with it; and it is worth while to dwell somewhat upon its details, first introducing the *dramatis personae.*

Denmark Vesey had come very near figuring as a revolutionist in Hayti, instead of South Carolina. Capt. Vesey, an old resident of Charleston, commanded a ship that traded between St. Thomas and Cape Français, during our Revolutionary War, in the slave-transportation line. In the year 1781 he took on board a cargo of three hundred and ninety slaves, and sailed for the Cape. On the passage, he and his officers were much attracted by the beauty and intelligence of a boy of fourteen, whom they unanimously adopted into the cabin as a pet. They gave him new clothes, and a new name, Télémaque, which was afterwards gradually corrupted into Telmak and Denmark. They amused themselves with him until their arrival at Cape Français, and then, "having no use for the boy," sold their pet as if he had been a macaw or a monkey. Capt. Vesey sailed for St. Thomas; and, presently making another trip to Cape Français, was surprised to hear from his consignee that Télémaque would be returned on his hands as being "unsound,"--not in theology nor in morals, but in body,-- subject to epileptic fits, in fact. According to the custom of that place, the boy was examined by the city physician, who required Capt. Vesey to take him back; and Denmark served him faithfully, with no trouble from epilepsy, for twenty years, travelling all over the world with him, and learning to speak various languages. In 1800 he drew a prize of fifteen hundred dollars in the East Bay-street Lottery, with which he bought his freedom from his master for six hundred dollars,--much less than his market value. From that time, the official report says, he worked as a carpenter in Charleston, distinguished for physical strength and energy. "Among those of his color he was looked up to with awe and respect. His temper was impetuous and domineering in the extreme, qualifying him for the despotic rule of which he was ambitious. All his passions were ungovernable and savage; and to his numerous wives and children he displayed the haughty and capricious cruelty of an Eastern bashaw."

"For several years before he disclosed his intentions to any one, he appears to have been constantly and assiduously engaged in endeavoring to imbitter the minds of the colored population against the white. He rendered himself perfectly familiar with all those parts of the Scriptures which he thought he could pervert to his purpose, and would readily quote them to prove that slavery was contrary to the laws of God; that slaves were bound to attempt their emancipation, however shocking and bloody might be the consequences; and that such efforts would not only be pleasing to the Almighty, but were absolutely enjoined, and their success predicted, in the Scriptures. His favorite texts when he addressed those of his own color were Zech. xiv. 1-3, and Josh. vi. 21; and in all his conversations he identified their situation with that of the Israelites. The number of inflammatory pamphlets on slavery brought into Charleston from some of our sister States within the last four years (and once from Sierra Leone), and distributed amongst the colored population of the city, for which there was a great facility, in consequence of the unrestricted intercourse allowed to persons of color between the different States in the Union, and the speeches in Congress of those opposed to the admission of Missouri into the Union, perhaps garbled and misrepresented, furnished him with ample means for inflaming the minds of the colored population of the State; and by distorting certain parts of those speeches, or selecting from them particular passages, he persuaded but too many that Congress had actually declared them free, and that they were held in bondage contrary to the laws of the land. Even whilst walking through the streets in company with another, he was not idle; for if his companion bowed to a white person, he would rebuke him, and observe that all men were born equal, and that he was surprised that any one would degrade himself by such conduct; that he would never cringe to the whites, nor ought any one who had the feelings of a man. When answered, 'We are slaves,' he would sarcastically and indignantly reply, 'You deserve to remain slaves;' and if he were further asked, 'What can we do?' he would remark, 'Go and buy a spelling-book, and read the fable of Hercules and the Wagoner,' which he would then repeat, and apply it to their situation. He also sought every opportunity of entering into conversation with white persons, when they could be overheard by negroes near by, especially in grog-shops,--during which conversation he would artfully introduce some bold remark on slavery; and sometimes, when, from the character he was conversing with, he found he might still be bolder, he would go so far, that, had not his declarations in such situations been clearly proved, they would scarcely have been credited. He continued this course until some time after the commencement of the last winter; by which time he had not only obtained incredible influence amongst persons of color, but many feared him more than their owners, and, one of them declared, even more than his God."

It was proved against him, that his house had been the principal place of meeting for the conspirators, that all the others habitually referred to him as the leader, and that he had shown great address in dealing with different temperaments and overcoming a variety of scruples. One witness testified that Vesey had read to him from the Bible about the deliverance of the children of Israel; another, that he had read to him a speech which had been delivered "in Congress by a Mr. King" on the subject of slavery, and Vesey had said that "this Mr. King was the black man's friend; that he, Mr. King, had declared he would continue to speak, write, and publish pamphlets against slavery the longest day he lived, until the Southern States consented to emancipate their slaves, for that slavery was a great disgrace to the country." But among all the reports there are only two sentences which really reveal the secret soul of Denmark Vesey, and show his impulses and motives. "He said he did not go with Creighton to Africa, because he had not a will; he wanted to stay and see what he could do for his fellow-creatures." The other takes us still nearer home. Monday Gell stated in his confession, that Vesey, on first broaching the plan to him, said "he was satisfied with his own condition, being free; but, as all his children were slaves, he wished to see what could be done for them."

It is strange to turn from this simple statement of a perhaps intelligent preference, on the part of a parent, for seeing his offspring in a condition of freedom, to the *naïve* astonishment of his judges. "It is difficult to imagine," says the sentence finally passed on Denmark Vesey, "what infatuation could have prompted you to attempt an enterprise so wild and visionary. You were a free man, comparatively wealthy, and enjoyed every comfort compatible with your situation. You had, therefore, much to risk and little to gain." Yet one witness testified: "Vesey said the negroes were living such an abominable life, they ought to rise. I said, I was living well; he said, though I was, others were not, and that 'twas such fools as I that were in the way and would not help them, and that after all things were well he would mark me." "His general conversation," said another witness, a white boy, "was about religion, which he would apply to slavery; as, for instance, he would speak of the creation of the world, in which he would say all men had equal rights, blacks as well as whites, etc.; all his religious remarks were mingled with slavery." And the firmness of this purpose did not leave him, even after the betrayal of his cherished plans. "After the plot was discovered," said Monday Gell, in his confession, "Vesey said it was all over, unless an attempt were made to rescue those who might be condemned, by rushing on the people and saving the prisoners, or all dying together."

The only person to divide with Vesey the claim of leadership was Peter Poyas. Vesey was the missionary of the cause, but Peter was the organizing mind. He kept the register of "candidates," and decided who should or should not be enrolled. "We can't live so," he often reminded his confederates; "we must break the yoke." "God has a hand in it; we have been meeting for four years, and are not yet betrayed." Peter was a ship-carpenter, and a slave of great value. He was to be the military leader. His plans showed some natural generalship: he arranged the night-attack; he planned the enrolment of a mounted troop to scour the streets; and he had a list of all the shops where arms and ammunition were kept for sale. He voluntarily undertook the management of the most difficult part of the enterprise,--the capture of the main guard-house,--and had pledged himself to advance alone and surprise the sentinel. He was said to have a magnetism in his eyes, of which his confederates stood in great awe; if he once got his eye upon a man, there was no resisting it. A white witness has since narrated, that, after his arrest, he was chained to the floor in a cell, with another of the conspirators. Men in authority came, and sought by promises, threats, and even tortures, to ascertain the names of other accomplices. His companion, wearied out with pain and suffering, and stimulated by the hope of saving his own life, at last began to yield. Peter raised himself, leaned upon his elbow, looked at the poor fellow, saying quietly, "Die like a man," and instantly lay down again. It was enough; not another word was extorted.

One of the most notable individuals in the plot was a certain Jack Purcell, commonly called Gullah Jack,--Gullah signifying Angola, the place of his origin. A conjurer by profession and by lineal heritage in his own country, he had resumed the practice of his vocation on this side the Atlantic. For fifteen years he had wielded in secret an immense influence among a sable constituency in Charleston; and as he had the reputation of being invulnerable, and of teaching invulnerability as an art, he was very good at beating up recruits for insurrection. Over those of Angolese descent, especially, he was a perfect king, and made them join in the revolt as one man. They met him monthly at a place called Bulkley's Farm, selected because the black overseer on that plantation was one of the initiated, and because the farm was accessible by water, thus enabling them to elude the patrol. There they prepared cartridges and pikes, and had primitive banquets, which assumed a melodramatic character under the inspiriting guidance of Jack. If a fowl was privately roasted, that mystic individual muttered incantations over it; and then they all grasped at it, exclaiming, "Thus we pull Buckra to pieces!" He gave them parched corn and ground-nuts to be eaten as internal safeguards on the day before the outbreak, and a consecrated *cullah*, or crab's claw, to be carried in the mouth by each, as an amulet. These rather questionable means secured him a power which was very unquestionable; the witnesses examined in his presence all showed dread of his conjurations, and referred to him indirectly, with a kind of awe, as "the little man who can't be shot."

When Gullah Jack was otherwise engaged, there seems to have been a sort of deputy seer employed in the enterprise, a blind man named Philip. He was a preacher; was said to have been born with a caul on his head, and so claimed the gift of second-sight. Timid adherents were brought to his house for ghostly counsel. "Why do you look so timorous?" he said to William Garner, and then quoted Scripture, "Let not your heart be troubled." That a blind man should know how he looked, was beyond the philosophy of the visitor; and this piece of rather cheap ingenuity carried the day.

Other leaders were appointed also. Monday Gell was the scribe of the enterprise; he was a native African, who had learned to read and write. He was by trade a harness-maker, working chiefly on his own account. He confessed that he had written a letter to President Boyer of the new black republic; "the letter was about the sufferings of the blacks, and to know if the people of St. Domingo would help them if they made an effort to free themselves." This epistle was sent by the black cook of a Northern schooner, and the envelope was addressed to a relative of the bearer.

Tom Russell was the armorer, and made pikes "on a very improved model," the official report admits. Polydore Faber fitted the weapons with handles. Bacchus Hammett had charge of the fire-arms and ammunition, not as yet a laborious duty. William Garner and Mingo Harth were to lead the horse-company. Lot Forrester was the courier, and had done, no one ever knew how much, in the way of enlisting country negroes, of whom Ned Bennett was to take command when enlisted. Being the governor's servant, Ned was probably credited with some official experience. These were the officers: now for the plan of attack.

It was the custom then, as later, for the country negroes to flock largely into Charleston on Sunday. More than a thousand came, on ordinary occasions, and a far larger number might at any time make their appearance without exciting any suspicion.

They gathered in, especially by water, from the opposite sides of Ashley and Cooper Rivers, and from the neighboring islands; and they came in a great number of canoes of various sizes,--many of which could carry a hundred men,--which were ordinarily employed in bringing agricultural products to the Charleston market. To get an approximate knowledge of the number, the city government once ordered the persons thus arriving to be counted,--and that during the progress of the trials, at a time when the negroes were rather fearful of coming into town; and it was found, that, even then, there were more than five hundred visitors on a single Sunday. This fact, then, was the essential point in the plan of insurrection. Whole plantations were found to have been enlisted among the "candidates," as they were termed; and it was proved that the city negroes, who lived nearest the place of meeting, had agreed to conceal these confederates in their houses to a large extent, on the night of the proposed outbreak.

The details of the plan, however, were not rashly committed to the mass of the confederates; they were known only to a few, and were finally to be announced only after the evening prayer-meetings on the appointed Sunday. But each leader had his own company enlisted, and his own work marked out. When the clock struck twelve, all were to move. Peter Poyas was to lead a party ordered to assemble at South Bay, and to be joined by a force from James's Island; he was then to march up and seize the arsenal and guard-house opposite St. Michael's Church, and detach a sufficient number to cut off all white citizens who should appear at the alarm-posts. A second body of negroes, from the country and the Neck, headed by Ned Bennett, was to assemble on the Neck, and seize the arsenal there. A third was to meet at Gov. Bennett's Mills, under command of Rolla, and, after putting the governor and intendant to death, to march through the city, or be posted at Cannon's Bridge, thus preventing the inhabitants of Cannonsborough from entering the city. A fourth, partly from the country, and partly from the neighboring localities in the city, was to rendezvous on Gadsden's Wharf, and attack the upper guard-house. A fifth, composed of country and Neck negroes, was to assemble at Bulkley's Farm, two miles and a half from the city, seize the upper powder-magazine, and then march down; and a sixth was to assemble at Denmark Vesey's, and obey his orders. A seventh detachment, under Gullah Jack, was to assemble in Boundary Street, at the head of King Street, to capture the arms of the Neck company of militia, and to take an additional supply from Mr. Duquercron's shop. The naval stores on Mey's Wharf were also to be attacked. Meanwhile, a horse-company, consisting of many draymen, hostlers, and butcher-boys, was to meet at Lightwood's Alley, and then scour the streets to prevent the whites from assembling. Every white man coming out of his own door was to be killed; and, if necessary, the city was to be fired in several places,--slow-match for this purpose having been purloined from the public arsenal, and placed in an accessible position.

Beyond this, the plan of action was either unformed or undiscovered; some slight reliance seems to have been placed on English aid,--more on assistance from St. Domingo. At any rate, all the ships in the harbor were to be seized; and in these, if the worst came to the worst, those most deeply inculpated could set sail, bearing with them, perhaps, the spoils of shops and of banks. It seems to be admitted by the official narrative, that they might have been able, at that season of the year, and with the aid of the fortifications on the Neck and around the harbor, to retain possession of the city for some time.

So unsuspicious were the authorities, so unprepared the citizens, so open to attack lay the city, that nothing seemed necessary to the success of the insurgents except organization and arms. Indeed, the plan of organization easily covered a supply of arms. By their own contributions they had secured enough to strike the first blow,--a few hundred pikes and daggers, together with swords and guns for the leaders. But they had carefully marked every place in the city where weapons were to be obtained. On King-street Road, beyond the municipal limits, in a common wooden shop, were left unguarded the arms of the Neck company of militia, to the number of several hundred stand; and these were to be secured by Bacchus Hammett, whose master kept the establishment. In Mr. Duquercron's shop there were deposited for sale as many more weapons; and they had noted Mr. Schirer's shop in Queen Street, and other gunsmiths' establishments. Finally, the State arsenal in Meeting Street, a building with no defences except ordinary wooden doors, was to be seized early in the outbreak. Provided, therefore, that the first moves proved successful, all the rest appeared sure.

Very little seems to have been said among the conspirators in regard to any plans of riot or debauchery, subsequent to the capture of the city. Either their imaginations did not dwell on them, or the witnesses did not dare to give testimony, or the authorities to print it. Death was to be dealt out, comprehensive and terrible; but nothing more is mentioned. One prisoner, Rolla, is reported in the evidence to have dropped hints in regard to the destiny of the women; and there was a rumor in the newspapers of the time, that he or some other of Gov. Bennett's slaves was to have taken the governor's daughter, a young girl of sixteen, for his wife, in the event of success; but this is all. On the other hand, Denmark Vesey was known to be for a war of immediate and total extermination; and when some of the company opposed killing "the ministers and the women and children," Vesey read from the Scriptures that all should be cut off, and said that "it was for their safety not to leave one white skin alive, for this was the plan they pursued at St. Domingo." And all this was not a mere dream of one lonely enthusiast, but a measure which had been maturing for four full years among several confederates, and had been under discussion for five months among multitudes of initiated "candidates."

As usual with slave-insurrections, the best men and those most trusted were deepest in the plot. Rolla was the only prominent conspirator who was not an active church-member. "Most of the ringleaders," says a Charleston letter-writer of that day, "were the rulers or class-leaders in what is called the African Society, and were considered faithful, honest fellows. Indeed, many of the owners could not be convinced, till the fellows confessed themselves, that they were concerned, and that the first object of all was to kill their masters." And the first official report declares that it would not be difficult to assign a motive for the insurrectionists, "if it had not been distinctly proved, that, with scarcely an exception, they had no individual hardship to complain of, and were among the most humanely treated negroes in the city. The facilities for combining and confederating in such a scheme were amply afforded by the extreme indulgence and kindness which characterize the domestic treatment of our slaves. Many slave-owners among us, not satisfied with ministering to the wants of their domestics by all the comforts of abundant food and excellent clothing, with a misguided benevolence have not only permitted their instruction, but lent to such efforts their approbation and applause."

"I sympathize most sincerely," says the anonymous author of a pamphlet of the period, "with the very respectable and pious clergyman whose heart must still bleed at the recollection that his confidential class-leader, but a week or two before his just conviction, had received the communion of the Lord's Supper from his hand. This wretch had been brought up in his pastor's family, and was treated with the same Christian attention as was shown to their own children." "To us who are accustomed to the base and proverbial ingratitude of these people, this ill return of kindness and confidence is not surprising; but they who are ignorant of their real character will read and wonder."

One demonstration of this "Christian attention" had lately been the closing of the African Church,--of which, as has been stated, most of the leading revolutionists were members,--on the ground that it tended to spread the dangerous infection of the alphabet. On Jan. 15, 1821, the city marshal, John J. Lafar, had notified "ministers of the gospel and others who keep night--and Sunday-schools for slaves, that the education of such persons is forbidden by law, and that the city government feel imperiously bound to enforce the penalty." So that there were some special as well as general grounds for disaffection among these ungrateful favorites of fortune, the slaves. Then there were fancied dangers. An absurd report had somehow arisen,--since you cannot keep men ignorant without making them unreasonable also,--that on the ensuing Fourth of July the whites were to create a false alarm, and that every black man coming out was to be killed, "in order to thin them;" this being done to prevent their joining an imaginary army supposed to be on its way from Hayti. Others were led to suppose that Congress had ended the Missouri Compromise discussion by making them all free, and that the law would protect their liberty if they could only secure it. Others, again, were threatened with the vengeance of the conspirators, unless they also joined; on the night of attack, it was said, the initiated would have a countersign, and all who did not know it would share the fate of the whites. Add to this the reading of Congressional speeches, and of the copious magazine of revolution to be found in the Bible,--and it was no wonder, if they for the first time were roused, under the energetic leadership of Vesey, to a full consciousness of their own condition.

"Not only were the leaders of good character, and very much indulged by their owners; but this was very generally the case with all who were convicted,--many of them possessing the highest confidence of their owners, and not one of bad character." In one case it was proved that Vesey had forbidden his followers to trust a certain man, because he had once been seen intoxicated. In another case it was shown that a slave named George had made every effort to obtain their confidence, but was constantly excluded from their meetings as a talkative fellow who could not be trusted,--a policy which his levity of manner, when examined in court, fully justified. They took no women into counsel,--not from any distrust apparently, but in order that their children might not be left uncared-for in case of defeat and destruction. House-servants were rarely trusted, or only when they had been carefully sounded by the chief leaders. Peter Poyas, in commissioning an agent to enlist men, gave him excellent cautions: "Don't mention it to those waiting-men who receive presents of old coats, etc., from their masters, or they'll betray us; I will speak to them." When he did speak, if he did not convince them, he at least frightened them. But the chief reliance was on those slaves who were hired out, and therefore more uncontrolled,--and also upon the country negroes.

The same far-sighted policy directed the conspirators to disarm suspicion by peculiarly obedient and orderly conduct. And it shows the precaution with which the thing was carried on, that, although Peter Poyas was proved to have had a list of some six hundred persons, yet not one of his particular company was ever brought to trial. As each leader kept to himself the names of his proselytes, and as Monday Gell was the only one of these leaders who turned traitor, any opinion as to the numbers actually engaged must be altogether conjectural.

One witness said nine thousand; another, six thousand six hundred. These statements were probably extravagant, though not more so than Gov. Bennett's assertion, on the other side, that "all who were actually concerned had been brought to justice,"--unless by this phrase he designates only the ringleaders. The avowed aim of the governor's letter, indeed, is to smooth the thing over, for the credit and safety of the city; and its evasive tone contrasts strongly with the more frank and thorough statements of the judges, made after the thing could no longer be hushed up. These high authorities explicitly acknowledge that they had failed to detect more than a small minority of those concerned in the project, and seem to admit, that, if it had once been brought to a head, the slaves generally would have joined in.

"We cannot venture to say," says the intendant's pamphlet, "to how many the knowledge of the intended effort was communicated, who without signifying their assent, or attending any of the meetings, were yet prepared to profit by events. That there are many who would not have permitted the enterprise to have failed at a critical moment, for the want of their co-operation, we have the best reason for believing." So believed the community at large; and the panic was in proportion, when the whole danger was finally made public. "The scenes I witnessed," says one who has since narrated the circumstances, "and the declaration of the impending danger that met us at all times and on all occasions, forced the conviction that never were an entire people more thoroughly alarmed than were the people of Charleston at that time.... During the excitement, and the trial of the supposed conspirators, rumor proclaimed all, and doubtless more than all, the horrors of the plot. The city was to be fired in every quarter; the arsenal in the immediate vicinity was to be broken open, and the arms distributed to the insurgents, and a universal massacre of the white inhabitants to take place. Nor did there seem to be any doubt in the mind of the people, that such would actually have been the result had not the plot fortunately been detected before the time appointed for the outbreak. It was believed, as a matter of course, that every black in the city would join in the insurrection, and that if the original design had been attempted, and the city taken by surprise, the negroes would have achieved a complete and easy victory. Nor does it seem at all impossible that such might have been, or yet may be, the case, if any well-arranged and resolute rising should take place."

Indeed, this universal admission, that all the slaves were ready to take part in any desperate enterprise, was one of the most startling aspects of the affair. The authorities say that the two principal State's evidence declared that "they never spoke to any person of color on the subject, or knew of any one who had been spoken to by the other leaders, who had withheld his assent." And the conspirators seem to have been perfectly satisfied that all the remaining slaves would enter their ranks upon the slightest success. "Let us assemble a sufficient number to commence the work with spirit, and we'll not want men; they'll fall in behind us fast enough." And as an illustration of this readiness, the official report mentions a slave who had belonged to one master for sixteen years, sustaining a high character for fidelity and affection, who had twice travelled with him through the Northern States, resisting every solicitation to escape, and who yet was very deeply concerned in the insurrection, though knowing it to involve the probable destruction of the whole family with whom he lived.

One singular circumstance followed the first rumors of the plot. Several white men, said to be of low and unprincipled character, at once began to make interest with the supposed leaders among the slaves, either from genuine sympathy, or with the intention of betraying them for money, or by profiting by the insurrection, should it succeed. Four of these were brought to trial; but the official report expresses the opinion that many more might have been discovered but for the inadmissibility of slave testimony against whites. Indeed, the evidence against even these four was insufficient for a capital conviction, although one was overheard, through stratagem, by the intendant himself, and arrested on the spot. This man was a Scotchman, another a Spaniard, a third a German, and the fourth a Carolinian. The last had for thirty years kept a shop in the neighborhood of Charleston; he was proved to have asserted that "the negroes had as much right to fight for their liberty as the white people," had offered to head them in the enterprise, and had said that in three weeks he would have two thousand men. But in no case, it appears, did these men obtain the confidence of the slaves; and the whole plot was conceived and organized, so far as appears, without the slightest co-operation from any white man.

The trial of the conspirators began on Wednesday, June 19. At the request of the intendant, Justices Kennedy and Parker summoned five freeholders (Messrs. Drayton, Heyward, Pringle, Legaré, and Turnbull) to constitute a court, under the provisions of the Act "for the better ordering and governing negroes and other slaves." The intendant laid the case before them, with a list of prisoners and witnesses. By a vote of the court, all spectators were excluded, except the owners and counsel of the slaves concerned. No other colored person was allowed to enter the jail, and a strong guard of soldiers was kept always on duty around the building. Under these general arrangements the trials proceeded with elaborate formality, though with some variations from ordinary usage,--as was, indeed, required by the statute.

For instance, the law provided that the testimony of any Indian or slave could be received, without oath, against a slave or free colored person, although it was not valid, even under oath, against a white. But it is best to quote the official language in respect to the rules adopted: "As the court had been organized under a statute of a peculiar and local character, and intended for the government of a distinct class of persons in the community, they were bound to conform their proceedings to its provisions, which depart in many essential features from the principles of the common law and some of the settled rules of evidence. The court, however, determined to adopt those rules, whenever they were not repugnant to nor expressly excepted by that statute, nor inconsistent with the local situation and policy of the State; and laid down for their own government the following regulations: First, that no slave should be tried except in the presence of his owner or his counsel, and that notice should be given in every case at least one day before the trial; second, that the testimony of one witness, unsupported by additional evidence or by circumstances, should lead to no conviction of a capital nature; third, that the witnesses should be confronted with the accused and with each other in every case, except where testimony was given under a solemn pledge that the names of the witnesses should not be divulged,--as they declared, in some instances, that they apprehended being murdered by the blacks, if it was known that they had volunteered their evidence; fourth, that the prisoners might be represented by counsel, whenever this was requested by the owners of the slaves, or by the prisoners themselves if free; fifth, that the statements or defences of the accused should be heard in every case, and they be permitted themselves to examine any witness they thought proper."

It is singular to observe how entirely these rules seem to concede that a slave's life has no sort of value to himself, but only to his master. His master, not he himself, must choose whether it be worth while to employ counsel. His master, not his mother or his wife, must be present at the trial. So far is this carried, that the provision to exclude "persons who had no particular interest in the slaves accused" seems to have excluded every acknowledged relative they had in the world, and admitted only those who had invested in them so many dollars. And yet the very first section of that part of the statute under which they were tried lays down an explicit recognition of their humanity: "And whereas natural justice forbids that any *person*, of what condition soever, should be condemned unheard." So thoroughly, in the whole report, are the ideas of person and chattel intermingled, that when Gov. Bennett petitions for mitigation of sentence in the case of his slave Batteau, and closes, "I ask this, gentlemen, as an individual incurring a severe and distressing loss," it is really impossible to decide whether the predominant emotion be affectional or financial.

It is a matter of painful necessity to acknowledge that the proceedings of most slave-tribunals have justified the honest admission of Gov. Adams of South Carolina, in his legislative message of 1855: "The administration of our laws, in relation to our colored population, by our courts of magistrates and freeholders, as these courts are at present constituted, calls loudly for reform. Their decisions are rarely in conformity with justice or humanity." This trial, as reported by the justices themselves, seems to have been no worse than the average,-- perhaps better. In all, thirty-five were sentenced to death, thirty-four to transportation, twenty-seven acquitted by the court, and twenty-five discharged without trial, by the

Committee of Vigilance,--making in all one hundred and twenty-one.

The sentences pronounced by Judge Kennedy upon the leading rebels, while paying a high tribute to their previous character, of course bring all law and all Scripture to prove the magnitude of their crime. "It is a melancholy fact," he says, "that those servants in whom we reposed the most unlimited confidence have been the principal actors in this wicked scheme." Then he rises into earnest appeals. "Are you incapable of the heavenly influence of that gospel, all whose paths are peace? It was to reconcile us to our destiny on earth, and to enable us to discharge with fidelity all our duties, whether as master or servant, that those inspired precepts were imparted by Heaven to fallen man."

To these reasonings the prisoners had, of course, nothing to say; but the official reports bear the strongest testimony to their fortitude. "Rolla, when arraigned, affected not to understand the charge against him, and, when it was at his request further explained to him, assumed, with wonderful adroitness, astonishment and surprise. He was remarkable, throughout his trial, for great presence and composure of mind. When he was informed he was convicted, and was advised to prepare for death, though he had previously (but after his trial) confessed his guilt, he appeared perfectly confounded, but exhibited no signs of fear. In Ned's behavior there was nothing remarkable; but his countenance was stern and immovable, even whilst he was receiving the sentence of death: from his looks it was impossible to discover or conjecture what were his feelings. Not so with Peter: for in his countenance were strongly marked disappointed ambition, revenge, indignation, and an anxiety to know how far the discoveries had extended; and the same emotions were exhibited in his conduct. He did not appear to fear personal consequences, for his whole behavior indicated the reverse; but exhibited an evident anxiety for the success of their plan, in which his whole soul was embarked. His countenance and behavior were the same when he received his sentence; and his only words were, on retiring, 'I suppose you'll let me see my wife and family before I die?' and that not in a supplicating tone. When he was asked, a day or two after, if it was possible he could wish to see his master and family murdered, who had treated him so kindly, he only replied to the question by a smile. Monday's behavior was not peculiar. When he was before the court, his arms were folded; he heard the testimony given against him, and received his sentence, with the utmost firmness and composure. But no description can accurately convey to others the impression which the trial, defence, and appearance of Gullah Jack made on those who witnessed the workings of his cunning and rude address. When arrested and brought before the court, in company with another African named Jack, the property of the estate of Pritchard, he assumed so much ignorance, and looked and acted the fool so well, that some of the court could not believe that this was the necromancer who was sought after. This conduct he continued when on his trial, until he saw the witnesses and heard the testimony as it progressed against him; when, in an instant, his countenance was lighted up as if by lightning, and his wildness and vehemence of gesture, and the malignant glance with which he eyed the witnesses who appeared against him, all indicated the savage, who indeed had been *caught*, but not *tamed*. His courage, however, soon forsook him. When he received sentence of death, he earnestly implored that a fortnight longer might be allowed him, and then a week longer, which he continued earnestly to solicit until he was taken from the court-room to his cell; and when he was carried to execution, he gave up his spirit without firmness or composure."

Not so with Denmark Vesey. The plans of years were frustrated; his own life and liberty were thrown away; many others were sacrificed through his leadership; and one more was added to the list of unsuccessful insurrections. All these disastrous certainties he faced calmly, and gave his whole mind composedly to the conducting of his defence. With his arms tightly folded, and his eyes fixed on the floor, he attentively followed every item of the testimony. He heard the witnesses examined by the court, and cross-examined by his own counsel; and it is evident from the narrative of the presiding judge, that he showed no small skill and policy in the searching cross-examination which he then applied. The fears, the feelings, the consciences, of those who had betrayed him, all were in turn appealed to; but the facts were quite overpowering, and it was too late to aid his comrades or himself. Then turning to the court, he skilfully availed himself of the point which had so much impressed the community: the intrinsic improbability that a man in his position of freedom and prosperity should sacrifice every thing to free other people. If they thought it so incredible, why not give him the benefit of the incredibility? The act being, as they stated, one of infatuation, why convict him of it on the bare word of men who, by their own showing, had not only shared the infatuation, but proved traitors to it? An ingenious defence,--indeed, the only one which could by any possibility be suggested, anterior to the days of Choate and somnambulism; but in vain. He was sentenced; and it was not, apparently, till the judge reproached him for the destruction he had brought on his followers, that he showed any sign of emotion. Then the tears came into his eyes. But he said not another word.

The executions took place on five different days; and, bad as they were, they might have been worse. After the imaginary Negro Plot of New York, in 1741, thirteen negroes had been judicially burned alive; two had suffered the same sentence at Charleston in 1808; and it was undoubtedly some mark of progress, that in this case the gallows took the place of the flames. Six were hanged on July 2, upon Blake's lands, near Charleston,--Denmark Vesey, Peter Poyas, Jesse, Ned, Rolla, and Batteau,--the last three being slaves of the governor himself. Gullah Jack and John were executed "on the Lines," near Charleston, on July 12; and twenty-two more on July 26. Four others suffered their fate on July 30; and one more, William Garner, effected a temporary escape, was captured, and tried by a different court, and was finally executed on Aug. 9.

The self-control of these men did not desert them at their execution. When the six leaders suffered death, the report says, Peter Poyas repeated his charge of secrecy: "Do not open your lips; die silent, as you shall see me do;" and all obeyed. And though afterwards, as the particulars of the plot became better known, there was less inducement to conceal, yet every one of the thirty-five seems to have met his fate bravely, except the conjurer. Gov. Bennett, in his letter, expresses much dissatisfaction at the small amount learned from the participators. "To the last hour of the existence of several who appeared to be conspicuous actors in the drama, they were pressingly importuned to make further confessions,"--this "importuning" being more clearly defined in a letter of Mr. Ferguson, owner of two of the slaves, as "having them severely corrected." Yet so little was obtained, that the governor was compelled to admit at last that the really essential features of the plot were not known to any of the informers.

It is to be remembered, that the plot failed because a man unauthorized and incompetent, William Paul, undertook to make enlistments on his own account. He happened on one of precisely that class of men,--favored house-servants,--whom his leaders had expressly reserved for more skilful manipulations. He being thus detected, one would have supposed that the discovery of many accomplices would at once have followed. The number enlisted was counted by thousands; yet for twenty-nine days after the first treachery, and during twenty days of official examination, only fifteen of the conspirators were ferreted out. Meanwhile the informers' names had to be concealed with the utmost secrecy; they were in peril of their lives from the slaves,--William Paul scarcely dared to go beyond the doorstep,--and the names of important witnesses examined in June were still suppressed in the official report published in October. That a conspiracy on so large a scale should have existed in embryo during four years, and in an active form for several months, and yet have been so well managed, that, after actual betrayal, the authorities were again thrown off their guard, and the plot nearly brought to a head again,--this certainly shows extraordinary ability in the leaders, and a talent for concerted action on the part of slaves generally, with which they have hardly been credited.

And it is also to be noted, that the range of the conspiracy extended far beyond Charleston. It was proved that Frank, slave of Mr. Ferguson, living nearly forty miles from the city, had boasted of having enlisted four plantations in his immediate neighborhood. It was in evidence that the insurgents "were trying all round the country, from Georgetown and Santee round about to Combahee, to get people;" and, after the trials, it was satisfactorily established that Vesey "had been in the country as far north as South Santee, and southwardly as far as the Euhaws, which is between seventy and eighty miles from the city." Mr. Ferguson himself testified that the good order of any gang was no evidence of their ignorance of the plot, since the behavior of his own initiated slaves had been unexceptionable, in accordance with Vesey's directions.

With such an organization and such materials, there was nothing in the plan which could be pronounced incredible or impracticable. There is no reason why they should not have taken the city. After all the governor's entreaties as to moderate language, the authorities were obliged to admit that South Carolina had been saved from a "horrible catastrophe." "For, although success could not possibly have attended the conspirators, yet, before their suppression, Charleston would probably have been wrapped in flames, many valuable lives would have been sacrificed, and an immense loss of property sustained by the citizens, even though no other distressing occurrences were experienced by them; while the plantations in the lower country would have been disorganized, and the agricultural interests have sustained an enormous loss." The Northern journals had already expressed still greater anxieties. "It appears," said the New-York *Commercial Advertiser*, "that, but for the timely disclosure, the whole of that State would in a few days have witnessed the horrid spectacle once witnessed in St. Domingo."

My friend, David Lee Child, has kindly communicated to me a few memoranda of a conversation held long since with a free colored man who had worked in Vesey's shop during the time of the insurrection; and these generally confirm the official narratives. "I was a young man then," he said; "and, owing to the policy of preventing communication between free colored people and slaves, I had little opportunity of ascertaining how the slaves felt about it. I know that several of them were abused in the street, and some put in prison, for appearing in sackcloth. There was an ordinance of the city, that any slave who wore a badge of mourning should be imprisoned and flogged. They generally got the law, which is thirty-nine lashes; but sometimes it was according to the decision of the court." "I heard, at the time, of arms being buried in coffins at Sullivan's Island." "In the time of the insurrection, the slaves were tried in a small room in the jail where they were confined. No colored person was allowed to go within two squares of the prison. Those two squares were filled with troops, five thousand of whom were on duty day and night. I was told, Vesey said to those that tried him, that the work of insurrection would go on; but as none but white persons were permitted to be present, I cannot tell whether he said it."

During all this time there was naturally a silence in the Charleston journals, which strongly contrasts with the extreme publicity at last given to the testimony. Even the *National Intelligencer*, at Washington, passed lightly over the affair, and deprecated the publication of particulars. The Northern editors, on the other hand, eager for items, were constantly complaining of this reserve, and calling for further intelligence. "The Charleston papers," said the Hartford *Courant* of July 16, "have been silent on the subject of the insurrection; but letters from this city state that it has created much alarm, and that two brigades of troops were under arms for some time to suppress any risings that might have taken place." "You will doubtless hear," wrote a Charleston correspondent of the same paper, just before, "many reports, and some exaggerated ones." "There was certainly a disposition to revolt, and some preparations made, principally by the plantation negroes, to take the city." "We hoped they would progress so far as to enable us to ascertain and punish the ringleaders." "Assure my friends that we feel in perfect security, although the number of nightly guards, and other demonstrations, may induce a belief among strangers to the contrary."

The strangers would have been very blind strangers, if they had not been more influenced by the actions of the Charleston citizens than by their words. The original information was given on May 25, 1822. The time passed, and the plot failed on June 16. A plan for its revival on July 2 proved abortive. Yet a letter from Charleston, in the Hartford *Courant* of Aug. 6, represented the panic as unabated: "Great preparations are making, and all the military are put in preparation to guard against any attempt of the same kind again; but we have no apprehension of its being repeated." On Aug. 10, Gov. Bennett wrote the letter already mentioned, which was printed and distributed as a circular, its object being to deprecate undue alarm. "Every individual in the State is interested, whether in regard to his own property, or the reputation of the State, in giving no more importance to the transaction than it justly merits." Yet, five days after this,--two months after the first danger had passed,--a re-enforcement of United-States troops arrived at Fort Moultrie; and, during the same month, several different attempts were made by small parties of armed negroes to capture the mails between Charleston and Savannah, and a reward of two hundred dollars was offered for their detection.

The first official report of the trials was prepared by the intendant, by request of the city council. It passed through four editions in a few months,--the first and fourth being published in Charleston, and the second and third in Boston. Being, however, but a brief pamphlet, it did not satisfy the public curiosity; and in October of the same year (1822), a larger volume appeared at Charleston, edited by the magistrates who presided at the trials,--Lionel H. Kennedy and Thomas Parker. It contains the evidence in full, and a separate narrative of the whole affair, more candid and lucid than any other which I have found in the newspapers or pamphlets of the day. It exhibits that rarest of all qualities in a slave-community, a willingness to look facts in the face. This narrative has been faithfully followed, with the aid of such cross-lights as could be secured from many other quarters, in preparing the present history.

The editor of the first official report racked his brains to discover the special causes of the revolt, and never trusted himself to allude to the general one. The negroes rebelled because they were deluded by Congressional eloquence; or because they were excited by a church squabble; or because they had been spoilt by mistaken indulgences, such as being allowed to learn to read,--"a misguided benevolence," as he pronounces it. So the Baptist Convention seems to have thought it was because they were not Baptists; and an Episcopal pamphleteer, because they were not Episcopalians. It never seems to occur to any of these spectators, that these people rebelled simply because they were slaves, and wished to be free.

No doubt, there were enough special torches with which a man so skilful as Denmark Vesey could kindle up these dusky powder-magazines; but, after all, the permanent peril lay in the powder. So long as that existed, every thing was incendiary. Any torn scrap in the street might contain a Missouri-

Compromise speech, or a report of the last battle in St. Domingo, or one of those able letters of Boyer's which were winning the praise of all, or one of John Randolph's stirring speeches in England against the slave-trade. The very newspapers which reported the happy extinction of the insurrection by the hanging of the last conspirator, William Garner, reported also, with enthusiastic indignation, the massacre of the Greeks at Constantinople and at Scio; and then the Northern editors, breaking from their usual reticence, pointed out the inconsistency of Southern journals in printing, side by side, denunciations of Mohammedan slave-sales, and advertisements of those of Christians.

Of course the insurrection threw the whole slavery question open to the public. "We are sorry to see," said the *National Intelligencer* of Aug. 31, "that a discussion of the hateful Missouri question is likely to be revived, in consequence of the allusions to its supposed effect in producing the late servile insurrection in South Carolina." A member of the Board of Public Works of South Carolina published in the Baltimore *American Farmer* an essay urging the encouragement of white laborers, and hinting at the ultimate abolition of slavery "if it should ever be thought desirable." More boldly still, a pamphlet appeared in Charleston, under the signature of "Achates," arguing with remarkable sagacity and force against the whole system of slave-labor *in towns*; and proposing that all slaves in Charleston should be sold or transferred to the plantations, and their places supplied by white labor. It is interesting to find many of the facts and arguments of Helper's "Impending Crisis" anticipated in this courageous tract, written under the pressure of a crisis which had just been so narrowly evaded. The author is described in the preface as "a soldier and patriot of the Revolution, whose name, did we feel ourselves at liberty to use it, would stamp a peculiar weight and value on his opinions." It was commonly attributed to Gen. Thomas Pinckney.

Another pamphlet of the period, also published in Charleston, recommended as a practical cure for insurrection the copious administration of Episcopal-Church services, and the prohibition of negroes from attending Fourth-of-July celebrations. On this last point it is more consistent than most pro-slavery arguments. "The celebration of the Fourth of July belongs *exclusively* to the white population of the United States. The American Revolution was a family quarrel among equals. In this the negroes had no concern; their condition remained, and must remain, unchanged. They have no more to do with the celebration of that day than with the landing of the Pilgrims on the rock at Plymouth. It therefore seems to me improper to allow these people to be present on these occasions. In our speeches and orations, much, and sometimes more than is politically necessary, is said about personal liberty, which negro auditors know not how to apply except by running the parallel with their own condition. They therefore imbibe false notions of their own personal rights, and give reality in their minds to what has no real existence. The peculiar state of our community must be steadily kept in view. This, I am gratified to learn, will in some measure be promoted by the institution of the South Carolina Association."

On the other hand, more stringent laws became obviously necessary to keep down the advancing intelligence of the Charleston slaves. Dangerous knowledge must be excluded from without and from within. For the first purpose the South Carolina Legislature passed, in December, 1822, the Act for the imprisonment of Northern colored seamen, which afterwards produced so much excitement. For the second object, the Grand Jury, about the same time, presented as a grievance "the number of schools which are kept within the city by persons of color," and proposed their prohibition. This was the encouragement given to the intellectual progress of the slaves; while, as a reward for betraying them, Pensil, the free colored man who advised with Devany, received a present of one thousand dollars; and Devany himself had what was rightly judged to be the higher gift of freedom, and was established in business, with liberal means, as a drayman. He lived long in Charleston, thriving greatly in his vocation, and, according to the newspapers, enjoyed the privilege of being the only man of property in the State whom a special statute exempted from taxation.

More than half a century has passed since the incidents of this true story closed. It has not vanished from the memories of South Carolinians, though the printed pages which once told it have gradually disappeared from sight. The intense avidity which at first grasped at every incident of the great insurrectionary plot was succeeded by a prolonged distaste for the memory of the tale; and the official reports which told what slaves had once planned and dared have now come to be among the rarest of American historical documents. In 1841, a friend of the writer, then visiting South Carolina, heard from her hostess, for the first time, the events which are recounted here. On asking to see the reports of the trials, she was cautiously told that the only copy in the house, after being carefully kept for years under lock and key, had been burnt at last, lest it should reach the dangerous eyes of the slaves. The same thing had happened, it was added, in many other families. This partially accounts for the great difficulty now to be found in obtaining a single copy of either publication; and this is why, to the readers of American history, Denmark Vesey and Peter Poyas have commonly been but the shadows of names.

NAT TURNER'S INSURRECTION

During the year 1831, up to the 23d of August, the Virginia newspapers seem to have been absorbed in the momentous problems which then occupied the minds of intelligent American citizens: What Gen. Jackson should do with the scolds, and what with the disreputables? should South Carolina be allowed to nullify? and would the wives of cabinet ministers call on Mrs. Eaton? It is an unfailing opiate to turn over the drowsy files of the Richmond *Enquirer*, until the moment when those dry and dusty pages are suddenly kindled into flame by the torch of Nat Turner. Then the terror flared on increasing, until the remotest Southern States were found shuddering at nightly rumors of insurrection; until far-off European colonies--Antigua, Martinique, Caraccas, Tortola--recognized by some secret sympathy the same epidemic alarms; until the very boldest words of freedom were reported as uttered in the Virginia House of Delegates with unclosed doors; until an obscure young man named Garrison was indicted at common law in North Carolina, and had a price set upon his head by the Legislature of Georgia.

Near the south-eastern border of Virginia, in Southampton

County, there is a neighborhood known as "The Cross Keys." It lies fifteen miles from Jerusalem, the county-town, or "court-house," seventy miles from Norfolk, and about as far from Richmond. It is some ten or fifteen miles from Murfreesborough in North Carolina, and about twenty-five from the Great Dismal Swamp. Up to Sunday, the 21st of August, 1831, there was nothing to distinguish it from any other rural, lethargic, slipshod Virginia neighborhood, with the due allotment of mansion-houses and log huts, tobacco-fields and "old-fields," horses, dogs, negroes, "poor white folks," so called, and other white folks, poor without being called so. One of these last was Joseph Travis, who had recently married the widow of one Putnam Moore, and had unfortunately wedded to himself her negroes also.

In the woods on the plantation of Joseph Travis, upon the Sunday just named, six slaves met at noon for what is called in the Northern States a picnic, and in the Southern a barbecue. The bill of fare was to be simple: one brought a pig, and another some brandy, giving to the meeting an aspect so cheaply convivial that no one would have imagined it to be the final consummation of a conspiracy which had been for six months in preparation. In this plot four of the men had been already initiated--Henry, Hark or Hercules, Nelson, and Sam. Two others were novices, Will and Jack by name. The party had remained together from twelve to three o'clock, when a seventh man joined them,--a short, stout, powerfully built person, of dark mulatto complexion, and strongly marked African features, but with a face full of expression and resolution. This was Nat Turner.

He was at this time nearly thirty-one years old, having been born on the 2nd of October, 1800. He had belonged originally to Benjamin Turner,--from whom he took his last name, slaves having usually no patronymic;--had then been transferred to Putnam Moore, and then to his present owner. He had, by his own account, felt himself singled out from childhood for some great work; and he had some peculiar marks on his person, which, joined to his mental precocity, were enough to occasion, among his youthful companions, a superstitious faith in his gifts and destiny. He had some mechanical ingenuity also; experimentalized very early in making paper, gunpowder, pottery, and in other arts, which, in later life, he was found thoroughly to understand. His moral faculties appeared strong, so that white witnesses admitted that he had never been known to swear an oath, to drink a drop of spirits, or to commit a theft. And, in general, so marked were his early peculiarities that people said "he had too much sense to be raised; and, if he was, he would never be of any use as a slave." This impression of personal destiny grew with his growth: he fasted, prayed, preached, read the Bible, heard voices when he walked behind his plough, and communicated his revelations to the awe-struck slaves. They told him, in return, that, "if they had his sense, they would not serve any master in the world."

The biographies of slaves can hardly be individualized; they belong to the class. We know bare facts; it is only the general experience of human beings in like condition which can clothe them with life. The outlines are certain, the details are inferential. Thus, for instance, we know that Nat Turner's young wife was a slave; we know that she belonged to a different master from himself; we know little more than this, but this is much. For this is equivalent to saying, that, by day or by night, her husband had no more power to protect her than the man who lies bound upon a plundered vessel's deck has power to protect his wife on board the pirate schooner disappearing in the horizon. She may be well treated, she may be outraged; it is in the powerlessness that the agony lies. There is, indeed, one thing more which we do know of this young woman: the Virginia newspapers state that she was tortured under the lash, after her husband's execution, to make her produce his papers: this is all.

What his private experiences and special privileges or wrongs may have been, it is therefore now impossible to say. Travis was declared to be "more humane and fatherly to his slaves than any man in the county;" but it is astonishing how often this phenomenon occurs in the contemporary annals of slave insurrections. The chairman of the county court also stated, in pronouncing sentence, that Nat Turner had spoken of his master as "only too indulgent;" but this, for some reason, does not appear in his printed Confession, which only says, "He was a kind master, and placed the greatest confidence in me." It is very possible that it may have been so, but the printed accounts of Nat Turner's person look suspicious: he is described in Gov. Floyd's proclamation as having a scar on one of his temples, also one on the back of his neck, and a large knot on one of the bones of his right arm, produced by a blow; and although these were explained away in Virginia newspapers as having been produced by fights with his companions, yet such affrays are entirely foreign to the admitted habits of the man. It must therefore remain an open question, whether the scars and the knot were produced by black hands or by white.

Whatever Nat Turner's experiences of slavery might have been, it is certain that his plans were not suddenly adopted, but that he had brooded over them for years. To this day there are traditions among the Virginia slaves of the keen devices of "Prophet Nat." If he was caught with lime and lampblack in hand, conning over a half-finished county-map on the barn-door, he was always "planning what to do if he were blind"; or, "studying how to get to Mr. Francis's house." When he had called a meeting of slaves, and some poor whites came eavesdropping, the poor whites at once became the subjects for discussion: he incidentally mentioned that the masters had been heard threatening to drive them away; one slave had been ordered to shoot Mr. Jones's pigs, another to tear down Mr. Johnson's fences. The poor whites, Johnson and Jones, ran home to see to their homesteads, and were better friends than ever to Prophet Nat.

He never was a Baptist preacher, though such vocation has often been attributed to him. The impression arose from his having immersed himself, during one of his periods of special enthusiasm, together with a poor white man named Brantley. "About this time," he says in his Confession, "I told these things to a white man, on whom it had a wonderful effect; and he ceased from his wickedness, and was attacked immediately with a cutaneous eruption, and the blood oozed from the pores of his skin, and after praying and fasting nine days he was healed. And the Spirit appeared to me again, and said, as the Saviour had been baptized, so should we be also; and when the white people would not let us be baptized by the church, we went down into the water together, in the sight of many who reviled us, and were baptized by the Spirit. After this I rejoiced greatly, and gave thanks to God."

The religious hallucinations narrated in his Confession seem to have been as genuine as the average of such things, and are very well expressed. The account reads quite like Jacob Behmen. He saw white spirits and black spirits contending in the skies; the sun was darkened, the thunder rolled. "And the Holy Ghost was with me, and said, 'Behold me as I stand in the heavens!' And I looked, and saw the forms of men in different attitudes. And there were lights in the sky, to which the children of darkness gave other names than what they really were; for they were the lights of the Saviour's hands, stretched forth from east to west, even as they were extended on the cross on Calvary, for the redemption of sinners." He saw drops of blood on the corn: this was Christ's blood, shed for man. He saw on the leaves in the woods letters and numbers and figures of men,--the same symbols which he had seen in the skies. On May 12, 1828, the Holy Spirit appeared to him, and proclaimed that the yoke of Jesus must fall on him, and he must fight against the serpent when the sign appeared. Then came an eclipse of the sun in February, 1831: this was the sign; then he must arise and prepare himself, and slay his enemies with their own weapons; then also the seal was removed from his lips, and then he confided his plans to four associates.

When he came, therefore, to the barbecue on the appointed

Sunday, and found not these four only, but two others, his first question to the intruders was, how they came thither. To this Will answered manfully, that his life was worth no more than the others, and "his liberty was as dear to him." This admitted him to confidence; and as Jack was known to be entirely under Hark's influence, the strangers were no bar to their discussion. Eleven hours they remained there, in anxious consultation: one can imagine those dusky faces, beneath the funereal woods, and amid the flickering of pine-knot torches, preparing that stern revenge whose shuddering echoes should ring through the land so long. Two things were at last decided: to begin their work that night; and to begin it with a massacre so swift and irresistible as to create in a few days more terror than many battles, and so spare the need of future bloodshed. "It was agreed that we should commence at home on that night, and, until we had armed and equipped ourselves and gained sufficient force, neither age nor sex was to be spared: which was invariably adhered to."

John Brown invaded Virginia with nineteen men, and with the avowed resolution to take no life but in self-defence. Nat Turner attacked Virginia from within, with six men, and with the determination to spare no life until his power was established. John Brown intended to pass rapidly through Virginia, and then retreat to the mountains. Nat Turner intended to "conquer Southampton County as the white men did in the Revolution, and then retreat, if necessary, to the Dismal Swamp." Each plan was deliberately matured; each was in its way practicable; but each was defeated by a single false step, as will soon appear.

We must pass over the details of horror, as they occurred during the next twenty-four hours. Swift and stealthy as Indians, the black men passed from house to house,--not pausing, not hesitating, as their terrible work went on. In one thing they were humaner than Indians, or than white men fighting against Indians: there was no gratuitous outrage beyond the death-blow itself, no insult, no mutilation; but in every house they entered, that blow fell on man, woman, and child,--nothing that had a white skin was spared. From every house they took arms and ammunition, and from a few money. On every plantation they found recruits: those dusky slaves, so obsequious to their master the day before, so prompt to sing and dance before his Northern visitors, were all swift to transform themselves into fiends of retribution now; show them sword or musket, and they grasped it, though it were an heirloom from Washington himself. The troop increased from house to house,--first to fifteen, then to forty, then to sixty. Some were armed with muskets, some with axes, some with scythes, some came on their masters' horses. As the numbers increased, they could be divided, and the awful work was carried on more rapidly still. The plan then was for an advanced guard of horsemen to approach each house at a gallop, and surround it till the others came up. Meanwhile, what agonies of terror must have taken place within, shared alike by innocent and by guilty! what memories of wrongs inflicted on those dusky creatures, by some,--what innocent participation, by others, in the penance! The outbreak lasted for but forty-eight hours; but, during that period, fifty-five whites were slain, without the loss of a single slave.

One fear was needless, which to many a husband and father must have intensified the last struggle. These negroes had been systematically brutalized from childhood; they had been allowed no legalized or permanent marriage; they had beheld around them an habitual licentiousness, such as can scarcely exist except under slavery; some of them had seen their wives and sisters habitually polluted by the husbands and the brothers of these fair white women who were now absolutely in their power. Yet I have looked through the Virginia newspapers of that time in vain for one charge of an indecent outrage on a woman against these triumphant and terrible slaves. Wherever they went, there went death, and that was all. It is reported by some of the contemporary newspapers, that a portion of this abstinence was the result of deliberate consultation among the insurrectionists; that some of them were resolved on taking the white women for wives, but were overruled by Nat Turner. If so, he is the only American slave-leader of whom we know certainly that he rose above the ordinary level of slave vengeance; and Mrs. Stowe's picture of Dred's purposes is then precisely typical of his: "Whom the Lord saith unto us, 'Smite,' them will we smite. We will not torment them with the scourge and fire, nor defile their women as they have done with ours.

But we will slay them utterly, and consume them from off the face of the earth."

When the number of adherents had increased to fifty or sixty, Nat Turner judged it time to strike at the county-seat, Jerusalem. Thither a few white fugitives had already fled, and couriers might thence be despatched for aid to Richmond and Petersburg, unless promptly intercepted. Besides, he could there find arms, ammunition, and money; though they had already obtained, it is dubiously reported, from eight hundred to one thousand dollars. On the way it was necessary to pass the plantation of Mr. Parker, three miles from Jerusalem. Some of the men wished to stop here and enlist some of their friends. Nat Turner objected, as the delay might prove dangerous; he yielded at last, and it proved fatal.

He remained at the gate with six or eight men; thirty or forty went to the house, half a mile distant. They remained too long, and he went alone to hasten them. During his absence a party of eighteen white men came up suddenly, dispersing the small guard left at the gate; and when the main body of slaves emerged from the house, they encountered, for the first time, their armed masters. The blacks halted; the whites advanced cautiously within a hundred yards, and fired a volley; on its being returned, they broke into disorder, and hurriedly retreated, leaving some wounded on the ground. The retreating whites were pursued, and were saved only by falling in with another band of fresh men from Jerusalem, with whose aid they turned upon the slaves, who in their turn fell into confusion. Turner, Hark, and about twenty men on horseback retreated in some order; the rest were scattered. The leader still planned to reach Jerusalem by a private way, thus evading pursuit; but at last decided to stop for the night, in the hope of enlisting additional recruits.

During the night the number increased again to forty, and they encamped on Major Ridley's plantation. An alarm took place during the darkness,--whether real or imaginary, does not appear,--and the men became scattered again. Proceeding to make fresh enlistments with the daylight, they were resisted at Dr. Blunt's house, where his slaves, under his orders, fired upon them; and this, with a later attack from a party of white men near Capt. Harris's, so broke up the whole force that they never re-united. The few who remained together agreed to separate for a few hours to see if any thing could be done to revive the insurrection, and meet again that evening at their original rendezvous. But they never reached it.

Gloomily came Nat Turner at nightfall into those gloomy woods where forty-eight hours before he had revealed the details of his terrible plot to his companions. At the outset all his plans had succeeded; every thing was as he predicted: the slaves had come readily at his call; the masters had proved perfectly defenceless. Had he not been persuaded to pause at Parker's plantation, he would have been master before now of the arms and ammunition at Jerusalem; and with these to aid, and the Dismal Swamp for a refuge, he might have sustained himself indefinitely against his pursuers.

Now the blood was shed, the risk was incurred, his friends were killed or captured, and all for what? Lasting memories of terror, to be sure, for his oppressors; but, on the other hand, hopeless failure for the insurrection, and certain death for him. What a watch he must have kept that night! To that excited imagination, which had always seen spirits in the sky and blood-drops on the corn and hieroglyphic marks on the dry leaves, how full the lonely forest must have been of signs and solemn warnings! Alone with the fox's bark, the rabbit's rustle, and the screech-owl's scream, the self-appointed prophet brooded over his despair. Once creeping to the edge of the wood, he saw men stealthily approach on horseback. He fancied them some of his companions; but before he dared to whisper their ominous names, "Hark" or "Dred,"--for the latter was the name, since famous, of one of his more recent recruits,--he saw them to be white men, and shrank back stealthily beneath his covert.

There he waited two days and two nights,--long enough to satisfy himself that no one would rejoin him, and that the insurrection had hopelessly failed. The determined, desperate spirits who had shared his plans were scattered forever, and longer delay would be destruction for him also. He found a spot which he judged safe, dug a hole under a pile of fence-rails in a field, and lay there for six weeks, only leaving it for a few moments at midnight to obtain water from a neighboring spring. Food he had previously provided, without discovery, from a house near by.

Meanwhile an unbounded variety of rumors went flying through the State. The express which first reached the governor announced that the militia were retreating before the slaves. An express to Petersburg further fixed the number of militia at three hundred, and of blacks at eight hundred, and invented a convenient shower of rain to explain the dampened ardor of the whites. Later reports described the slaves as making three desperate attempts to cross the bridge over the Nottoway between Cross Keys and Jerusalem, and stated that the leader had been shot in the attempt. Other accounts put the number of negroes at three hundred, all well mounted and armed, with two or three white men as leaders. Their intention was supposed to be to reach the Dismal Swamp, and they must be hemmed in from that side.

Indeed, the most formidable weapon in the hands of slave insurgents is always this blind panic they create, and the wild exaggerations which follow. The worst being possible, every one takes the worst for granted. Undoubtedly a dozen armed men could have stifled this insurrection, even after it had commenced operations; but it is the fatal weakness of a rural slaveholding community, that it can never furnish men promptly for such a purpose. "My first intention was," says one of the most intelligent newspaper narrators of the affair, "to have attacked them with thirty or forty men; but those who had families here were strongly opposed to it."

As usual, each man was pinioned to his own hearth-stone. As usual, aid had to be summoned from a distance; and, as usual, the United-States troops were the chief reliance. Col. House, commanding at Fort Monroe, sent at once three companies of artillery under Lieut.-Col. Worth, and embarked them on board the steamer "Hampton" for Suffolk. These were joined by detachments from the United States ships "Warren" and "Natchez," the whole amounting to nearly eight hundred men. Two volunteer companies went from Richmond, four from Petersburg, one from Norfolk, one from Portsmouth, and several from North Carolina. The militia of Norfolk, Nansemond, and Princess Anne Counties, and the United States troops at Old Point Comfort, were ordered to scour the Dismal Swamp, where it was believed that two or three thousand fugitives were preparing to join the insurgents. It was even proposed to send two companies from New York and one from New London to the same point.

When these various forces reached Southampton County, they found all labor paralyzed and whole plantations abandoned. A letter from Jerusalem, dated Aug. 24, says, "The oldest inhabitant of our county has never experienced such a distressing time as we have had since Sunday night last.... Every house, room, and corner in this place is full of women and children, driven from home, who had to take the woods until they could get to this place." "For many miles around their track," says another "the county is deserted by women and children." Still another writes, "Jerusalem is full of women, most of them from the other side of the river,--about two hundred at Vix's." Then follow descriptions of the sufferings of these persons, many of whom had lain night after night in the woods. But the immediate danger was at an end, the short-lived insurrection was finished, and now the work of vengeance was to begin. In the frank phrase of a North Carolina correspondent, "The massacre of the whites was over, and the white people had commenced the destruction of the negroes, which was continued after our men got there, from time to time, as they could fall in with them, all day yesterday." A postscript adds, that "passengers by the Fayetteville stage say, that, by the latest accounts, one hundred and twenty negroes had been killed,"-- this being little more than one day's work.

These murders were defended as Nat Turner defended his: a fearful blow must be struck. In shuddering at the horrors of the insurrection, we have forgotten the far greater horrors of its suppression.

The newspapers of the day contain many indignant protests against the cruelties which took place. "It is with pain," says a correspondent of the *National Intelligencer*, Sept. 7, 1831, "that we speak of another feature of the Southampton Rebellion; for we have been most unwilling to have our sympathies for the sufferers diminished or affected by their misconduct. We allude to the slaughter of many blacks without trial and under circumstances of great barbarity.... We met with an individual of intelligence who told us that he himself had killed between ten and fifteen.... We [the Richmond troop] witnessed with surprise the sanguinary temper of the population, who evinced a strong disposition to inflict immediate death on every prisoner."

There is a remarkable official document from Gen. Eppes, the officer in command, to be found in the Richmond *Enquirer* for Sept. 6, 1831. It is an indignant denunciation of precisely these outrages; and though he refuses to give details, he supplies their place by epithets: "revolting,"--"inhuman and not to be justified,"--"acts of barbarity and cruelty,"--"acts of atrocity,"--"this course of proceeding dignifies the rebel and the assassin with the sanctity of martyrdom." And he ends by threatening martial law upon all future transgressors. Such general orders are not issued except in rather extreme cases. And in the parallel columns of the newspaper the innocent editor prints equally indignant descriptions of Russian atrocities in Lithuania, where the Poles were engaged in active insurrection, amid profuse sympathy from Virginia.

The truth is, it was a Reign of Terror. Volunteer patrols rode in all directions, visiting plantations. "It was with the greatest difficulty," said Gen. Brodnax before the House of Delegates, "and at the hazard of personal popularity and esteem, that the coolest and most judicious among us could exert an influence sufficient to restrain an indiscriminate slaughter of the blacks who were suspected." A letter from the Rev. G. W. Powell declares, "There are thousands of troops searching in every direction, and many negroes are killed every day: the exact number will never be ascertained." Petition after petition was subsequently presented to the Legislature, asking compensation for slaves thus assassinated without trial.

Men were tortured to death, burned, maimed, and subjected to nameless atrocities. The overseers were called on to point out any slaves whom they distrusted, and if any tried to escape they were shot down. Nay, worse than this. "A party of horsemen started from Richmond with the intention of killing every colored person they saw in Southampton County. They stopped opposite the cabin of a free colored man, who was hoeing in his little field. They called out, 'Is this Southampton County?' He replied, 'Yes, sir, you have just crossed the line, by yonder tree.' They shot him dead, and rode on." This is from the narrative of the editor of the Richmond *Whig*, who was then on duty in the militia, and protested manfully against these outrages. "Some of these scenes," he adds, "are hardly inferior in barbarity to the atrocities of the insurgents."

These were the masters' stories. If even these conceded so much, it would be interesting to hear what the slaves had to report. I am indebted to my honored friend, Lydia Maria Child, for some vivid recollections of this terrible period, as noted down from the lips of an old colored woman, once well known in New York, Charity Bowery. "At the time of the old Prophet Nat," she said, "the colored folks was afraid to pray loud; for the whites threatened to punish 'em dreadfully, if the least noise was heard. The patrols was low drunken whites; and in Nat's time, if they heard any of the colored folks praying, or singing a hymn, they would fall upon 'em and abuse 'em, and sometimes kill 'em, afore master or missis could get to 'em. The brightest and best was killed in Nat's time. The whites always suspect such ones. They killed a great many at a place called Duplon. They killed Antonio, a slave of Mr. J. Stanley, whom they shot; then they pointed their guns at him, and told him to confess about the insurrection. He told 'em he didn't know any thing about any insurrection. They shot several balls through him, quartered him, and put his head on a pole at the fork of the road leading to the court." (This is no exaggeration, if the Virginia newspapers may be taken as evidence.) "It was there but a short time. He had no trial. They never do. In Nat's time, the patrols would tie up the free colored people, flog 'em, and try to make 'em lie against one another, and often killed them before anybody could interfere. Mr. James Cole, high sheriff, said, if any of the patrols came on his plantation, he would lose his life in defence of his people. One day he heard a patroller boasting how many niggers he had killed. Mr. Cole said, 'If you don't pack up, as quick as God Almighty will let you, and get out of this town, and never be seen in it again, I'll put you where dogs won't bark at you.' He went off, and wasn't seen in them parts again."

These outrages were not limited to the colored population; but other instances occurred which strikingly remind one of more recent times. An Englishman, named Robinson, was engaged in selling books at Petersburg. An alarm being given, one night, that five hundred blacks were marching towards the town, he stood guard, with others, on the bridge. After the panic had a little subsided, he happened to remark, that "the blacks, as men, were entitled to their freedom, and ought to be emancipated." This led to great excitement, and he was warned to leave town. He took passage in the stage, but the stage was intercepted. He then fled to a friend's house; the house was broken open, and he was dragged forth. The civil authorities, being applied to, refused to interfere. The mob stripped him, gave him a great number of lashes, and sent him on foot, naked, under a hot sun, to Richmond, whence he with difficulty found a passage to New York.

Of the capture or escape of most of that small band who met with Nat Turner in the woods upon the Travis plantation, little can now be known. All appear among the list of convicted, except Henry and Will. Gen. Moore, who occasionally figures as second in command, in the newspaper narratives of that day, was probably the Hark or Hercules before mentioned; as no other of the confederates had belonged to Mrs. Travis, or would have been likely to bear her previous name of Moore. As usual, the newspapers state that most, if not all the slaves, were "the property of kind and indulgent masters."

The subordinate insurgents sought safety as they could. A free colored man, named Will Artist, shot himself in the woods, where his hat was found on a stake and his pistol lying by him;

another was found drowned; others were traced to the Dismal Swamp; others returned to their homes, and tried to conceal their share in the insurrection, assuring their masters that they had been forced, against their will, to join,--the usual defence in such cases. The number shot down at random must, by all accounts, have amounted to many hundreds, but it is past all human registration now. The number who had a formal trial, such as it was, is officially stated at fifty-five; of these, seventeen were convicted and hanged, twelve convicted and transported, twenty acquitted, and four free colored men sent on for further trial and finally acquitted. "Not one of those known to be concerned escaped." Of those executed, one only was a woman, "Lucy, slave of John T. Barrow."

There is one touching story, in connection with these terrible retaliations, which rests on good authority, that of the Rev. M. B. Cox, a Liberian missionary, then in Virginia. In the hunt which followed the massacre, a slaveholder went into the woods, accompanied by a faithful slave, who had been the means of saving his life during the insurrection. When they had reached a retired place in the forest, the man handed his gun to his master, informing him that he could not live a slave any longer, and requesting him either to free him or shoot him on the spot. The master took the gun, in some trepidation, levelled it at the faithful negro, and shot him through the heart. It is probable that this slaveholder was a Dr. Blunt,--his being the only plantation where the slaves were reported as thus defending their masters. "If this be true," said the Richmond *Enquirer*, when it first narrated this instance of loyalty, "great will be the desert of these noble-minded Africans."

Meanwhile the panic of the whites continued; for, though all others might be disposed of, Nat Turner was still at large. We have positive evidence of the extent of the alarm, although great efforts were afterwards made to represent it as a trifling affair. A distinguished citizen of Virginia wrote, three months later, to the Hon. W. B. Seabrook of South Carolina, "From all that has come to my knowledge during and since that affair, I am convinced most fully that every black preacher in the country east of the Blue Ridge was in the secret." "There is much reason to believe," says the Governor's Message on Dec. 6, "that the spirit of insurrection was not confined to Southampton. Many

convictions have taken place elsewhere, and some few in distant counties." The withdrawal of the United States troops, after some ten days' service, was a signal for fresh excitement; and an address, numerously signed, was presented to the United States Government, imploring their continued stay. More than three weeks after the first alarm, the governor sent a supply of arms into Prince William, Fauquier, and Orange Counties. "From examinations which have taken place in other counties," says one of the best newspaper historians of the affair (in the Richmond *Enquirer* of Sept. 6), "I fear that the scheme embraced a wider sphere than I at first supposed." Nat Turner himself, intentionally or otherwise, increased the confusion by denying all knowledge of the North Carolina outbreak, and declaring that he had communicated his plans to his four confederates within six months; while, on the other hand, a slave-girl, sixteen or seventeen years old, belonging to Solomon Parker, testified that she had heard the subject discussed for eighteen months, and that at a meeting held during the previous May some eight or ten had joined the plot.

It is astonishing to discover, by laborious comparison of newspaper files, how vast was the immediate range of these insurrectionary alarms. Every Southern State seems to have borne its harvest of terror. On the eastern shore of Maryland, great alarm was at once manifested, especially in the neighborhood of Easton and Snowhill; and the houses of colored men were searched for arms even in Baltimore. In Delaware, there were similar rumors through Sussex and Dover Counties; there were arrests and executions; and in Somerset County great public meetings were held, to demand additional safeguards. On election-day in Seaford, Del., some young men, going out to hunt rabbits, discharged their guns in sport; the men being absent, all the women in the vicinity took to flight;

the alarm spread like the "Ipswich Fright"; soon Seaford was thronged with armed men; and when the boys returned from hunting, they found cannon drawn out to receive them.

In North Carolina, Raleigh and Fayetteville were put under military defence, and women and children concealed themselves in the swamps for many days. The rebel organization was supposed to include two thousand. Forty-six slaves were imprisoned in Union County, twenty-five in Sampson County, and twenty-three at least in Duplin County, some of whom were executed. The panic also extended into Wayne, New Hanover, and Lenoir Counties. Four men were shot without trial in Wilmington,--Nimrod, Abraham, Prince, and "Dan the Drayman," the latter a man of seventy,--and their heads placed on poles at the four corners of the town. Nearly two months afterwards the trials were still continuing; and at a still later day, the governor in his proclamation recommended the formation of companies of volunteers in every county.

In South Carolina, Gen. Hayne issued a proclamation "to prove the groundlessness of the existing alarms,"--thus implying that serious alarms existed. In Macon, Ga., the whole population were roused from their beds at midnight by a report of a large force of armed negroes five miles off. In an hour, every woman and child was deposited in the largest building of the town, and a military force hastily collected in front. The editor of the Macon *Messenger* excused the poor condition of his paper, a few days afterwards, by the absorption of his workmen in patrol duties and describes "dismay and terror" as the condition of the people of "all ages and sexes." In Jones, Twiggs, and Monroe Counties, the same alarms were reported; and in one place "several slaves were tied to a tree, while a militia captain hacked at them with his sword."

In Alabama, at Columbus and Fort Mitchell, a rumor was spread of a joint conspiracy of Indians and negroes. At Claiborne the panic was still greater: the slaves were said to be thoroughly organized through that part of the State, and multitudes were imprisoned; the whole alarm being apparently founded on one stray copy of the Boston *Liberator*.

In Tennessee, the Shelbyville *Freeman* announced that an insurrectionary plot had just been discovered, barely in time for its defeat, through the treachery of a female slave. In Louisville, Ky., a similar organization was discovered or imagined, and arrests were made in consequence. "The papers, from motives of policy, do not notice the disturbance," wrote one correspondent to the Portland *Courier*. "Pity us!" he added.

But the greatest bubble burst in Louisiana. Capt. Alexander, an English tourist, arriving in New Orleans at the beginning of September, found the whole city in tumult. Handbills had been issued, appealing to the slaves to rise against their masters, saying that all men were born equal, declaring that Hannibal was a black man, and that they also might have great leaders among them. Twelve hundred stand of weapons were said to have been found in a black man's house; five hundred citizens were under arms, and four companies of regulars were ordered to the city, whose barracks Alexander himself visited.

If such was the alarm in New Orleans, the story, of course, lost nothing by transmission to other slave States. A rumor reached Frankfort, Ky., that the slaves already had possession of the coast, both above and below New Orleans. But the most remarkable circumstance is, that all this seems to have been a mere revival of an old terror once before excited and exploded. The following paragraph had appeared in the Jacksonville, Ga., *Observer*, during the spring previous:--

"FEARFUL DISCOVERY.--We were favored, by yesterday's mail, with a letter from New Orleans, of May 1, in which we find that an important discovery had been made a few days previous in that city. The following is an extract: 'Four days ago, as some planters were digging under ground, they found a square room containing eleven thousand stand of arms and fifteen thousand cartridges, each of the cartridges containing a bullet.' It is said the negroes intended to rise as soon as the sickly season began, and obtain possession of the city by massacring the white population. The same letter states that the mayor had prohibited the opening of Sunday schools for the instruction of blacks, under a penalty of five hundred dollars for the first offence, and, for the second, death."

Such were the terrors that came back from nine other slave States, as the echo of the voice of Nat Turner. And when it is also known that the subject was at once taken up by the legislatures of other States, where there was no public panic, as in Missouri and Tennessee; and when, finally, it is added that reports of insurrection had been arriving all that year from Rio Janeiro, Martinique, St. Jago, Antigua, Caraccas, and Tortola,-- it is easy to see with what prolonged distress the accumulated terror must have weighed down upon Virginia during the two months that Nat Turner lay hid.

True, there were a thousand men in arms in Southampton County, to inspire security. But the blow had been struck by only seven men before; and unless there were an armed guard in every house, who could tell but any house might at any moment be the scene of new horrors? They might kill or imprison negroes by day, but could they resist their avengers by night? "The half cannot be told," wrote a lady from another part of Virginia, at this time, "of the distresses of the people. In Southampton County, the scene of the insurrection, the distress beggars description. A gentleman who has been there says that even here, where there has been great alarm, we have no idea of the situation of those in that county.... I do not hesitate to believe that many negroes around us would join in a massacre as horrible as that which has taken place, if an opportunity should offer."

Meanwhile the cause of all this terror was made the object of desperate search. On Sept. 17 the governor offered a reward of five hundred dollars for his capture; and there were other rewards, swelling the amount to eleven hundred dollars,--but in vain. No one could track or trap him. On Sept. 30 a minute account of his capture appeared in the newspapers, but it was wholly false. On Oct. 7 there was another, and on Oct. 18 another; yet all without foundation. Worn out by confinement in his little cave, Nat Turner grew more adventurous, and began to move about stealthily by night, afraid to speak to any human being, but hoping to obtain some information that might aid his escape. Returning regularly to his retreat before daybreak, he might possibly have continued this mode of life until pursuit had ceased, had not a dog succeeded where men had failed. The creature accidentally smelt out the provisions hid in the cave, and finally led thither his masters, two negroes, one of whom was named Nelson. On discovering the formidable fugitive, they fled precipitately, when he hastened to retreat in an opposite direction. This was on Oct. 15; and from this moment the neighborhood was all alive with excitement, and five or six hundred men undertook the pursuit.

It shows a more than Indian adroitness in Nat Turner to have escaped capture any longer. The cave, the arms, the provisions, were found; and, lying among them, the notched stick of this miserable Robinson Crusoe, marked with five weary weeks and six days. But the man was gone. For ten days more he concealed himself among the wheat-stacks on Mr. Francis's plantation, and during this time was reduced almost to despair. Once he decided to surrender himself, and walked by night within two miles of Jerusalem before his purpose failed him. Three times he tried to get out of that neighborhood, but  in vain: travelling by day was of course out of the question, and by night he found it impossible to elude the patrol. Again and again, therefore, he returned to his hiding-place; and, during his whole two months' liberty, never went five miles from the Cross Keys. On the 25th of October, he was at last discovered by Mr. Francis as he was emerging from a stack. A load of buckshot was instantly discharged at him, twelve of which passed through his hat as he fell to the ground. He escaped even then; but his pursuers were rapidly concentrating upon him, and it is perfectly astonishing that he could have eluded them for five days more.

On Sunday, Oct. 30, a man named Benjamin Phipps, going out for the first time on patrol duty, was passing at noon a clearing in the woods where a number of pine-trees had long since been felled. There was a motion among their boughs; he stopped to watch it; and through a gap in the branches he saw, emerging from a hole in the earth beneath, the face of Nat Turner. Aiming his gun instantly, Phipps called on him to surrender. The fugitive, exhausted with watching and privation, entangled in the branches, armed only with a sword, had nothing to do but to yield,--sagaciously reflecting, also, as he afterwards explained, that the woods were full of armed men, and that he had better trust fortune for some later chance of escape, instead of desperately attempting it then. He was correct in the first impression, since there were fifty armed scouts within a circuit of two miles. His insurrection ended where it began; for this spot was only a mile and a half from the house of Joseph Travis.

Tom, emaciated, ragged, "a mere scarecrow," still wearing the hat perforated with buckshot, with his arms bound to his sides, he was driven before the levelled gun to the nearest house, that of a Mr. Edwards. He was confined there that night; but the news had spread so rapidly that within an hour after his arrival a hundred persons had collected, and the excitement became so intense "that it was with difficulty he could be conveyed alive to Jerusalem." The enthusiasm spread instantly through Virginia; M. Trezvant, the Jerusalem postmaster, sent notices of it far and near; and Gov. Floyd himself wrote a letter to the Richmond *Enquirer* to give official announcement of the momentous capture.

When Nat Turner was asked by Mr. T. R. Gray, the counsel assigned him, whether, although defeated, he still believed in his own Providential mission, he answered, as simply as one who came thirty years after him, "Was not Christ crucified?" In the same spirit, when arraigned before the court, "he answered, 'Not guilty,' saying to his counsel that he did not feel so." But apparently no argument was made in his favor by his counsel, nor were any witnesses called,--he being convicted on the testimony of Levi Waller, and upon his own confession, which was put in by Mr. Gray, and acknowledged by the prisoner before the six justices composing the court, as being "full, free, and voluntary." He was therefore placed in the paradoxical position of conviction by his own confession, under a plea of "Not guilty." The arrest took place on the 30th of October, 1831, the confession on the 1st of November, the trial and conviction on the 5th, and the execution on the following Friday, the 11th of November, precisely at noon. He met his death with perfect composure, declined addressing the multitude assembled, and told the sheriff in a firm voice that he was ready. Another account says that he "betrayed no emotion, and even hurried the executioner in the performance of his duty." "Not a limb nor a muscle was observed to move. His body, after his death, was given over to the surgeons for dissection."

The confession of the captive was published under authority of Mr. Gray, in a pamphlet, at Baltimore. Fifty thousand copies of it are said to have been printed; and it was "embellished with an accurate likeness of the brigand, taken by Mr. John Crawley, portrait-painter, and lithographed by Endicott & Swett, at Baltimore." The newly established *Liberator* said of it, at the time, that it would "only serve to rouse up other leaders, and hasten other insurrections," and advised grand juries to indict Mr. Gray. I have never seen a copy of the original pamphlet; it is not easily to be found in any of our public libraries; and I have heard of but one as still existing, although the Confession itself has been repeatedly reprinted. Another small pamphlet, containing the main features of the outbreak, was published at New York during the same year, and this is in my possession. But the greater part of the facts which I have given were gleaned from the contemporary newspapers.

Who now shall go back thirty years, and read the heart of this extraordinary man, who, by the admission of his captors, "never was known to swear an oath, or drink a drop of spirits"; who, on the same authority, "for natural intelligence and quickness of apprehension was surpassed by few men," "with a mind capable of attaining any thing"; who knew no book but his Bible, and that by heart; who devoted himself soul and body to the cause of his race, without a trace of personal hope or fear; who laid his plans so shrewdly that they came at last with less warning than any earthquake on the doomed community around; and who, when that time arrived, took the life of man, woman, and child, without a throb of compunction, a word of exultation, or an act of superfluous outrage? Mrs. Stowe's "Dred" seems dim and melodramatic beside the actual Nat Turner, and De Quincey's "Avenger" is his only parallel in imaginative literature. Mr. Gray, his counsel, rises into a sort of bewildered enthusiasm with the prisoner before him. "I shall not attempt to describe the effect of his narrative, as told and commented on by himself, in the condemned-hole of the prison.

The calm, deliberate composure with which he spoke of his late deeds and intentions, the expression of his fiend-like face when excited by enthusiasm, still bearing the stains of the blood of helpless innocence about him, clothed with rags and covered with chains, yet daring to raise his manacled hands to heaven, with a spirit soaring above the attributes of man,--I looked on him, and the blood curdled in my veins."

But, the more remarkable the personal character of Nat Turner, the greater the amazement felt that he should not have appreciated the extreme felicity of his position as a slave. In all insurrections, the standing wonder seems to be that the slaves most trusted and best used should be most deeply involved. So in this case, as usual, men resorted to the most astonishing theories of the origin of the affair. One attributed it to Free-Masonry, and another to free whiskey,--liberty appearing dangerous, even in these forms. The poor whites charged it upon the free colored people, and urged their expulsion; forgetting that in North Carolina the plot was betrayed by one of this class, and that in Virginia there were but two engaged, both of whom had slave wives. The slaveholding clergymen traced it to want of knowledge of the Bible, forgetting that Nat Turner knew scarcely any thing else. On the other hand, "a distinguished citizen of Virginia" combined in one sweeping denunciation "Northern incendiaries, tracts, Sunday schools, religion, reading, and writing."

But whether the theories of its origin were wise or foolish, the insurrection made its mark; and the famous band of Virginia emancipationists, who all that winter made the House of Delegates ring with unavailing eloquence,--till the rise of slave-exportation to new cotton regions stopped their voices,-- were but the unconscious mouthpieces of Nat Turner. In January, 1832, in reply to a member who had called the outbreak a "petty affair," the eloquent James McDowell thus described the impression it left behind:--

"Now, sir, I ask you, I ask gentlemen in conscience to say, was that a 'petty affair' which startled the feelings of your whole population; which threw a portion of it into alarm, a portion of it into panic; which wrung out from an affrighted people the thrilling cry, day after day, conveyed to your executive, 'We are in peril of our lives; send us an army for defence'? Was that a 'petty affair' which drove families from their homes,--which assembled women and children in crowds, without shelter, at places of common refuge, in every condition of weakness and infirmity, under every suffering which want and terror could inflict, yet willing to endure all, willing to meet death from famine, death from climate, death from hardships, preferring any thing rather than the horrors of meeting it from a domestic assassin? Was that a 'petty affair' which erected a peaceful and confiding portion of the State into a military camp; which outlawed from pity the unfortunate beings whose brothers had offended; which barred every door, penetrated every bosom with fear or suspicion; which so banished every sense of security from every man's dwelling, that, let but a hoof or horn break upon the silence of the night, and an aching throb would be driven to the heart, the husband would look to his weapon, and the mother would shudder and weep upon her cradle? Was it the fear of Nat Turner, and his deluded, drunken handful of followers, which produced such effects? Was it this that induced distant counties, where the very name of Southampton was strange, to arm and equip for a struggle? No, sir: it was the suspicion eternally attached to the slave himself,--the suspicion that a Nat Turner might be in every family; that the same bloody deed might be acted over at any time and in any place; that the materials for it were spread through the land, and were always ready for a like explosion. Nothing but the force of this withering apprehension,--nothing but the paralyzing and deadening weight with which it falls upon and prostrates the heart of every man who has helpless dependants to protect,-- nothing but this could have thrown a brave people into consternation, or could have made any portion of this powerful Commonwealth, for a single instant, to have quailed and trembled."

While these things were going on, the enthusiasm for the Polish Revolution was rising to its height. The nation was ringing with a peal of joy, on hearing that at Frankfort the Poles had killed fourteen thousand Russians. The *Southern Religious Telegraph* was publishing an impassioned address to Kosciuszko; standards were being consecrated for Poland in the larger cities; heroes like Skrzynecki, Czartoryski, Rozyski, Raminski, were choking the trump of Fame with their complicated patronymics. These are all forgotten now; and this poor negro, who did not even possess a name, beyond one abrupt monosyllable,--for even the name of Turner was the master's property,--still lives, a memory of terror, and a symbol of wild retribution.

Endnotes

THE MAROONS OF JAMAICA

1. Dallas, R. C. "The History of the Maroons, from their origin to the establishment of their chief tribe at Sierra Leone: including the expedition to Cuba, for the purpose of procuring Spanish chasseurs; and the state of the Island of Jamaica for the last ten years, with a succinct history of the island previous to that period." In two volumes. London, 1803. [8vo.]

2. Edwards, Bryan. "The History, Civil and Commercial, of the British Colonies in the West Indies. To which is added a general description of the Bahama Islands, by Daniel M'Kinnen, Esq." In four volumes. Philadelphia, 1806. [8vo.]

3. Edwards, Bryan. "Proceedings of the Governor and Associates of Jamaica in regard to the Maroon Negroes, with an account of the Maroons." London, 1796. 8vo.

4. Edwards, Bryan. "Historical Survey of St. Domingo, with an account of the Maroon Negroes, a history of the war in the West Indies, 1793-94" [etc.]. London, 1801. 4to.

5. *Edinburgh Review*, ii. 376. [Review of Dallas and Edwards, by Henry Lord Brougham.]

Also Annual Register, Hansard's Parliamentary Debates, etc.

[There appeared in *Once a Week* (1865) a paper entitled "The Maroons of Jamaica," and reprinted in *Every Saturday* (i. 50, Jan. 31, 1866), in which Gov. Eyre is quoted as having said, in the London *Times*, "To the fidelity and loyalty of the Maroons it is due that the negroes did not commit greater devastation" in the recent insurrection; thus curiously repeating the encomium given by Lord Balcarres seventy years before.]

THE MAROONS OF SURINAM

1. "Narrative of a Five Years' Expedition against the revolted negroes of Surinam, in Guiana, on the wild coast of South America, from the year 1772 to 1777 ... by Capt. J. G. Stedman." London. Printed for J. Johnson, St. Paul's Churchyard, and J. Edwards, Pall Mall. 1790. [2 vols. 4to.]

2. "Transatlantic Sketches, comprising visits to the most interesting scenes in North and South America and the West Indies. With notes on negro slavery and Canadian emigration. By Capt. J. E. Alexander, 42 Royal Highlanders." London: Richard Bentley, New Burlington St., 1833. [2 vols. 8vo.]

Also Annual Register, etc.

[The best account of the present condition of the Maroons, or, as they are now called, bush-negroes, of Surinam, is to be found in a graphic narrative of a visit to Dutch Guiana, by W. G. Palgrave, in the *Fortnightly Review*, xxiv. 801; xxv. 194, 536. These papers are reprinted in *Littell's Living Age*, cxxviii. 154, cxxix. 409. He estimates the present numbers of these people as approaching thirty thousand. The "Encyclopaedia Britannica" gives the names of several publications relating to their peculiar dialect, popularly known as Negro-English, but including many Dutch words.]

GABRIEL'S DEFEAT

The materials for the history of Gabriel's revolt are still very fragmentary, and must be sought in the contemporary newspapers. No continuous file of Southern newspapers for the year 1800 was to be found, when this narrative was written, in any Boston or New-York library, though the Harvard-College Library contained a few numbers of the Baltimore *Telegraphe* and the Norfolk *Epitome of the Times*. My chief reliance has therefore been the Southern correspondence of the Northern newspapers, with the copious extracts there given from Virginian journals. I am chiefly indebted to the Philadelphia *United-States Gazette*, the Boston *Independent Chronicle*, the Salem *Gazette* and Register, the New-York *Daily Advertiser*, and the Connecticut *Courant*. The best continuous narratives that I have found are in the *Courant* of Sept. 29, 1800, and the Salem *Gazette* of Oct. 7, 1800; but even these are very incomplete. Several important documents I have been unable to discover,--the official proclamation of the governor, the description of Gabriel's person, and the original confession of the slaves as given to Mr. Sheppard. The discovery of these would no doubt have enlarged, and very probably corrected, my narrative.

DENMARK VESEY

1. "Negro Plot. An Account of the late intended insurrection among a portion of the blacks of the city of Charleston, S.C. Published by the Authority of the Corporation of Charleston." Second edition. Boston: printed and published by Joseph W. Ingraham. 1822. 8vo, pp. 50.

[A third edition was printed at Boston during the same year, a copy of which is in the library of the Massachusetts Historical Society. The first and fourth editions, which were printed at Charleston, S.C., I have never seen.]

2. "An Official Report of the trials of sundry negroes, charged with an attempt to raise an insurrection in the State of South Carolina: preceded by an introduction and narrative; and in an appendix, a report of the trials of four white persons, on indictments for attempting to excite the slaves to insurrection. Prepared and published at the request of the court. By Lionel H. Kennedy and Thomas Parker, members of the Charleston bar, and the presiding magistrates of the court." Charleston: printed by James R. Schenck, 23 Broad St. 1822. 8vo, pp. 188x4.

3. "Reflections occasioned by the late disturbances in Charleston, by Achates." Charleston: printed and sold by A. E. Miller, No. 4 Broad St. 1822. 8vo, pp. 30.

4. "A Refutation of the Calumnies circulated against the Southern and Western States, respecting the institution and existence of slavery among them. To which is added a minute and particular account of the actual state and condition of their Negro Population, together with Historical Notices of all the Insurrections that have taken place since the settlement of the country.--Facts are stubborn things.--*Shakspeare*. By a South Carolinian." [Edwin C. Holland.] Charleston: printed by A. E. Miller, No. 4 Broad St. 1822. 8vo, pp. 86.

5. "Rev. Dr. Richard Furman's Exposition of the views of the Baptists relative to the colored population in the United States, in a communication to the Governor of South Carolina." Second edition. Charleston: printed by A. E. Miller, No. 4 Broad St. 1833. 8vo, pp. 16.

[The first edition appeared in 1823. It relates to a petition offered by a Baptist Convention for a day of thanksgiving and humiliation, in reference to the insurrection, and to a violent hurricane which had just occurred.]

6. "Practical Considerations, founded on the Scriptures, relative to the Slave Population of South Carolina. Respectfully dedicated to the South Carolina Association. By a South Carolinian." Charleston: printed and sold by A. E. Miller, No. 4 Broad St. 1823. 8vo, pp. 38.

7. [The letter of Gov. Bennett, dated Aug. 10, 1822, was evidently printed originally as a pamphlet or circular, though I have not been able to find it in that form. It may be found reprinted in the *Columbian Centinel* (Aug. 31, 1822), *Connecticut Courant* (Sept. 3), and Worcester *Spy* (Sept. 18). It is also printed in Lundy's *Genius of Universal Emancipation* for September, 1822 (ii. 42), and reviewed in subsequent numbers (pp. 81, 131, 142).]

8. "The Liberty Bell, by Friends of Freedom. Boston: Anti-Slavery Bazaar. 1841. 12mo." [This contains an article on p. 158, entitled "Servile Insurrections," by Edmund Jackson, including brief personal reminiscences of the Charleston insurrection, during which he resided in that city.]

[Of the above-named pamphlets, all now rare, Nos. 1 and 2 are in my own possession. Nos. 3, 4, 5, 6, are in the Wendell Phillips collection of pamphlets in the Boston Public Library.]

NAT TURNER'S INSURRECTION

1. "The Confessions of Nat Turner, the leader of the late Insurrection in Southampton, Va., as fully and voluntarily made to Thomas R. Gray, in the prison where he was confined, and acknowledged by him to be such when read before the Court of Southampton, with the certificate under

seal of the court convened at Jerusalem, Nov. 5, 1831, for this trial. Also an authentic account of the whole insurrection, with lists of the whites who were murdered, and of the negroes brought before the Court of Southampton, and there sentenced, etc." New York: printed and published by C. Brown, 211 Water Street, 1831.

[This pamphlet was reprinted in the *Anglo-African Magazine* (New York), December, 1859. Whether it is identical with the work said by the newspapers of the period to have been published at Baltimore, I have been unable to ascertain. But if, as was alleged, forty thousand copies of the Baltimore pamphlet were issued, it seems impossible that they should have become so scarce. The first reprint of the Confession, so far as I know, was a partial one in Abdy's "Journal in the United States." London. 1835. 3 vols. 8vo.]

2. "Authentic and Impartial Narrative of the Tragical Scene which was witnessed in Southhampton County (Va.), on Monday, the 22d of August last, when Fifty-five of its inhabitants (mostly women and children) were inhumanly massacred by the blacks! Communicated by those who were eye-witnesses of the bloody scene, and confirmed by the confessions of several of the Blacks, while under Sentence of Death." [By Samuel Warner, New York.] Printed for Warner & West. 1831. 12mo, pp. 36 [or more, copy incomplete. With a frontispiece]. Among the Wendell Phillips tracts in the Boston Public Library.

3. "Slave Insurrection in 1831, in Southampton County, Va., headed by Nat Turner. Also a conspiracy of slaves in Charleston, S.C., in 1822." New York: compiled and published by Henry Bibb, 9 Spruce St. 1849. 12mo, pp. 12.

[The contemporary newspaper narratives may be found largely quoted in the first volume of the *Liberator* (1831), and in Lundy's *Genius of Universal Emancipation* (September, 1831). The files of the Richmond *Enquirer* have also much information on the subject.]

"STABBED ONE OF THE NEGROES" (p. 125).

SLAVE INSURRECTIONS

Joshua Coffin

Joshua Coffin (October 12, 1792 – June 24, 1864) was an American antiquary and abolitionist. Coffin was a headstrong proponent of emancipation, and was one of the founders of the New-England Anti-Slavery Society in 1832, being its first recording secretary. The following is the complete text of Coffin's work, An Account of Some of the Principal Slave Insurrections: And others, which have occurred, or been attempted, in the United States and elsewhere, during the last two centuries, with various remarks. The book was originally published by the American Anti-Slavery Society in 1860.

NOTE TO THE READER

The subsequent collection of facts is presented to your notice, with the hope that they will have that effect which facts always have on every candid and ingenuous mind. They exhibit clearly the dangers to which slaveholders are always liable, as well as the safety of immediate emancipation. They furnish, in both cases, a rule which admits of no exception, as it is always dangerous to do wrong, and safe to do right. Please examine carefully the whole account of the revolution in St. Domingo, beginning in March, 1790, and ending in 1802. That exhibits a different picture from that presented in a speech made at the Union-saving meeting lately held in Boston. A part of the truth may be so told as to have all the effect of a deliberate lie.

SLAVE INSURRECTIONS

"And they said one to another, We are verily guilty concerning our brother, in that we saw the anguish of his soul when he besought us, and we would not hear; therefore is this distress come upon us."— Gen. 42:21.

"Thus said the Lord my God, Feed the flock of the slaughter, whose pastors slay them, and hold themselves not guilty; and they that sell them say, Blessed be the Lord, for I am rich; and their own shepherds pity them not."—Zech. 11:4, 5.

"He that stealeth a man, and selleth him, or if he be found in his hand, he shall surely be put to death."—Ex. 21:16.

The late invasion of Virginia by Capt. John Brown and his company has, with all its concomitant circumstances, excited more attention and aroused a more thorough spirit of inquiry on the subject of slavery, than was ever before known. As this is pre-eminently a moral question, and as there is no neutral ground in morals, all intelligent men must ultimately take sides. Every such man must either cherish and defend slavery, or oppose and condemn it, and his vote, if he is an honest man, must accord with his belief. On a question of so momentous importance, "Silence is crime." It demands and will have a thorough investigation, and all attempts to stifle discussion will only accelerate the triumph of the cause they were designed to crush. Thus the denunciation in Congress of Mr. Helper's book, which is in substance only an abstract of facts taken from the last census of the United States, has operated as an extensive advertisement, and will be the means of circulating thousands of copies, where, without such denunciation, it would never have been known. There is in the North, as well as the South, a class of men who act, apparently, on the supposition that those who foresee and foretell any calamity are as guilty as those who create it, and that the only way to obviate any impending danger is not to see it. Such persons not only refuse to see and hear themselves, but do what they can to keep their neighbors in like ignorance.

It has been truly said that "the power of slavery lies in the ignorance, the degradation, the servility of the slaves, and of the non-slaveholding whites of the South, and of the corresponding classes in the Free States. It is through this ignorance and servility that the slaveholders manage to dictate to ecclesiastical bodies, to have power to control pulpits, presses, Colleges, Theological Seminaries, and Missionary and Tract Societies." To keep the blacks and non-slaveholding whites in ignorance is, doubtless, the reason why such pains are taken in Congress to prevent the circulation of Helper's book at the South, which was compiled by a non-slaveholder for the special benefit of the men of his class. The population of the Free States is now about eighteen millions; of the Slave States, eight millions. The slaves number about four millions, who are held as property by only 347,545 persons, men, women and children. This number, small as it is, constituting about one sixth part of the United States, have thus far controlled the legislation of the country. How this power has been acquired is easily understood when we examine the false ideas respecting slavery which are everywhere prevalent; such as the weakness of the public conscience, in the absence of a practical and experimental knowledge of the truth of God's word—in the atheistic notion, prevailing even in the Church and in the ministry, that the unrighteous enactments of wicked me are paramount in authority to the commandments of the Great Jehovah. Hundreds of clergymen, in all parts of the Union, profess to believe that the Bible sanctions American slavery,—a system which, of necessity, cannot exist without a continual violation of every commandment of the Decalogue.

If the Bible sanctions slavery, (as many profess to believe,) why does not the God of the Bible sanction it? In other words, if slavery is sanctioned by the revealed will of God, why are not the dispensations of his providence in accordance with that will? Could it be fairly proved that slavery is in accordance with the will of God, it must necessarily follow that obedience to his will is not only highly advantageous, but perfectly safe; for, surely, no Christian can, for a moment, believe that the providence of God ever militates against the precepts of his word. As, however, the consequences of slavery have been, in all cases, when not averted by timely repentance, disastrous in the extreme, it is therefore undeniably evident that slavery is in direct opposition to the revealed will of God, and, consequently, that those who so violently oppose the abolition of slavery, for fear of supposed dangerous consequences, may truly be said "to know not what they do." The truth on this subject is so plain, and the facts so abundant, that he who runs may read, and know to a certainty the entire safety of immediate emancipation; and that danger arises from liberty withheld, and not from liberty granted. The general opinion seems to be, that the moment you proclaim "liberty to the captive," and make the slave a freeman, be the conditions and restrictions what they may, that moment you make him a vagabond, a thief, and a murderer, whom nothing will satisfy but the blood of those who had been so "fanatical and insane" as to treat him like a human being. Whence this opinion is derived, no one can tell; for it is in direct opposition to reason, common sense, the nature of the human mind, and is entirely unsustained by facts. Indeed, so far as the evidence of facts is concerned, the advocates of immediate abolition have a complete monopoly. All experience proves two things, viz., the entire safety of immediate emancipation, and that all danger has arisen from its indefinite postponement; for this is really the true definition of gradual emancipation.

We all know the results of slavery in Greece and Rome. Troy perished by her slaves in a single night; and as like causes always produce like effects, our obligations to our slaveholding brethren imperiously demand that we should urge on them, in the most earnest manner, the duty of immediately abolishing slavery as their only hope of safety,—the only means by which they can escape the just judgments of God. The safety of immediate emancipation has been proved by Buenos Ayres in 1816, Colombia in 1821, Guatemala in 1824, Peru and Chili in 1828, Mexico in 1829, and especially on the 1st of August, 1834, when 800,000 slaves were set free in a single day in the British West India Islands; and thus far, not a single life has been lost, not a drop of blood shed, in consequence of that beneficent and righteous act. The consequences of holding slaves in bondage, and refusing to emancipate them, have always been disastrous. In our present exemption from slavery in the Free States, we have no cause of boasting, but rather of deep humiliation. We are all involved in the guilt, and must share in the punishment, unless timely and thorough repentance avert the impending blow. To do this effectually, information must be spread, the spirit of inquiry aroused, the temple of God be purified, and "the book of law be read in the ears of all the people," that thus the gross mistakes and misapprehensions which everywhere exist on the subject of slavery and its abolition may be corrected.

Of these mistakes, no one is more prevalent or more dangerous than the one just mentioned, that insurrection, rapine and bloodshed are the necessary consequences of immediate emancipation; and that the only way to avert the evils and the curse of slavery, is to continue in the sin for the present, promise future repentance, and in the meantime, whilst we are preparing to get ready to begin to repent, do every thing that in us lies to extinguish every good feeling, and cultivate and bring into action every bad feeling of the human heart. That such is the belief, and consequent practice, to an alarming extent, throughout our country, and that such a course is impolitic, because it is wicked and dangerous, because it is unjust, facts abundantly show.

Since the abolition of slavery in the British dominions, no trouble has arisen, no danger been feared or apprehended. A thousand John Browns, each with nineteen white men and five black men, could not cause any tumult in any part of the British West Indies. Why is it, then, that one John Brown and company have created so wide-spread an alarm and consternation throughout the Slave States? The Governor of South Carolina has sent a dispatch (Nov. 21) to Gov. Wise, tendering any amount of *military aid to the defence of Virginia!* Gov. Wise had several companies of the military present on the day of the execution of John Brown and others, and assured the Governor of South Carolina that Virginia is able to defend herself. What causes all this tumult and apprehension? SLAVERY! And yet, strange as it may seem, the Virginians, with a stupidity and infatuation which no language can describe, are seriously discussing the propriety of enslaving the free negroes of that State. Such a proceeding would resemble a physician who should order a dose of arsenic to cure a patient who had taken strychnine, or attempt to extinguish a conflagration by throwing oil on the flames.

How the consequences of abolishing slavery would be dreadful and horrible, neither history nor experience informs us. Let us, then, see what they tell us of the consequences of holding men in bondage. In every instance which has fallen under my notice, insurrections have always been projected and carried on by slaves, and never (with the exception of Denmark Vesey in 1822, in Charleston, S. C.) by the free blacks.

The contest between truth and falsehood, right and wrong, justice and injustice, has always continued from the earliest ages to the present moment. More especially is it true concerning American slavery, that "sum of all villanies," a crime which involves the continual violation of every one of the Ten Commandments. I propose, therefore, to give, with other incidents, an abstract of some of the attempts of the oppressed to throw off the yoke which held them, or threatened to hold them, in bondage.

The first instance which has come to my knowledge in this country of an insurrection on a small scale, occurred on Noddle's Island, now East Boston, in 1638. In John Josselyn's account of his first voyage to New England may be found the following. Having previously stated that he was a guest of "Mr. Samuel Maverick, the only hospitable man (as he says) in all the country, giving entertainment to all comers gratis," he thus writes:—

> "The second of October about 9 of the clock in the morning Mr. Maverick's negro came to my chamber window, and in her own Countrey language and tune sung very loud and shrill. Going out to her she used a great deal of respect towards me, and willingly would have expressed her grief in English, but I apprehended it by her countenance and deportment, whereupon I repaired to my host to learn of him the cause, and resolved to intreat him on her behalf for that I understood before that she had been a Queen in her own Countrey, and observed a very dutiful garb used toward her by another Negro who was her main. Mr. Maverick was desirous to have a breed of Negroes, and therefore seeing she would not yield by persuasion to company with a Negro young man he had in his house, he commanded him, will'd she, nill'd she, to go to bed with her, but she kickt him out again. This she took in high disdain beyond her slavery, and this was the cause of her grief."

From this statement it appears that Maverick had at least three slaves: but the number held in the Province, no record informs us. In 1641, the Massachusetts Colony passed the following law:—

> "There shall never be any bond slaverie, villinage or captivitie amongst us unless it be lawfull captives taken in just warres, and such strangers as *willingly sell themselves*. And these shall have all the liberties and christian usuages, which the law of God established in Isreal concerning such persons doth morally require. This exempts none from *servitude*, who shall be judged thereto by authority."

"He that stealeth a man, and selleth him, or if he be found in his hand, he shall surely be put to death."—Ex. 21:16.

In 1646, one James Smith, a member of Boston church, brought home two negroes from the Coast of Guinea, and had been the means of killing near a hundred more. In consequence of this conduct, the General Court passed the following order:—

"The General Court conceiving themselves bound by the first opportunity to bear witness against the heinous and crying sin of man- stealing, as also to prescribe such timely redress for what is past and such a law for the future, as may sufficiently deter all others belonging to us to have to do in such vile and odious courses, justly abhorred of all good and just men, do order that the negro interpreter with others unlawfully taken, be by the first opportunity at the charge of the country for the present, sent to his native country (Guinea) and a letter with him of the indignation of the Court thereabouts, and justice thereof desiring our honored Governor would please put this order in execution."

From this time till about 1700, the number of slaves imported into Massachusetts was not large. In 1680, Governor Simon Bradstreet, in answer to inquiries from "the lords of his Majesties privy council," thus writes:—

"There had been no company of blacks or slaves brought into the country since the beginning of this plantation, for the space of 50 years, only one small vessell about two yeares since after 20 month's voyage to Madagasca brought hither betwixt 40 and 50 negros, most women and children, sold for 10 pounds, 15 pounds and 20 pounds apiece, which stood the merchants in near 40 pounds apiece one with another: now and then two or three negros are brought hither from Barbados and other of his majesties plantations, and sold her for about 20 pounds apiece, so that there may bee within our government about 100 or 120, and it may bee as many Scots brought hither and sold for servants in the time of the war with Scotland, and most now married and living here, and about halfe so many Irish brought hither at several times as servants."

The number of slaves at this period in the middle and southern colonies is not easily ascertained, as few books, and no newspapers, were published in North America prior to 1704. In that year, the *Weekly News Letter* was commenced, and in the same year the "Society for the propagation of the Gospel in foreign parts opened a catechising school for the slaves at New York, in which city there were then computed to be about 1500 negro and Indian slaves," a sufficient number to furnish materials for the *"irrepressible conflict,"* which had long before begun. The catechist, whom the Society employed, was "Mr.

Elias Neau, by nation a Frenchman, who, having made a confession of the Protestant religion in France, for which he had been confined several years in prison, and seven years in the gallies." Mr. Neau entered upon his office "with great diligence, and his labors were very successful; but the negroes were much discouraged from embracing the Christian religion upon account of the very little regard showed them in any religious respect. Their marriages were performed by mutual consent only, without the blessing of the Church; they were buried by those of their own country and complexion, in the common field, without any Christian office; perhaps some ridiculous heathen rites were performed at the grave by some of their own people. No notice was given of their being sick, that they might be visited; on the contrary, frequent discourses were made in conversation, that they had no souls, and perished as the beasts," and "that they grew worse by being taught, and made Christians."

In 1711, May 15, Gov. Gibbes, of South Carolina, in his address to the Legislature of that Province, thus speaks:—

"And, gentlemen, I desire you will consider the great *quantities* of negroes that are daily brought into the government, and the small *number* of whites that comes amongst us: how insolent and mischievous the negroes are become, and to consider the Negro Act already made, doth not reach up to some of the crimes they have lately been guilty of, therefore it might be convenient by some additional clause of said Negro Act to appoint either by gibbets or some such like way, that after executed, they may remain more exemplary than any punishment that hath been inflicted on them."

In the next month, June, the Governor thus writes:—

"We further recommend unto you the repairs of the fortifications about Charleston, and the amending of the Negro Act, who are of late grown to that height of impudence, that there is scarce a day passes without some robbery or insolence, committed by them in one part or other of this province."

"In the year 1712," says the Rev. D. Humphreys, "a considerable number of negroes of the Carmantee and Pappa Nations formed a plot to destroy all the English, *in order to obtain their liberty;* and kept their conspiracy so secret, that there was no suspicion of it till it came to the very execution.

However, the plot was by God's Providence happily defeated. The plot was this. The negroes sat fire to a house in York city, and Sunday night in April, about the going down of the moon. The fire alarmed the town, who from all parts ran to it; the conspirators planted themselves in several streets and lanes leading to the fire, and shot or stabbed the people as they were running to it. Some of the wounded escaped, and acquainted the Government, and presently by the firing of a great gun from the fort, the inhabitants were called under arms and pretty easily scattered the negroes; they had killed about 8 and wounded 12 more. In their flight some of them shot themselves, others their wives, and then themselves; some absconded a few days, and then killed themselves for fear of being taken; but a great many were taken, and 18 of them suffered death. This wicked conspiracy was at first apprehended to be general among all the negroes, and opened the mouths of many to speak against giving the negroes instruction. Mr. Neau durst hardly appear abroad for some days; his school was blamed as the main occasion of this barbarous plot. On examination, only two of all his school were so much as charged with the plot, and on full trial the guilty negroes were found to be such as never came to Mr. Neau's school; and what is very observable, the persons, whose negroes were found to be most guilty, were such as were the declared opposers of making them Christians. However a great jealousy was now raised, and the common cry very loud against instructing the negroes."

From the *Boston Weekly Journal*, of April 8th, 1724, I make the following extract:—

"Every reasonable man ought to remember their *first* villanous attempt at New York, and how many good innocent people were murdered by tem, and had it not been for the garrison there, that city would have been reduced to ashes, and the greatest part of the inhabitants murdered."

On the 6th of May, 1720, the negroes of South Carolina murdered Mr. Benjamin Cattle, a white woman, and a negro boy. Forces were immediately raised, and sent after them, twenty-three of whom were taken, six convicted, three executed, and three escaped.

In October, 1722, about two hundred negroes near the mouth

of the Rappahannock river, Virginia, got together in a body, armed with an intent to kill the people in church, but were discovered, and fled.

On the 13th of April, 1723, Gov. Dummer issued a proclamation with the following preamble, viz.:—

> "Whereas within some short time past, many fires have broke out within the town of Boston, and divers buildings have thereby been consumed: which fires have been designedly and industriously kindled by some villanous and desperate Negroes, or other dissolute people, as appears by the confession of some of them (who have been examined by authority) and many concurring circumstances; and it being vehemently suspected that they *have entered into a combination to burn and destroy the town,* I have therefore thought fit, with the advice of his Majesty's Council, to issue forth this Proclamation," &c.

On the 18th of April, 1723, Rev. Joseph Sewall preached a discourse, particularly occcasioned "by the late fires yet have broke out in Boston, supposed to be purposely set by ye Negroes."

On the next day, April 19th, the Selectmen of Boston made a report to the town on the subject, consisting of nineteen articles, of which the following is No. 9:—

> "That if more than Two Indians, Negro or Molatto Servants or Slaves be found in the Streets or Highways in or about the Town, idling or lurking together unless in the service of their Master or Employer, every one so found shall be punished at the House of Correction."

So great at that time were the alarm and danger in Boston, occasioned by the slaves, that in addition to the common watch, a military force was not only kept up, but at the breaking out of every fire, a part of the militia were ordered out under arms to keep the slaves in order!!

The report of nineteen articles, submitted to the town of Boston, was finally embodied in a Negro Act of fifteen sections, of which the 15th was as follows:—

> "That no Indian, negro or mullatto, upon the breaking out of fire and the continuance thereof during the night season, shall depart from his or her master's house, nor be found in the streets at or near the place where the fire is, upon pain of being forthwith seized and sent to the common gaol, and afterwards

whipt, three days following before dismist, &c."

From the *N. E. Courant*, Nov. 1724, I take the following extract:—

"It is well known what loss the town of Boston sustained by fire not long since, *when almost every night* for a considerable time together, some building or other and sometimes several in the same night were either burned to the ground or some attempts made to do it. It is likewise well known that those villanies were carried on by Negro servants, the like whereof we never felt before from unruly servants, nor ever heard of the like happening in any place attended with the like circumstances."

Like causes produce like effects. Since the abolition of slavery in Massachusetts, no one has felt alarmed at seeing "two or more colored men lurking together" in Boston. Prior to the abolition of slavery in the British West Indies, the militia were always called out under arms on the Christmas holidays, in order to prevent any attempts at insurrection among the slaves. Since that time, there has been no apprehension of any disturbances, and, of course, no calling out of the militia.

In 1728, an insurrection of slaves occurred in Savannah, Georgia, who were fired on twice before they fled. They had formed a plot to destroy all the whites, and nothing prevented them but a disagreement about the mode. At that time, the population consisted of 3000 whites and 2700 blacks.

In January, 1729, the slaves in Antigua conspired to destroy the English, which was discovered two or three days before the intended assault. Of the three conspirators, *two were burnt alive!!* "'Twas admirable," says the account, "to see how long they stood before they died, the great wood not readily burning, and their cry was water, water!"

In August, 1730, an insurrection of blacks occurred in

Williamsburgh, Va., occasioned by a report, on Col. Spotswood's arrival, that he had direction from his Majesty to free all baptized persons. The negroes improved this to a great height. Five counties were in arms pursuing them, with orders to kill them if they did not submit.

In August, 1730, the slaves in South Carolina conspired to destroy all the whites. This was the first open rebellion in that State, where the negroes were actually armed and embodied, and took place on the Sabbath.

In the same month, a negro man plundered and burned a house in Malden, (Mass.) and gave this reason for his conduct, that his master had sold him to a man in Salem, whom he did not like.

In 1731, Capt. George Scott, of R. I. was returning from Guinea with a cargo of slaves, who rose upon the ship, murdered three of the crew, all of whom soon after died, except the captain and boy.

In 1732, Capt. John Major, of Portsmouth, N. H., was murdered, with all his crew, and the schooner and cargo seized by the slaves.

In December, 1734, Jamaica was under martial law, and two thousand soldiers ordered out after the "rebellious negroes."

In the same year, an insurrection occurred in Burlington, (Pa.) among the blacks, whom the account styles *"intestine and inhuman enemies, who in some places have been too much indulged."* Their design was as soon as the season was advanced, so that they could lie in the woods, on a certain night, agreed on by some hundreds of them, and kept secret a long time, that every negro and negress should rise at midnight, kill every master and his sons, sparing the women, kill all the draught horses, set all their houses and barns on fire, and secure all their saddle horses for flight towards the Indians in the French interest.

In 1735, the slaves of the ship Dolphin, of London, on the coast of Africa, rose upon the crew; but being overpowered, they got into the powder room, and to be revenged, blew up themselves with the crew.

In 1739, there were three formidable insurrections of the

slaves in South Carolina—one in St. Paul's Parish, one in St. Johns, and one in Charleston. In one of these, which occurred in September, they killed in one night twenty-five whites, and burned six houses. They were pursued, attacked, and fourteen killed. In two days, twenty more were killed, and forty were taken, some of whom were shot, some hanged, and some gibbeted alive! This "more exemplary" punishment, as Gov. Gibbes called it, failed of its intended effect, for the next year there was another insurrection in South Carolina. There were then above 40,000 slaves, and about twenty persons were killed before it was quelled.

In 1741, there was a formidable insurrection among the slaves in New York. At that time the population consisted of 12,000 whites and 2,000 blacks. Of the conspirators, thirteen were burned alive, eighteen hung, and eighty transported.

Those who were transported were sent to the West India Islands. As a specimen of the persons who were suitable for transportation, I give the following from the Boston Gazette, Aug. 17, 1761:—

"To be sold, a parcel of likely young negroes, imported from Africa, cheap for cash. Inquire of John Avery. Also, if any person have any negro men, strong and hearty, though not of the best moral character, which are proper subjects for transportation, they may have an exchange for small negroes."

In 1747, the slaves on board of a Rhode Island ship commanded by Capt. Beers, rose, when off Cape Coast Castle, and murdered the captain and all the crew, except the two mates, who swam ashore.

In 1754, C. Croft, Esq., of Charleston, S. C., had his buildings burned by his female negroes, two of whom were burned alive!!

In September, 1755, Mark and Phillis, slaves, were put to death at Cambridge, (Mass.) for poisoning their master, Mr. John Codman of Charlestown. Mark was hanged, and Phillis burned alive! Having ascertained that their master had, by his will, made them free at his death, they poisoned him in order to obtain their liberty so much the sooner.

In August, 1759, another insurrection was contemplated in

Charleston, S. C.

In October, 1761, there was a rebellion among the slaves in Kingston, Jamaica; and in the next December, the slaves in Bermuda rebelled, and threatened to destroy all the whites. All were engaged in the plot, which was accidentally discovered. *One was burned alive*, one hanged, and eleven condemned.

In the same year, Capt. Nichols, of Boston, lost forty of his slaves by an insurrection, but saved his vessel.

In 1763, the Dutch settlement at Barbetias was surprised and destroyed by the negroes.

In 1764, the slaves in Jamaica projected a rebellion, and intended to destroy all the whites on the island.

In 1767, there was a rebellion among the slaves in Grenada.

In 1768, when Gen. Gage was in command of the British troops in Massachusetts, one Capt. John Wilson, of the 59th regiment, made an attempt to excite the few slaves in Boston (about 300) to rise against their masters. He assured the slaves that the foreign troops had come to procure their freedom, and that "with their assistance, they would be able to drive the Liberty Boys to the devil." In October, the Selectmen made a complaint against him; had him arrested, and bound over for trial, but by the influence of British officials, the indictment was quashed, and Wilson fled, satisfied that Boston would not be a safe place for *him*.

In 1765, symptoms of a rebellious and insurrectionary spirit were manifested in various parts of the thirteen colonies, then nominally at least subjects of King George. This spirit was aroused by the passage, by the British Parliament, of the Stamp Act on the 22d of March of that year. As the British government were unable to enforce this Act, it was graciously repealed on the 22d of February, 1766, but coupled with the declaratory Act, that "the Legislature of Great Britain had authority to bind the colonies in all cases whatsoever." On the 20th of November, 1767, the Act previously passed, imposing a duty of three pence per pound on tea, was to take effect. From this Act, with other causes combined, many commotions were excited anew among the people. On the 5th of March, 1770, the Boston massacre occurred. The skirmish at Lexington and Concord on the 19th of April, and the battle on Breed's hill on the 17th of June, 1775, greatly increased the excitement. About the middle of July, the year Lord Dunmore, the royal governor of Virginia, ceased to exercise the functions of his office, having with his wife and children, for fear of the people, taken refuge on board the Fowey man of war. With the hope that he should succeed in reducing the Virginians to subjection, Lord Dunmore gave out that he should instigate the slaves, who were extremely numerous, to revolt against their masters. The dread of the consequences of such a revolt decided the Virginians to form a convention, in which they placed great confidence. The governor expected, but in vain, that the people would rise, and take arms in favor of the king. Hoping, however, that with such force as he had, and the frigates on that station, he should make some impression on the surrounding country, he surprised the town of Hampton, situated on the bay of the same name, and devoted it to the flames. He then proclaimed martial law, "declared free all slaves or servants, black or white, belonging to rebels, provided they would take up arms and join the royal troops." The governor again came on shore at Norfolk, where some hundreds of loyalists and negroes joined the governor. With this motley force, aided by two hundred soldiers of the line, he made an unsuccessful attack on the provincials on the 9th of December. He again repaired on board of one of the ships, and on the first of January, 1776, the frigate Liverpool, two corvettes and the governor's armed sloop, opened a terrible fire on the city; and at the same time, a detachment of marines landed, and set fire to the houses. In this manner was destroyed on of the most opulent and flourishing cities of Virginia.

On the 4th of July, 1776, after eleven years of unavailing negotiation and some fighting, the delegates of the thirteen Colonies, not believing the modern dogma that, however bad the laws may be, they must be obeyed till they are repealed, raised the standard of rebellion, and bade defiance to the colossal power of Great Britain, declaring that they were, and of right ought to be, free and independent, and making the following declaration, viz.:—

"We hold these truths to be self-evident: that all men are created equal; that they are endowed by their Creator with certain inalienable rights; that among these are life, liberty, and the pursuit of happiness."

This was an insurrection on a great scale; and as the insurgents were *white* men, and were successful, they were, of course, right. Says Jefferson, in 1814, "What an incomprehensible machine is man! who can endure toil, famine, stripes, imprisonment, and death itself, in vindication of his own liberty; and the next moment be deaf to all those motives, whose power supported him through his trials, and inflict on his fellow-man a bondage, *one hour of which is fraught with more misery than ages of that which he rose in rebellion to oppose.*"

The insurrection of the people of France against their king, which is generally called the French revolution, is with all its horrors too well known to require notice.

The scenes of St. Domingo next claim our attention. The incidents are given in the language of an author, whose name I do not recollect.

When the French Revolution, which decreed equality of rights to all citizens, had taken place, the *free people of color* of St. Domingo, many of whom were persons of large property and liberal education, petitioned the General Assembly that they might enjoy the same political privileges as the whites. At length, in March, 1790, the subject of the petition was discussed, when the Assembly adopted a decree concerning it. The decree, however, was worded so ambiguously, that the two parties in St. Domingo—the *whites* and the *people of color*—interpreted each in their own favor. This difference of interpretation gave rise to animosities between them, which were augmented by political party spirit, according as they were royalists, or partisans of the French revolution, so that disturbances took place, and blood was shed.

In the year 1791, the people of color petitioned the Assembly again, but principally for an explanation of the decree in question.

On the 15th of May, the subject was taken into consideration, and the result was another decree in more explicit terms, which determined that the people of color in all the French islands were entitled to all the rights of citizens, provided they were born of *free parents on both sides*. The news of this decree no sooner arrived at the Cape, than it produce an indignation almost amounting to frenzy among the whites. They directly trampled under foot the national cockade, and with difficulty were prevented from seizing all the merchant ships in the roads. After this, the two parties armed against each other. Even camps began to be formed. Horrible massacres and conflagrations followed, the reports of which, when brought to the mother country, were so terrible that the Assembly rescinded the decree in favor of the people of color in the same year.

In 1792, the news of this new decree reached St. Domingo, and produced as much irritation among the people of color, as the news of the former had done among the whites; and hostilities were renewed on both sides.

As soon as these events became known in France, the Conventional Assembly, which had then succeeded the Legislature, seeing no hope of reconciliation on either side, knew not what other course to take than to do justice, whatever the consequences might be. They resolved accordingly, in the month of April, that the decree of 1791, which had been first made and reversed by the preceding Assembly, should be made good; thus restoring to the people of color the privileges which had been voted to them; and they appointed Santhonax, Polverel, and another to repair as Commissioners to St. Domingo, with a large body of troops, in order to enforce the decree, and to keep the peace.

In the year 1793, the same division and bloodshed continuing, notwithstanding the arrival of the commissioners, a very trivial matter, a quarrel between a mulatto and a white man, (an officer in the French marines,) gave rise to new disasters. The quarrel took place at Cape Francois on the 20th of June. On the same day, the seamen left their ships in the roads, and came on shore, and made common cause with the white inhabitants of the town. On the other side were ranged the mulattoes and other people of color, and these were afterwards joined by some insurgent blacks. The battle lasted nearly two days. During this time, the arsenal was taken and plundered, some thousands were killed in the streets, and more than half of the town was burned. The commissioners, who were witnesses of the horrible scene, and who had done all that they could to restore peace, escaped unhurt; but they were left upon a heap of ruins, and with little more power than the authority which their commission gave them. They had only about a thousand troops left in the place. They determined, therefore, under these circumstances, to call in the slaves in their neighborhood to their assistance. They issued a proclamation in consequence, by which they promised to give *freedom to all the blacks who were willing to range themselves under the banner of the republic.*

This was the first proclamation made by public authority for emancipating slaves in St. Domingo, and was usually called the proclamation of Santhonax. The result of it was, that a considerable number of slaves came in, and were enfranchised.

Soon after this transaction, Polverel left his colleague, Santhonax, at the Cape, and went in his capacity of commissioner to Port au Prince, the capital of the West. Here he found every thing quiet, and cultivation in a flourishing state. From Port au Prince he visited Aux Cayes, the capital of the South. He had not, however, been long there, before he found that the minds of the slaves began to be in an unsettled state. They had become acquainted with what had taken place in the North; not only with the riots at the Cape, but the proclamation of Santhonax. Polverel, therefore, seeing the impression which it had begun to make on the minds of the slaves in these parts, was convinced that emancipation could neither be prevented, nor even retarded; and that it was absolutely necessary, for *the personal safety of the white planters,* that it should be extended to *the whole island.* He was so convinced of the necessity of this, that in September, 1793, *he drew up a proclamation without further delay to that effect,* and put it into circulation. He dated it from Aux Cayes. He exhorted the planters to patronise it. He advised them, if they wished to avoid the most serious calamities, to concur themselves in the proposition of giving freedom to their slaves. He then caused a registry to be opened at the government house, to receive the signatures of those who should approve of his advice. It was remarkable that all the proprietors in these parts inscribed their names in this book. He then caused a similar registry to be opened at Port au Prince for the West. Here the same disposition was found to prevail. All the planters, except one, gave in their signatures. They had become pretty generally convinced, by this time, that their own personal safety was connected with the measure. We may now add that, in the month of February, 1794, the Conventional Assembly of France passed a decree for the abolition of slavery *throughout the whole of the French Colonies*. Thus the government of the mother country confirmed freedom to those, on whom it had been bestowed by the commissioners. This decree, therefore, *put the finishing stroke to the whole*. It completed the emancipation of *the whole slave population of St. Domingo*.

With regard to the conduct of those who were emancipated by Santhonax in the North, I find nothing particular to communicate. With respect to those emancipated in the South and West by Polverel, we are enabled to give a pleasing account. Colonel Malenfant, who was residing in the island at the time, has made us acquainted with their general conduct and character. "After the public act of emancipation," says he, (by Polverel,) "the *negroes remained quiet, both in the South and in the West, and they continued to work on all the plantations*. There were, indeed, estates which had neither owners nor managers resident on them. Some of these had been put in prison by Mount Brun; and others, fearing the same fate, had fled to the quarter which had just been given up to the English. Yet on these estates, though abandoned, *the negroes continued their labors*, where there were any (even inferior) agents to guide them; and on those estates where no white men were left to direct them, they betook themselves to the planting of provisions; but on all the plantations where the *whites* resided, the *blacks continued to labor as quietly as before*."

A little further on, in the same work, ridiculing the notion entertained in France, that the negroes would not work without compulsion, he takes occasion to allude to other negroes who had been liberated by the same proclamation, but who were more immediately under his own eye. "If," says he, "you will take care not to speak to them of their return to slavery, but talk to them about their liberty, you may, with this latter word, chain them down to labor. How did Toussaint succeed? How did I succeed also, before his time, in the plain of the Cul de Sac, and on the plantation Gouraud, more than eight months after liberty had been granted (by Polverel) to the slaves? Let those who knew me at the time, and even the blacks themselves, be asked. They will all reply that *not a single negro* on that plantation, consisting of more than 460 laborers, *refused to work;* and yet this plantation was thought to be under the worst discipline, and the slaves the most idle in the plain. I, myself, inspired the same activity into three other plantations, of which I had the management."

The above account is far beyond any thing that could have been reasonably expected; indeed, it is most gratifying. We find that the liberated negroes, *both in the South and West,* continued to work on *their old plantations,* and for *their old masters;* so that there was also a spirit of industry among them; for they are described as continuing to work *as quietly as before.* Such was the conduct of the negroes for the first nine months after their liberation, up to the middle of 1794. Of the conduct of the negroes during the year 1795, and part of 1796, I find no account. Had there been any outrages, they would have been mentioned. Let no one connect the outrages, which assuredly took place in St. Domingo in 1791 and 1792, *with the effects of the emancipation of the slaves.* The great massacres and conflagrations which at that time made so frightful a picture in the history of this unhappy island, occurred *in the days of slavery,* before the proclamation of Santhonax and Polverel, and before the great conventional decree of the mother country was known. They had been occasioned, too, *not originally by the slaves themselves,* but by quarrels between the *white* and *colored* planters, and between the *royalists* and the *revolutionists,* who, for the purpose of wreaking their vengeance on each other, called in the aid of their slaves; and as to the insurgent negroes of the North, who filled that part of the colony in those years with terror and dismay, they were originally put in motion, according to Malenfant, *by the royalists themselves,* to strengthen their own cause, and to put down *the partisans of the French revolution.*

When Jean Francois and Brasson commenced the insurrection, there were many white royalists among them, and the negroes were made to wear the white cockade.

I now come to the latter part of the year 1796, and we shall find that there was no want of industry or of obedience in those who had been emancipated. *"The colony,"* says Malenfant, *"was flourishing under Toussaint; the whites lived happily on their estates, and the negroes continued to work for them."* Now, Toussaint came into power, being General-in-chief of the armies of St. Domingo, near the end of the year 1796, and remained in power till the year 1802, or till the invasion of the island by the French expedition by Bonaparte, under Le Clerc. Malenfant, therefore, means to state that from 1796 to 1802, a period of six years, the planters and farmers kept possession of their estates; that they lived on them peacefully, and without interruption or disturbance; and that the negroes, though they had all been set free, continued to be their laborers.

Gen. La Croix, who published his "Memoirs for a History of St. Domingo" at Paris in 1819, informs us that when Santhonax returned to the colony in 1796, *"he was astonished at the state in which he found it on his return."* This, says, La Croix, was owing to Toussaint, who, while he had succeeded in establishing perfect order and discipline among the black troops, had succeeded in making the black laborer return to the plantation, there to resume the drudgery of cultivation.

But the same author tells us that, in the next year, 1797, the most wonderful progress had been made in agriculture. He uses these remarkable words:—*"The colony marched as by enchantment to its former splendor; cultivation prospered; every day produced perceptible proofs of its progress. The city of the Cape and the plantations of the North rose up again visibly to the eye."* To effect this wonderful improvement, many circumstances conspired, but principally the fact that the negroes, being free, had a powerful motive to be industrious and obedient.

The next witness is Gen. Vincent, who was a colonel, and afterwards a general of brigade of artillery at St. Domingo, and was there during the time of Santhonax and Toussaint. He was called to Paris by Toussaint, when he arrived just at the moment of the peace of Amiens, and found, to his inexpressible surprise and grief, that Bonaparte was preparing an immense armament, to be commanded by Le Clerc, for the purpose of *restoring slavery in St. Domingo!* Against this expedition, the General remonstrated with the First Consul, telling him that, though the army destined for this purpose was composed of the brilliant conquerors of Europe, it would do nothing in the Antilles, and would assuredly be destroyed by the climate of St. Domingo, if not destroyed by the blacks. He stated that every thing was going on well in St. Domingo and therefore conjured him, in the name of humanity, not to attempt to reverse this beautiful order of things. His efforts were ineffectual. The armament sailed, and, arriving on the shores of St. Domingo, a scene of blood and torture followed, *such as history had seldom if ever before disclosed,* which, though *planned and executed by whites,* all the barbarities said to have been perpetrated *by the insurgent blacks of the North* amounted comparatively to nothing. At length, the survivors of that vast army were driven from the island, with the loss of sixty thousand lives. Till that time, the planters had retained their estates; and then it was, and not till then, that they lost their all. The question may be asked, why did the First Consul make this frightful invasion? It was owing, not to the emancipated negroes, who were *peaceful, industrious, and beyond example happy,* but to the prejudices of their former masters—prejudices common to almost all slaveholders. Accustomed to the use of arbitrary power, they could not brook the loss of their whips. Accustomed to look down on the negroes as an inferior race of beings, as mere reptiles of the earth, they could not bear, peaceably as these had conducted themselves, to come into that familiar contact with them as free laborers, which the change in their condition required. They considered them, too, as property lost, and which was to be recovered. In an evil hour, they prevailed on Bonaparte, by false representations and *promises of pecuniary support,* to undertake to restore things to their former state; and the result is before the world as an example and a warning. When will our slaveholding brethren learn that the advocates of immediate emancipation are the only true friends of both slaveholders and slaves, and that the only path of safety is the path of duty, which demands the immediate repentance of all sin, and especially that "sum of all villanies," slavery?

In the year 1800, the city of Richmond, Va., and indeed the whole slaveholding country were thrown into a state of intense excitement, consternation and alarm, by the discovery of an intended insurrection among the slaves. The plot was laid by a slave named Gabriel, who was claimed as the property of Mr. Thomas Prosser. A full and true account of this General Gabriel, and of the proceedings consequent on the discovery of the plot, has never yet been published. In 1831 a short account, which is false in almost every particular, appeared in the Albany *Evening Journal* under the head of "Gabriel's Defeat." It was the same year republished in the first volume of the *Liberator*, and during the last year (1859) has been extensively republished in many other papers. The following is the copy of a letter dated Sept. 21, 1800, written by a gentleman of Richmond, Va., and published in the Boston *Gazette*, Oct. 6th:—

"By this time, you have no doubt heard of the conspiracy, formed in this country by the negroes, which, but for the interposition of Providence, would have put the metropolis of the State, and even the State itself, into their possession. A dreadful storm with a deluge of rain, which carried away the bridges and rendered the water courses every where impassable, prevented the execution of their plot. *It was extensive and vast in its design. Nothing could have been better contrived. The conspirators were to have seized on the magazine, the treasury, the mills, and the bridges across James river.* They were to have entered the city of Richmond in three places with fire and sword, to commence an indiscriminate slaughter, the French only excepted. They were then to have called on their fellow negroes and the friends of humanity throughout the continent, by proclamation, to rally round their standard. The magazine, which was defenceless, would have supplied them with arms for many thousand men. The treasury would have given them money, the mills bread, and the bridges would have enabled them to let in their friends, and keep out their enemies. Never was there a more propitious season for the accomplishment of their purpose. The country is covered with rich harvests of Indian corn; flocks and herds are every where fat in the fields; and the liberty and equality doctrine, nonsensical and wicked as it is, (in this land of tyrants and slaves,) is for electioneering purposes sounding and resounding through our valleys and mountains in every direction. The city of Richmond and the circumjacent country are in arms, and have been so for ten or twelve days past. The patrollers are doubled through the State, and the Governor, impressed with the magnitude of the danger, has appointed for himself three Aids de Camp. A number of conspirators have been hung, *and a great many more are yet to be hung.* The trials and executions are going on day by day. Poor deluded wretches! *Their democratic deluders, conscious of their own guilt, and fearful of the public vengeance, are most active in bringing them to punishment.* "*Quicquid delirant reges, plectuntur Achivi*"! Two important facts have been established by the witnesses on the different trials. First, that the plan of the plot was drawn by two Frenchmen in Richmond, and by them given to the negro General Gabriel, who is not yet caught; and secondly, that in the meditated massacre, *not one Frenchman* was to be touched. It is moreover believed, though not positively known, that a great many of our profligate and abandoned whites (who are distinguished by the burlesque appellation of *democrats*) are implicated with the blacks, and would have joined them if they had commenced their operations. The particulars of this horrid affair you will probably see detailed in Davis' paper from Richmond, but certainly in Stewart's paper in Washington. The Jacobin printers and their friends are panic struck. Never was terror more strongly depicted in the countenances of men. They see, they feel, the fatal mischiefs that their preposterous principles and ferocious party spirit have brought upon us."

The Virginia *Gazette* of Sept. 12th thus writes:—

"The public mind has been much involved in dangerous apprehensions concerning an insurrection of the negroes in several of the adjoining counties. Such a thing has been in agitation by an ambitious and insidious fellow named Gabriel, the property of Mr. Thomas Prossor. * * * * Yesterday a Court was held at the Court House in this city, when six of them were convicted, and condemned to be executed this day, Sept. 12th."

"On Thursday, Sept. 18th," says the New York *Spectator,* "five more were executed near the city of Richmond, who were concerned in the insurrection."

These eleven negroes were executed before the apprehension of Gen. Gabriel, for whose arrest Gov. Monroe offered a reward of $300. The following is a copy of a letter dated Norfolk, Sept. 25th, 1800:—

"Last Tuesday, on information being given that Gen. Gabriel was on board the three-masted schooner Mary, Richardson

Taylor skipper, just arrived from Richmond, he was committed to prison in irons. It appeared on his examination that he went on board on the 14th inst., four miles below Richmond, and remained on board eleven days; that when he went first on board, he was armed with a bayonet and bludgeon, both of which he threw into the river."

"On Saturday last," (Sept. 27th,) says a Richmond paper, "the noted Gabriel arrived here by water, under guard from Norfolk, and was committed to the Penitentiary for trial. We understand that when he was apprehended, he manifested the greatest marks of firmness and composure, showing not the least disposition to equivocate, or screen himself from justice. He denied the charge of being the first in exciting the insurrection, although he was to have had the chief command, but that there were four or five persons more materially concerned in the conspiracy, and said that he could mention several in Norfolk; but being conscious of meeting with the fate of those before him, he was determined to make no confession."

"It was stated," says a New York paper, "to be the best planned and most matured of any before attempted." "Gabriel was condemned," says another paper, "on the 3d of October, and executed on the 7th, (having been respited from the 4th,) without making any *useful* confession. On the 3d of October, ten more negroes were executed, and on the 7th, fifteen more— viz.: five at the Brook, five at Four Mile Creek, and four with Gabriel at the Richmond gallows."

These fifteen, as far as we have any account, were the last who were either executed or tried. The Court, in their eager haste to apprehend and punish the conspirators, of whom five, six, ten and fifteen at a time were executed, and that only the day after trial, of whom not one had committed any overt act, and against whom no testimony appears to have been furnished by any white witness, found, after the apprehension of General Gabriel, that they had made some sad mistakes. This fact, with others, caused such a revulsion of feeling, and excited so great a sympathy in behalf of the poor creatures, that they were obliged, by a moral necessity, to pause in their course.

Under date of Oct. 13th, the *Commercial Advertiser* thus writes:—

"The trials of the negroes concerned in the late insurrection are suspended until the opinion of the Legislature can be had on the subject. *This measure is said to be owing to the immense numbers, who are implicated in the plot, whose death, should they all be found guilty and be executed, will nearly produce the annihilation of the blacks in this part of the country.*"

The next day, Oct. 14th, a correspondent from Richmond makes a similar statement with this addition:—

"A conditional amnesty is perhaps expected. At the next session of the Legislature of Virginia, they took into consideration the subject referred to them, *in secret session, with closed doors.* The *whole* result of their deliberations has never yet been made public, as the injunction of secrecy has never been removed. To satisfy the Court, the public, and themselves, they had a task so difficult to perform, that it is not surprising that their deliberations were in secret."

From 1800 till 1816, nothing was divulged. In the spring of 1816, the Hon. Charles Fenton Mercer, in a speech delivered by him in 1833, says, "The intelligence broke in upon me, like a ray of light through the profoundest gloom, and by a mere accident, which occurred in the spring of 1816, that, upon two several occasions, the General Assembly of Virginia had invited the United States to obtain a territory beyond their limits, whereon to colonize *certain portions* of our colored population. For the evidence of these facts, *then new to me*, I was referred to the Clerk of the Senate; and in the *private records* I found them verified."

On the 21st of December, 1800, the Virginia House of Delegates passed, in *secret session*, the following resolution:—

"Resolved, That the Governor [Monroe] be requested to correspond with the President of the United States, on the subject of purchasing land without the limits of this State, *whither persons obnoxious to the laws, or dangerous to the peace of society, may be removed.*"

The General Assembly of Virginia, having through their agent, Mr. Jefferson, failed in 1800, 1802 and 1804, to obtain a place of *banishment* for that portion of their colored population whom they were afraid to hang, and unwilling to pardon, passed on Jan. 22, 1805, still in *secret session*, the following resolution:—

"Resolved, That the Senators of this State in the Congress of the United States be instructed, and the Representatives be requested, to exert their best efforts for the obtaining from the General Government a competent portion of territory in the country of Louisana, to be appropriated to the residence of *such people of color as have been, or shall be, emancipated, or may hereafter become dangerous to the public safety,*" &c.—[See African Repository, June, 1832, and November, 1833.]

The Legislature of Virginia having failed in all their attempts to find a suitable Botany Bay, to which the free people of color, convicts, and other dangerous persons could be banished, passed in 1805 a law prohibiting emancipation, except on the condition that the emancipated should leave the State; or, if remaining in the State more than twelve months, should be sold by the overseers of the poor for the benefit of the Literary Fund.

Here we see another consequence of the attempt of slaves to obtain their freedom, viz., an increased persecution of the free people of color, a law to prevent their increase, and a desire to banish all of them from the State. The conspiracy of Gen. Gabriel and his coadjutors was, therefore, the occasion, if not the cause, of the formation, in 1817, of the Colonization Society, whose great object was, by removing all disturbing causes, to make slavery secure, lucrative, and perpetual. Another noticeable fact, made manifest by the intended insurrection, is the state of fearful insecurity in which the residents of a slaveholding community must feel that they are living. The late assertion of Gov. Wise, that "We, the Virginians, are in no danger from our slaves or the colored people,"— or that of Senator Mason, "We can take care of ourselves,"—or that of Miles, of South Carolina, "We are impregnable,"—betrays the depth and extent of their fear by the very attempt to conceal it; like timid boys "ejaculating through white lips and chattering teeth," *Who's afraid?* In the wide-spread panic of 1800, the slaveholders appear to have been excessively puzzled to ascertain what could have induced their slaves to engage in such a conspiracy. They, of course, could not have originated such a plot, and had been, in their opinion, so well-treated that *they* could have no motive to wish for their freedom. It was at first rumored that Gabriel had in his possession letters written by white men; then, that the conspiracy of the negroes was "occasioned by the circulation of some artfully written hand-bills, drawn up by the noted Callender in prison, and circulated by two French people of color from Guadaloupe, aided by a United Irish pretended Methodist preacher"; then, "that the instigators of the diabolical plan wished thereby to insure the elections of Adams and Pinckney, and that the blacks, as far as they were capable, reasoned on the Jeffersonian principles of emancipation." They were, at last, unwillingly compelled to believe that the whole plot originated with slaves, and was confined to them exclusively, and that, like all other human beings, deprived by arbitrary power of all their just rights, they were determined to be free.

In a letter written in 1800, by Judge St. George Tucker, of Virginia, and published in Baltimore, he thus speaks:—

"The love of freedom is an inborn sentiment, which the God of nature has planted deep in the heart. Long may it be kept under by the arbitrary institutions of society; but, at the first favorable moment, it springs forth with a power which defies all check. This celestial spark, which fires the breast of the savage, which glows in that of the philosopher, is not extinguished in the bosom of the slave. It may be buried in the embers, but it *still lives,* and the breath of knowledge kindles it into a flame. Thus we find there never have been slaves in any country, who have not seized the first favorable opportunity to revolt. These, our hewers of wood and drawers of water, possess the power of doing us mischief, and are prompted to it by *motives which self-love dictates, which reason justifies.* Our sole security, then, consists in their ignorance of this power, and their means of using it—a security which we have lately found is not to be relied on, and which, small as it is, every day diminishes. Every year adds to the number of those who can read and write; and *the increase of knowledge is the principal agent in evolving the spirit we have to fear.* * * * By way of marking the prodigious change which a few years have made among that class of men, compare the late conspiracy with the revolt under Lord Dunmore. In the one case, a few solitary individuals flocked to that standard, under which they were sure to find protection. In the other, they, in a body, of their own accord, combine a plan for asserting their freedom, and rest their safety on success alone. The difference is, that then they sought freedom merely as a good; now they also claim it as a right. * * * Ignorant and illiterate as they yet are, they have maintained a correspondence, which, whether we consider its extent or duration, is truly astonishing."

Thus far Judge Tucker.

Monday, Sept. 1st, was the day set by General Gabriel and his associates to make the attack on Richmond with fire and sword. The plot was, however, discovered only the day previous, and, as I have been informed, was made known by a slave named Ben, who was unwilling that his master (a Mr. W. who had been very kind to him) should lose his life.

The incidents of this conspiracy were embodied in a song, and set to a tune, both of which were composed by a colored man. The song is still sung.

In the New York *Spectator*, of Sept. 24th, 1800, is a letter dated CHARLESTON, S. C., Sept. 13th, which says that "the negroes have rose in arms against the whites in this country, and have killed several. All the troops of light horse are ordered out by the Governor to suppress the insurrection. Some reports state the number of insurgents, who were embodied about thirty miles from the city, to be about four or five thousand strong. Others decreased this number to seven or eight hundred."

In June, 1816, a conspiracy was formed in Camden, South Carolina; but information of the intent was given by a favorite and confidential slave of Col. Chestnut.

On May 30th, 1822, a "faithful and confidential slave" disclosed to the Intendant of Charleston, S. C., that, on Sunday evening, June 16th, the slaves had determined to rise in rebellion against the whites, "set fire to the Governor's house, seize the Guard-house and Arsenal, and sweep the town with fire and sword, not permitting a white soul to escape." Of the supposed conspirators, one hundred and thirty-one were committed to prison, thirty-five executed, and thirty- seven banished. Of the six ringleaders, Ned Bennet, Peter Poyas, Rolla, Batteau, Jesse, and Denmark Vesey, all were slaves, except Vesey, who had been a slave thirty-eight years, a few man twenty-two years, having in 1800 purchased his freedom.

On July 12th, two slaves were executed; July 26th, twenty-two; July 30th, four; and August 9th, one.

In 1826, the inhabitants of Newbern, Targorough and Hillsborough were alarmed by insurrectionary movements among their slaves. The people of Newbern, being informed that forty slaves were assembled in a swamp, surrounded it, and killed the whole party!!

In August, 1831, there was an insurrection of slaves in Southampton, Virginia, headed by a slave, who called himself Gen. Nat. Turner, who declared to his associates that he was acting under inspired directions, and that the singular appearance of the sun at that time was the signal for them to commence the work of destruction; which resulted in the murder of sixty-four white persons, and more than one hundred slaves were killed. The excitement extended throughout Virginia and the Carolinas. "Another such insurrection," says the Richmond Whig, "will be followed by *putting the whole race to the sword.*" In the same year, insurrections occurred in Martinique, Antigua, St. Jago, Caraccas, and Tortola.

In January, 1832, James McDowell, Jr., in reply to a member who called the Nat. Turner insurrection a "petty affair," thus spoke in the Virginia House of Delegates:—

"Now, sir, I ask you, I ask gentlemen, in conscience to say, was that a 'petty affair' which startled the feelings of your whole population; which threw a portion of it into alarm, a portion of it into panic; which wrung out from an affrigted people the thrilling cry, day after day, conveyed to your executive, '*We are in peril of our lives—send us an army for defence!*' Was that a 'petty affair,' which drove families from their homes; which assembled women and children in crowds, without shelter, at places of common refuge, in every condition of weakness and infirmity, under every suffering which want and terror could inflict, yet willing to endure all, willing to meet death from famine, death from climate, death from hardships, preferring any thing rather than the horrors of meeting it from a domestic assassin? Was that a 'petty affair,' which erected a peaceful and confiding portion of the State into a military camp; which *outlawed from pity the unfortunate beings whose brothers had offended;* which barred every door, penetrated every bosom with fear or suspicion; which so banished every sense of security from every man's dwelling, that, let but a hoof or horn break upon the silence of the night, and an aching throb would be driven to the heart? The husband would look to his weapon, and the mother would shudder, and weep upon her cradle! Was it the fear of Nat. Turner and his deluded, drunken handful of followers, which produced such effects? Was it this that induced distant counties, where the very name of Southampton was strange, to arm and equip for a struggle? No, sir, it was the *suspicion eternally attached to the slave himself;* the suspicion that a Nat. Turner might be in every family—that the same bloody deed might be acted over at any time, and in any place—that the materials for it were spread through the land, and were always ready for a like explosion. Nothing but the force of this withering apprehension, nothing but the paralyzing and deadening weight with which it falls upon and prostrates the heart of every man who has helpless dependants to protect, nothing but this could have thrown a brave people into consternation, or could have made any portion of this powerful Commonwealth, for a single instant, to have quailed and trembled."

In the same year and month, Henry Berry, Esq., another delegate, thus spoke:—

"Sir, I believe that no cancer on the physical body was ever more certain, steady and fatal in its progress, than this cancer on the political body of Virginia. It is eating into her very vitals. And shall we admit that the evil is past remedy? Shall we act the part of a puny patient, suffering under the ravages of a fatal disease, who would say the remedy is too painful? Pass as severe laws as you will to keep these unfortunate creatures in ignorance, it is in vain, unless you can extinguish that spark of intellect which God has given them. Sir, we have, as far as possible, closed *every avenue by which light might enter their minds.* We have only to go one step further— to extinguish the capacity to see the light—and our work will be completed. They would then be reduced to the level of the beasts of the field, and we should be safe; and I am not certain that we would not do it, if we could find out the necessary process, and that under the plea of necessity. But, sir, this is impossible; and can man be in the midst of freemen, and not know what freedom is? Can he feel that he has the power to assert his liberty, and *will he not do it?* Yes, sir, *with the certainty of Time's current, he will do it whenever he has the power.* The data are before us all, and every man can work out the process for himself. Sir, a *death-struggle must come between the two classes, in which one or the other will be extinguished forever.* Who can contemplate such a catastrophe as even possible, and be indifferent?"

In an essay written by Judge St. George Tucker, and published in 1796, he expresses similar sentiments, in language equally forcible, and concludes by saying:—

"I presume it is possible that an effectual remedy for the evils

of slavery may at length be discovered. Whenever that happens, *the golden age of our country will begin.* Till then,—
"Non hospes a hospite tutus, Non Herus a Famulis, fratrum quoque gratia rara."

"I tremble for my country when I reflect that God is just, that his justice cannot sleep forever," and "that the Almighty has no attribute that can take sides with us in such a contest," viz., "an exchange of situation" [with the slaves,] are the well-known words of Jefferson.

In 1832, a general insurrection of the slaves occurred in Jamaica, when between two and three thousand slaves were killed, and a large number of whites. The loss occasioned by the rebellion was estimated at five millions of dollars, a part of which was occasioned by the burning of one hundred and fifty plantations. *Now,* the British West Indies are forever exempted from all danger of insurrection, while the danger of a servile war in America will, until slavery is abolished, every year increase.

In the month of June, 1839, a vessel, called the Amistad, Ramon Ferrer, Captain, sailed from Havana for Principe, about one hundred leagues distant, with fifty-four negroes and two white passengers, (Spaniards,) viz., Pedro Montez and Jose Ruiz, one of whom claimed to be the owner of the negroes, who were all natives of Africa. While on board, they "suffered much from hunger and thirst." In addition to this, there was much whipping, and "the cook told them that, when they reached land, they would all be eaten." This "made their hearts burn." To avoid being eaten, and to escape the bad treatment, they rose upon the crew with the design of returning to Africa. This was on June 27th, four days after leaving Havana. After killing the captain and the cook, and permitting the crew to escape, they under command of Cinque, who compelled Montez to steer the ship for Africa, which he did in the day time, because the negroes could tell his course by the sun, but put the vessel about in the night. In this manner, the vessel drifted about till August 26th, when she was taken possession of by Capt. Gedney, U. S. N. After an interesting trial in Connecticut, the negroes were set free, and, under the American Missionary Association, were sent to their native country, Africa, and of whom many are now receiving religious instruction by means of missionaries who accompanied them to the Mendi country. It is in relation to these blacks that President Buchanan, in his late message, thus speaks:—"I again recommend that an appropriation be made to be paid to the Spanish Government for the purpose of distribution among the claimants in the Amistad case"!!

On the 27th of October, 1841, the Creole sailed from Richmond with one hundred and thirty-five slaves, bound for New Orleans. On November 7th, they rose on the crew, killed a passenger named Howell, and on November 9th, arrived at Nassau, New Providence, where they were all set free by the British authorities. The leader in this successful attempt to secure their freedom was Madison Washington. "The sagacity, bravery and humanity of this man," says the Hon. William Jay, "do honor to his name, and, but for his complexion, would excite universal admiration."

In 1846, the slaves in Santa Cruz rose in rebellion against their masters, took possession of the island, and thus obtained their freedom, but did no injury to any white person. This was remarkable, as the whites numbered 3,000, and the blacks 25,000.

Now, what is the inference from this list of conspiracies and insurrections, and scores of others which could be collected? Why, (1,) that all danger arises from the continuance of slavery, and not from its abolition. And, (2,) that if the Bible sanctions slavery, the God of the Bible does not. The language of God's providence is one and uniform, and too explicit to be misunderstood. It assures us, and writes the assurance in lines of blood, that the way of the transgressor is hard, and that though hand join in hand, the violators of God's law shall not go unpunished. All history, ancient and modern, is full of examples and warnings on this point. Shall we slight these warnings, shut our eyes against the light, and madly rush on our own destruction? Let us remember that slavery is an unnatural state; that Nature, when her eternal principles are violated, always struggles to restore them to her true estate; and that the natural feelings accord with the sentiment of the poet,

"If I'm designed yon lordling's slave,
By Nature's laws designed,
Why was an independent wish
E'er planted in my mind?"

"If the Bible," says the Rev. Albert Barnes, "could be shown to defend and countenance slavery as a good institution, it would make thousands of infidels; for there are multitudes of minds that will see more clearly that slavery is against all the laws which God has written on the human soul, than they would see that a book, sanctioning such a system, had evidence of divine origin."

Says Charles Alcott, of Medina, Ohio, in his very able lectures on slavery:—

> "It is easy to show that slavery has, from first to last, been supported directly and solely by crimes, and that the commission of nearly every crime in the Bible calendar, and many crimes against the common law, are absolutely necessary to support it, and give it full effect. It is a fact equally curious and true, that crime of any kind can only be supported by crime; and that, in order to persevere in the commission of one crime, and prevent its detection and punishment, it is necessary to commit still further crimes."

This being true, it follows conclusively that immediate repentance of the sin of slavery is the duty of every master, and immediate emancipation the right of every slave. Says Charles Alcott, "A man cannot stir, or move, or begin to act, either in support of slavery, or in opposition to its immediate abolition, without committing crimes or sins of some sort or other." He cannot be neutral. Therefore, gentle reader, in the *"irrepressible conflict"* that is now agitating the country, and will continue to agitate it till slavery is abolished, which side have you chosen, or do you intend to choose? Will you take the "higher law," which is in harmony with God's providence and his word, or act in favor of the "lower law," which opposes both? If slavery is right, sustain, defend and justify it; but if it is a crime, do all in your power, by moral means, to overthrow the execrable system. If you are a professed Christian, remember the words of Rev. Albert Barnes:—

> "There is not vital energy enough, there is not power of numbers and influence enough, *out of the Church,* to sustain it. Let every religious denomination in the land detach itself from all connection with slavery. All that is needful is, for each Christian man, for every Christian church, to stand up in the sacred majesty of such a solemn testimony, and to free themselves from all connection with the evil, and utter a calm, deliberate voice to the world, *and the work is done."*

THE STONO REBELLION

THE NEGRO INSURRECTION IN SOUTH CAROLINA

Originally titled "An Account of the Negroe Insurrection in South Carolina," this account – written by an unidentified white official – begins with a summary of Spain's promise of protection and freedom to slaves in the British colonies, then proceeds to relate the events of the uprising.[1]

Sometime since there was a Proclamation published at Augustine [Spanish Florida], in which the King of Spain (then at Peace with Great Britain) promised Protection and freedom to all Negroes Slaves that would resort thither. Certain Negroes belonging to Captain Davis escaped to Augustine, and were received there. . . The good reception of the Negroes at Augustine was spread about. Several attempted to escape to the Spaniards, & were taken, one of them was hanged at Charles Town. . . .

On the 9th day of September last, being Sunday, which is the day the Planters allow them to work for themselves, Some Angola Negroes assembled to the number of Twenty; and one who was called Jemmy was their Captain. They surprised a Warehouse belonging to Mr. Hutchenson at a place called Stonehow [Stono]; they there killed Mr. Robert Bathurst and Mr. Gibbs, plundered the House and took a pretty many small Arms and Powder, which were there for Sale. Next they plundered and burnt Mr. Godfrey's house and killed him, his Daughter and Son. They then turned back and marched Southward along Pons Pons, which is the Road through Georgia to Augustine.

They passed Mr. Wallace's Tavern towards daybreak, and said they would not hurt him, for he was a good Man and kind to his Slaves, but they broke open and plundered Mr. Lemy's House and killed him, his wife and Child. They marched on towards Mr. Rose's resolving to kill him; but he was saved by a Negroe who, having hid him, went out and pacified the others. Several Negroes joined them, they calling out Liberty, marched on with Colors displayed and two Drums beating, pursuing all the white people they met with, and killing Man Woman and Child when they could come up to them.

Colonel Bull, Lieutenant Governor of South Caro-lina, who was then riding along the Road, discovered them, was pursued, and with much difficulty escaped & raised the Country. They burnt Colonel Hext's house and killed his Overseer and his Wife. They then burnt Mr. Sprye's house, then Mr. Sacheverell's, and then Mr. Nash's house, all lying upon the Pons Pons Road, and killed all the white People they found in them. Mr. Bullock got off, but they burnt his House.

By this time many of them were drunk with the Rum they had taken in the Houses. They increased every minute by new Negroes coming to them, so that they were above Sixty, some say a hundred, on which they halted in a field and set to dancing, Singing and beating Drums, to draw more Negroes to them, thinking they were now victorious over the whole Province, having marched ten miles & burnt all before them without Opposition, but the Militia being raised, the Planters with great briskness pursued them and when they came up, dismounting, charged them on foot. The Negroes were soon routed though they behaved boldly, several being killed on the Spot, many ran back to their Plantations thinking they had not been missed, but they were there taken and Shot, Such as were taken in the field also, were, after being examined, shot on the Spot; and this is to be said to the honor of the Carolina Planters, that notwithstanding the Provocation they had received from so many Murders, they did not torture one Negroe, but only put them to an easy death.

All [slaves] that proved to be forced & were not concerned in the Murders & Burnings were pardoned. And this sudden Courage in the field, & the Humanity afterwards hath had so good an Effect that there hath been no farther Attempt, and the very Spirit of Revolt seems over. About 30 escaped from the fight, of which ten marched about 30 miles Southward, and being overtaken by the Planters on horseback, fought stoutly for some time and were all killed on the Spot. The rest are yet untaken. In the whole action about 40 Negroes and 20 whites were killed.

The Lieutenant Governor sent an account of this to General

Oglethorpe, who met the advices on his return from the Indian Nation. He immediately ordered a Troop of Rangers to be ranged, to patrol through Georgia, placed some Men in the Garrison at Palichocolas, which was before abandoned, and near which the Negroes formerly passed, being the only place where Horses can come to swim over the River Savannah for near 100 miles, ordered out the Indians in pursuit, and a Detachment of the Garrison at Port Royal to assist the Planters on any Occasion, and published a Proclamation ordering all the Constables &c. [etc.] of Georgia to pursue and seize all Negroes, with a Reward for any that should be taken. It is hoped these measures will prevent any Negroes from getting down to the Spaniards.

A FAMILY ACCOUNT OF THE STONO UPRISING

In most accounts of slave uprisings from the slave's perspective - such as formulaic legal confessions or dramatic narratives transcribed as "fully and voluntarily made" by the captured rebel (e.g., The Confessions of Nat Turner) - the slave's experience is heavily filtered through the white recorder's pen. In contrast, this 1937 interview with a direct descendant of Cato, a leader of the 1739 Stono Rebellion in South Carolina, may be the closest we get to an unfiltered first-person account of a slave rebellion.[2]

George Cato, the great-great-grandson of Cato, relates the slaves' account as passed down for two centuries in the Cato family (and as transcribed by a white interviewer in the WPA Federal Writers' Project). The narrative is presented as transcribed. It is important to note that some white interviewers, despite project guidelines for transcribing the narratives, used stereotypical patterns of representing black speech, as is the case below.[3]

George Cato, a Negro laborer, residing at the rear of 1010 Lady Street, Columbia, S.C., says he is a great-great-grandson of the late Cato slave who commanded the Stono Insurrection in 1739, in which 21 white people and 44 Negroes were slain. George, now 50 years old, states that this Negro uprising has been a tradition in his family for 198 years.

When asked for the particulars, he smiled, invited the caller to be seated, and related the following story:

"Yes sah! I sho' does come from dat old stock who had de misfortune to be slaves but who decide to be men, at one and de same time, and I's right proud of it. De first Cato slave we knows 'bout, was plum willin' to lay down his life for de right, as he see it. Dat is pow'ful fine for de Catoes who has come after him. My granddaddy and my daddy tell me plenty 'bout it, while we was livin' in Orangeburg County, not far from where de fightin' took place in de long ago.

"My granddaddy was a son of de son of de Stono slave commander. He say his daddy often take him over de route of de rebel slave march, dat time when dere was sho' big trouble all 'bout dat neighborhood. As it come down to me, I thinks de first Cato take a darin' chance on losin' his life, not so much for his own benefit as it was to help others. He was not lak some slaves, much 'bused by deir masters. My kinfolks not 'bused.

Da[t] why, I reckons, de captain of de slaves was picked by them. Cato was teached how to read and write by his rich master.

"How it all start? Dat what I ask but nobody ever tell me how 100 slaves between de Combahee and Edisto rivers come to meet in de woods not far from de Stono River on September 9, 1739. And how they elect a leader, my kinsman, Cato, and late dat day march to Stono town, break in a warehouse, kill two white men in charge, and take all de guns and ammunition they wants. But they do it. Wid dis start, they turn south and march on.

"They work fast, coverin' 15 miles, passin' many fine plantations, and in every single case, stop, and break in de house and kill men, women, and children. Then they take what they want 'cludin' arms, clothes, liquor and food. Near de Combahee swamp, Lieutenant Governor Bull, drivin' from Beaufort to Charleston, see them and he small a rat. Befo' he was seen by de army he detour into de big woods and stay 'til de slave rebels pass.

"Governor Bull and some planters, between de Combahee and Edisto [rivers], ride fast and spread de alarm and it wasn't long 'til de militiamen was on de trail in pursuit of de slave army. When found, many of de slaves was singin' and dancin' and Cap. Cato and some of de other leaders was cussin' at them sumpin awful. From dat day to dis, no Cato has tasted whiskey, 'less he go 'against his daddy's warnin'. Dis war last less than two days but it sho' was pow'ful hot while it last.

"I reckon it was hot, 'cause in less than two days, 21 white men, women, and chillun, and 44 Negroes, was slain. My granddaddy say dat in de woods and at Stono, where de war start, dere was more than 100 Negroes in line. When de militia come in sight of them at Combahee swamp, de drinkin' dancin' Negroes scatter I de brush and only 44 stand deir ground.

"Commander Cato speak for de crowd. He say: 'We don't lak slavery. We start to jine [join] de Spanish in Florida. We surrender but we not whipped yet and we is not converted.' De other 43 men say: 'Amen.' They was taken, unarmed, and hanged by de militia. Long befo' dis uprisin', de Cato slave wrote passes for slaves and do all he can to send them to freedom. He die but he die for doin' de right, as he see it."

Endnotes

1. The Colonial Records of the State of Georgia, ed. Allen D. Candler, et al. (Atlanta: Byrd, 1913), vol. 22, pt. 2, pp. 232-236. Paragraphing added and some spelling and punctuation modernized by the National Humanities Center for clarity. Some scholars credit the account to Gen. James Oglethorpe, founder and leader of the Georgia colony.

2. According to Mark M. Smith's Stono: Documenting and Interpreting a Southern Slave Revolt:

> Although such narratives must be treated with care as historical sources – they are, after all, interviews conducted in the 1930s about slave life before 1865 and are far removed in time and place from slavery – a good deal of what George Cato says – roughly two hundred years after the event – is corroborated by other sources. Oral tradition among nonliterate or barely literate peoples is often reliable. George Cato stresses matters in his account that historians have come to see as critical to a full understanding of the revolt: masculinity, drink, religion, military fighting, timing. The document is the only source we have from a nonwhite perspective, and it is worth reading carefully. (p. 55)

2. According to the "A Note on the Language of the Narratives" from the Library of Congress:

> The Slave Narrative Collection in the Manuscript Division at the Library of Congress consists of narrative texts derived from oral interviews. The narratives usually involve some attempt by the interviewers to reproduce in writing the spoken language of the people they interviewed, in accordance with instructions from the project's headquarters, the national office of the Federal Writers' Project in Washington, D.C.
>
> The interviewers were writers, not professionals trained in the phonetic transcription of speech. And the instructions they received were not altogether clear. "I recommend that truth to idiom be paramount, and exact truth to pronunciation secondary," wrote the project's editor, John Lomax, in one letter to interviewers in sixteen states. Yet he also urged that "words that definitely have a notably different pronunciation from the usual should be recorded as heard," evidently assuming that "the usual" was self-evident.

In fact, the situation was far more problematic than the instructions from project leaders recognized. All the informants were of course black, most interviewers were white, and by the 1930s, when the interviews took place, white representations of black speech already had an ugly history of entrenched stereotype dating back at least to the early nineteenth century. What most interviewers assumed to be "the usual" patterns of their informants' speech was unavoidably influenced by preconceptions and stereotypes.

TOUSSAINT LOUVERTURE

THE HAITIAN REVOLUTION

AN 1805 ACCOUNT

Marcus Rainsford

Toussaint Louverture, as described in an excerpt by Marcus Rainsford, in one of the earliest published and positive accounts of the Haitian revolution. The excerpt comes from Rainsford's 1805 *An Historical Account of the Black Empire of Hayti: Comprehending a View of the Principal Transactions in the Revolution of Saint-Domingo; with its Ancient and Modern State.*

The close of the eighteenth century, a period marked by the grandest operations and the most gigantic projects, presented to the world a new and organized empire, where it was not only supposed to be impossible to exist, but, where even its existence was denied, although it was known by those connected with that quarter of the globe to have taken place, and under the most flourishing auspices. The beneficent and able black, Toussaint L'Ouverture, devoid of the extraneous policy of the governors of ancient states, no sooner found himself at ease from the complicated warfare with which, from the first moment of his government he had been surrounded, than he evinced equal talents for the arts of peace, with those which he had invariably displayed in the field; and that mercy which had ever accompanied him in victory, now transfused itself in a mild and humane policy in the legislature. His first care was to establish, on a firm foundation, the ordinances of religion, according to the existing constitutions of society, to watch over the morals, and excite the industry of those who had committed themselves to his charge.

The effects of these exertions were quickly evident throughout his dominion. Such was the progress of agriculture from this period, that the succeeding crop produced (notwithstanding the various impediments, in addition to the ravages of near a ten years war) full one third of the quantity of sugar and coffee, which had ever been produced at its most prosperous period. The increase of population was such, as to astonish the planters resident in the mother country who could not conceive the possibility of preventing that falling off, in the numbers of the negroes, which formed their absolute necessity for supplying them by the by slave trade. Health, became prevalent throughout the country, with its attendant, cheerfulness, that exhilarator of labor.

Having introduced in a prominent fashion the surprising character, to whose talents and energies, the inhabitants of this regenerated island were indebted for their then existing advantages, it becomes necessary to present the reader with a view of the circumstances which accompanied a life so important in the history of St. Domingo.

TOUSSAINT L'OUVERTURE was born a slave in the year 1745[2], on the estate of the Count de Noe, at a small distance from Cape François, in the northern province of St. Domingo, a spot since remarkable as the very source of revolution, and site of a camp, (that Breda,) from whence its native general has issued mandates more powerful than those of any monarch on the earth.

While tending his master's flocks, the genius of Toussaint began to expand itself, by an attention towards objects beyond the reach of his comprehension; and without any other opportunity than was equally possessed by those around him, who remained nearly in impenetrable ignorance, he learnt to read, write, and use figures. Encouraged by the progress he rapidly made in these arts, and fired with the prospect of higher attainments, he employed himself assiduously in the further cultivation of his talents. His acquirements, as is oftentimes the case, under such circumstances, excited the admiration of his fellow slaves, and fortunately attracted the attention of the attorney, or manager of the estate, M. Bayou de Libertas. This gentleman, with a discrimination honorable to his judgment, withdrew Toussaint from the labor of the fields, to his own house, and began the amelioration of his fortune, by appointing him his postilion, an enviable situation among slaves, for its profit, and comparative respectability.

This instance of patronage by M. Bayou, impressed itself strongly on the susceptible mind of Toussaint. True genius and elevated sentiments are inseparable; the recollection of the most trivial action, kindly bestowed in obscurity, or under the pressure of adverse circumstances, warms the heart of sensibility, even in the hour of popular favor, more than the proudest honors. This truth was exemplified by the subsequent gratitude of Toussaint towards his master. He continued to deserve and receive promotion, progressively, to offices of considerable confidence.

Among other traits fondly preserved in St. Domingo of the conduct of Toussaint during the early period of his life, are his remarkable benevolence towards the brute creation, and an unconquerable patience. Of the former, many instance related which evince a mind endowed with every good quality. He knew how to avail himself so well of the sagacity of the horse, as to perform wonders with that animal; without those cruel methods used to extort from them the docility exhibited in Europe; he was frequently seen musing amongst the different cattle, seemingly holding a species of dumb converse, which they evidently understood, and produced in them undoubted marks of attention. They knew and manifested their acquaintance, whenever he appeared; and he has been frequently seen attending with the anxiety of a nurse any accident which had befallen them; the only instance in which he could be roused to irritation, was when a slave had revenged the punishment he received from his owner upon his harmless and unoffending cattle. Proverbial became his patience, insomuch that it was a favorite amusement of the young and inconsiderate upon the same estate, to endeavor to provoke him by wanton tricks and affected malignity. But so perfectly he had regulated his temper, that he constantly answered with a meek smile, and accounted for their conduct by such means, as would render it strictly pardonable. To the law of self-preservation, or the misfortune of not knowing the delight of philanthropy, he would attribute an act of brutal selfishness; while he imputed to a momentary misapprehension an inclination to rude and malicious controversy. Thus was his passive disposition never in the smallest degree affected, being ready on all occasions to conciliate and to bear, in circumstances whether frivolous or of the, highest importance.

At the age of twenty-five Toussaint attached himself to a female of similar character to his own, and their union cemented by marriage, which does not appear to have been violated, conferred respectability on their offspring. Still he continued a slave; nor did the goodness of M. Bayou, although it extended to render him as happy as the state of servitude would admit, ever contemplate the manumission of one who was to become a benefactor to him and his family. Such is the effect of ancient prejudice, in obscuring, the highest excellence of our nature; he who would perform godlike actions without hesitation, from any other cause, shrinks from a breach of etiquette, or a violation of custom!

Continuing on the estate on which he was born, when the deliberations preceding the actual rebellion of the slaves were taking place upon the plantation of Noe the opinion of him who was always regarded with esteem and admiration was solicited. His sanction was of importance, as he had a number of slaves under his command, and a general influence over his fellow negroes. Among the leaders of this terrible revolt were several of his friends, who he had deemed worthy to make his associates for mutual intelligence; yet, from whatever cause is not ascertained, he forbore in the first instance to join in the contest of liberty. It is probable that his manly heart revolted from cruelties attendant on the first burst of revenge in slaves about to retaliate their wrongs and sufferings on their owners. He saw that the innocent would suffer with the guilty; and that the effects of revolution regarded future, more than present justice. When the cloud charged with electric fluid becomes too ponderous, it selects not the brooding murderer on the barren heath, but bursts, perhaps, indiscriminately, in wasteful vengeance, o'er innocent flocks reposing in verdant fields.

There were ties which connected Toussaint more strongly than the consideration of temporary circumstances. These were gratitude for the benefits received from his master, and, generosity to those who were about to fall,—not merely beneath the stroke of the assassin, for that relief from their sufferings was not to be allowed to all, but likewise the change of situations of luxury and splendor, to an exile of danger, contempt, and poverty, with all the miseries such a reverse can accumulate.

Toussaint prepared for the emigration of M. Bayou de Libertas, as if he had only removed for his pleasure, to the American continent. He found means to embark produce that should form a useful provision for the future; procured his escape with his family, and contrived every plan for his convenience: nor did his care end here, for after M. Bayou's establishment in safety at Baltimore, in Maryland, he availed himself of every opportunity to supply any conceived deficiency, and, as he rose in circumstances, to render those of his protégés more qualified to his situation, and equal to that warm remembrance of the services he owed him, which would never expire.

Having provided for the safety of his master in the first instance, Toussaint no longer resisted the temptations to join the army of his country, which had (at this period) assumed a regular form. He attached himself to the corps under the command of a courageous black chief, named Biassou, and was appointed next in command to him. Though possessed of striking abilities the disposition of this general rendered him unfit for the situation which he held; his cruelty caused him to be deprived of a power which he abused. No one was found equally calculated, to supply his place, with the new officer, Toussaint; therefore, quitting for ever a subordinate situation, he was appointed to the command of a division.

If during this early period of his life, the black general had shone conspicuously, through every disadvantage, with the brightest talents and the milder virtues, he now rose superior to all around him, with the qualities and rank of an exalted chief. Every part of his conduct was marked by judgment and benevolence. By the blacks, who had raised him to the dignity he enjoyed, he was beloved with enthusiasm; and, by the public characters of other nations, with whom he had occasion to communicate, he was regarded with every mark of respect and esteem. General Laveaux called him "the negro, the Spartacus, foretold by Raynal, whose destiny it was to avenge the wrongs committed on his race": and the Spanish Marquis d'Hermona declared, in the hyperbole of admiration, that "if the Supreme had descended on earth, he could not inhabit a heart more apparently good, than that of Toussaint L'Ouverture."

His powers of invention in the art of war, and domestic government, the wonder of those who surrounded, or opposed him, had not previously an opportunity for exhibition as at the period to which we have arrived in this history. Embarrassed by a variety of contending factions among the blacks, and by enemies of different nations and characters, he was too much occupied in evading the blows constantly meditated in different quarters, to find leisure for the display of that wisdom and magnanimity which he so eminently exercised. Nevertheless a variety of incidents are recorded in the fleeting memorials of the day to corroborate the excellence of his character, and still more are impressed on the memory of all who have visited the scene of his government. Notwithstanding the absoluteness of military jurisdiction, which existed with extra power, no punishment ever took place without the anxious endeavors of the General-in-Chief to avoid it, exerted in every way that could be devised. No object was too mean for his remonstrance, or advice; nor any crime too great to be subjected to the rules he had prescribed to himself.

AN 1823 ACCOUNT

Thomas Clarkston

The following is an excerpt from Thomas Clarkson's 1823 *Thoughts on the Necessity for improving the Condition of the Slaves in the British Colonies: With a view to their ultimate emancipation: And on the practicability, the safety, and the advantages of the latter measure.* It illustrates the importance many observers gave to the Haitian Revolution. Clarkson, a British abolitionist, was not only a contemporary of Jean-Jacques Dessalines and Toussaint Louverture, but was also directly involved in the struggle in Saint-Domingue, for example, through his support of Vincent Ogé in the years leading up to the start of the Haitian Revolution after the 1791 vodou ceremonies of Bois Caïman, also known as Boukman.

To do justice to this case [the end of slavery in Haiti], I must give a history of the different circumstances connected with it. It may be remembered, then, that when the French Revolution, which decreed equality of rights to all citizens, had taken place, the free People of Color of St. Domingo, many of whom were persons of large property and liberal education, petitioned the National Assembly, that they might enjoy the same political privileges as the *Whites* there. At length the subject of the petition was discussed, but not till the 8th of March 1790, when the Assembly agreed upon a decree concerning it. The decree, however, was worded so ambiguously, that the two parties in St. Domingo, the Whites and the *People of Color*, interpreted it each of them in its own favor. This difference of interpretation gave rise to animosities between them, and these animosities were augmented by political party-spirit, according as they were royalists or partisans of the French Revolution, so that disturbances took place and blood was shed.

In the year 1791, the People of Color petitioned the Assembly again, but principally for an explanation of the decree in question. On the 15th of May, the subject was taken into consideration, and the result was another decree in explicit terms, which determined, that the People of Color in all the French islands were entitled to all the rights of citizenship, provided *they were born of free parents on both sides*. The news of this decree had no sooner arrived at the Cape, than it produced an indignation almost amounting to frenzy among the Whites. They directly trampled under foot the national cockade, and with difficulty were prevented from seizing all the French merchant ships in the roads. After this the two parties armed against each other. Even camps began to be formed. Horrible massacres and conflagrations followed, the reports of which, when brought to the mother-country, were so terrible, that the Assembly abolished the decree in favor of the *Free People of Color* in the same year.

In the year 1792, the news of the rescinding of the decree as now stated, produced, when it reached St. Domingo, as much irritation among the People of Color, as the news of the passing of it had done among the Whites, and hostilities were renewed between them, so that new battles, massacres, and burnings, took place. Suffice it to say, that as soon as these events became known in France, the Conventional Assembly, which had then succeeded the Legislative, took them into consideration. Seeing, however, nothing but difficulties and no hope of reconciliation on either side, they knew not what other course to take than to do justice, whatever the consequences might be. They resolved, accordingly, in the month of April, that the decree of 1791, which had been both made and reversed by the preceding Assembly in the same year, should stand good. They restored therefore the People of Color to the privileges which had been before voted to them, and appointed Santhonax, Polverel, and another, to repair in person to St. Domingo, with a large body of troops, and to act there as commissioners, and, among other things, to enforce the decree and to keep the peace.

In the year 1793, the same divisions and the same bad blood continuing, notwithstanding the arrival of the commissioners, a very trivial matter, viz. a quarrel between a Mulatto and a *White man* (an officer in the French marine), gave rise to new disasters. This quarrel took place on the 20th of June. On the same day the seamen left their ships in the roads, and came on shore, and made common cause of the affair with the white inhabitants of the town. On the other side were opposed the Mulattos and other People of Color, and these were afterwards joined by some insurgent Blacks. The battle lasted nearly two days. During this time the arsenal was taken and plundered, and some thousands were killed in the streets, and more than half the town was burnt. The commissioners, who were spectators of this horrible scene, and who had done all they could to restore peace, escaped unhurt, but they were left upon a heap of ruins, and with but little more power than the authority which their commission gave them. They had only about a thousand troops left in the place. They determined, therefore, under these circumstances, to call in the Negro Slaves in the neighbourhood to their assistance. They issued a proclamation in consequence, by which *they promised to give freedom to all the Blacks who were willing to range themselves under the banners of the Republic*. This was the first proclamation made by public authority for emancipating slaves in St. Domingo. It is usually called the Proclamation of Santhonax [Sonthonax], though both commissioners had a hand in it; and sometimes, in allusion to the place where it was issued (the Cape), the Proclamation of the North. The result of it was, that a considerable number of slaves came in and were enfranchised.

Soon after this transaction Polverel left his colleague Santhonax at the Cape, and went in his capacity of commissioner to Port au Prince, the capital of the West. Here he found every thing quiet, and cultivation in a flourishing state. From Port au Prince he visited Les Cayes, the capital of the South. He had not, however, been long there, before he found that the minds of the slaves began to be in an unsettled state. They had become acquainted with what had taken place in the north, not only with the riots at the Cape, but the proclamation of Santhonax. Now this proclamation, though it sanctioned freedom only for a particular or temporary purpose, did not exclude it from any particular quarter. The terms therefore appeared to be open to all who would accept them. Polverel therefore, seeing the impression which it had begun to make upon the minds of the slaves in these parts, was convinced that emancipation could be neither stopped nor retarded, and that it was absolutely necessary for *the personal safety of the white planters*, that it should be extended to the whole island. He was so convinced of the necessity of this, that *he drew up a proclamation* without further delay *to that effect*, and *put it into circulation*. He dated it from Les Cayes. He exhorted the planters to patronize it. He advised them, if they wished to avoid the most serious calamities, to concur themselves in the proposition of giving freedom to their slaves. He then caused a register to be opened at the Government house to receive the signatures of all those who should approve of his advice. It was remarkable that all the proprietors in these parts inscribed their names in the book. He then caused a similar register to be opened at Port au Prince for the West. Here the same disposition was found to prevail. All the planters, except one, gave in their signatures. They had become pretty generally convinced by this time, that their own personal safety was connected with the measure. It may be proper to observe here, that the proclamation last mentioned, which preceded these registries, though it was the act of Polverel alone, was sanctioned afterwards by Santhonax. It is, however, usually called the Proclamation of Polverel or of Les Cayes. It came out in September 1793. We may now add, that in the month of February 1794, the Conventional Assembly of France, though probably ignorant of what the commissioners had now done, passed a decree for the abolition of slavery throughout the *whole of the French colonies*. Thus the Government of the mother-country, without knowing it, confirmed freedom to those upon whom it had been bestowed by the commissioners. This decree put therefore the finishing stroke to the whole. It completed the emancipation of the *whole* slave *population of St. Domingo*.

Having now given a concise history of the abolition of slavery in St. Domingo, I shall inquire how those who were

liberated on these several occasions conducted themselves after this change in their situation. It is of great importance to us to know, whether they used their freedom properly, or whether they abused it.

With respect to those emancipated by Santhonax in the North, we have nothing to communicate. They were made free for military purposes only; and we have no clue whereby we can find out what became of them afterwards.

With respect to those who were emancipated next in the South, and those directly afterwards in the West, by the proclamation of Polverel, we are enabled to give a very pleasing account. Fortunately for our views, Colonel Malenfant, who was resident in the island at the time, has made us acquainted with their general conduct and character. His account, though short, is quite sufficient for our purpose. Indeed it is highly satisfactory. "After this public act of emancipation," says he, (by Polverel,) "the Negroes *remained quiet* both in the South and in the West, and they *continued to work upon all the plantations.* There were estates, indeed, which had neither owners nor managers resident upon them, for some of these had been put into prison by Montbrun; and others, fearing the same fate, had fled to the quarter which had just been given up to the English. Yet upon these estates, though abandoned, the Negroes *continued their labors*, where there were any, even inferior, agents to guide them; and on those estates, where no white men were left to direct them, they betook themselves to the planting of provisions; but upon *all the plantations* where the Whites resided, the Blacks *continued to labor as quietly as before.*" A little further on in the work, ridiculing the notion entertained in France, that the Negroes would not work without compulsion, he takes occasion to allude to other Negroes, who had been liberated by the same proclamation, but who were more immediately under his own eye and cognizance. "If," says he, "you will take care not to speak to them of their return to slavery, but talk to them about their liberty, you may with this latter word chain them down to their labor. How did Toussaint succeed? How did I succeed also before his time in the plain of the Cul de Sac, and on the Plantation Gouraud, more than eight months after liberty had been granted (by Polverel) to the slaves? Let those who knew me at that time, and even the Blacks themselves, be asked. They will all reply, that *not a single Negro* upon that plantation, consisting of more than four hundred and fifty laborers, *refused to work*; and yet this plantation was thought to be under the worst discipline, and the slaves the most idle, of any in the plain. I, myself, inspired the same activity into three other plantations, of which I had the management."

The above account is far beyond any thing that could have been expected. Indeed, it is most gratifying. We find that the liberated Negroes, *both in the South and the West*, continued to work upon their *old plantations*, and for their *old masters*; that there was also a *spirit of industry* among them, and that they gave no uneasiness to their employers; for they are described as continuing to work *as quietly as before.* Such was the conduct of the Negroes for the first nine months after their liberation, or up to the middle of 1794. Let us pursue the subject, and see how they conducted themselves after this period.

During the year 1795 and part of 1796 I learn nothing about them, neither good, nor bad, nor indifferent, though I have ransacked the French historians for this purpose. Had there, however, been any thing in the way of *outrage*, I should have heard of it; and let me take this opportunity of setting my readers right, if, for want of knowing the dates of occurrences, they should have connected *certain outrages*, which assuredly took place in St. Domingo, *with the emancipation of the slaves.* The great massacres and conflagrations, which have made so frightful a picture in the history of this unhappy island, had been all effected *before the proclamations* of Santhonax and Polverel. They had all taken place *in the days of slavery*, or before the year 1794, that is, before the great conventional decree of the mother country was known. They had been occasioned, too, *not originally by the slaves themselves*, but by quarrels between the *white* and colored planters, and between the royalists and the *revolutionists*, who, for the purpose of reeking their vengeance upon each other, called in the aid of their respective slaves; and as to the insurgent Negroes of the North, who filled that part of the colony so often with terror and dismay, they were originally put in motion, according to Malenfant, under *the auspices of the royalists themselves*, to strengthen their own cause, and *to put down the partisans of the* French revolution. When Jean François and Biassou commenced the insurrection, there were many white royalists with them, and the Negroes were made to wear the white cockade. I repeat, then, that during the years 1795 and 1796, I can find nothing in the History of St. Domingo, wherewith to reproach the emancipated Negroes in the way of outrage. There is every reason, on the other hand, to believe, that they conducted themselves, during this period, in as orderly a manner as before.

I come now to the latter part of the year 1796; and here happily a clue is furnished me, by which I have an opportunity of pursuing my inquiry with pleasure. We shall find, that from this time there was no want of industry in those who had been emancipated, nor want of obedience in them as hired servants: they maintained, on the other hand, a respectable character. Let us appeal first to Malenfant. "The colony," says he, "was flourishing under Toussaint. The Whites *lived happily and in peace upon their estates, and the Negroes continued to work for them.*" Now Toussaint came into power, being general-in-chief of the armies of St. Domingo, a little before the end of the year 1796, and remained in power till the year 1802, or till the invasion of the island by the French expedition of Bonaparte [Bonaparte] under Leclerc. Malenfant means therefore to state, that from the latter end of 1796 to 1802, a period of six years, the planters or farmers kept possession of their estates; that they lived upon them, and that they lived upon them peaceably, that is, without interruption or disturbance from any one; and, finally, that the Negroes, though they had been all set free, continued to be their laborers. Can there be any account more favorable to our views than this, after so sudden an emancipation.

I may appeal next to General Lacroix, who published his "Memoirs for a History of St. Domingo," at Paris, in 1819. He informs us, that when Santhonax, who had been recalled to France by the Government there, returned to the colony in 1796, *"he was astonished at the state in which he found it on his return."* This, says Lacroix, "was owing to Toussaint, who, while he had succeeded in establishing perfect order and discipline among the black troops, had succeeded also in making the black laborers return to the plantations, there to resume the drudgery of cultivation."

But the same author tells us, that in the next year (1797) the most wonderful progress had been made in agriculture. He uses these remarkable words: *"The colony,"* says he, *"marched, as by enchantment, towards its ancient splendour; cultivation prospered; every day produced perceptible proofs of its progress. The city of the*

Cape *and the plantations of the North rose up again visibly to the eye.*" Now I am far from wishing to attribute all this wonderful improvement, this daily visible progress in agriculture, to the mere act of the emancipation of the slaves in St. Domingo. I know that many other circumstances which I could specify, if I had room, contributed towards its growth; but I must be allowed to maintain, that unless the Negroes, who were then free, *had done their part as laborers,* both by working regularly and industriously, and by obeying the directions of their superintendents or masters, the colony could never have gone on, as relates to cultivation, with the rapidity described.

The next witness to whom I shall appeal, is the estimable General Vincent, who lives now at Paris, though at an advanced age. Vincent was a colonel, and afterwards a general of brigade of artillery in St. Domingo. He was stationed there during the time both of Santhonax and Toussaint. He was also a proprietor of estates in the island. He was the man who planned the renovation of its agriculture after the abolition of slavery, and one of the great instruments in bringing it to the perfection mentioned by Lacroix. In the year 1801, he was called upon by Toussaint to repair to Paris, to lay before the Directory the new constitution, which had been agreed upon in St. Domingo. He obeyed the summons. It happened, that he arrived in France just at the moment of the peace of Amiens; here he found, to his inexpressible surprise and grief, that Buonaparte was preparing an immense armament, to be commanded by Leclerc, for the purpose of *restoring* slavery in St. Domingo. He lost no time in seeing the First Consul, and he had the courage to say at this interview what, perhaps, no other man in France would have dared to say at this particular moment. He remonstrated against the expedition; he told him to his face, that though the army destined for this purpose was composed of the brilliant conquerors of Europe, it could do nothing in the Antilles. It would most assuredly be destroyed by the climate of St. Domingo, even though it should be doubtful, whether it would not be destroyed by the Blacks. He stated, as another argument against the expedition, that it was totally unnecessary, and therefore criminal; for that every thing was going on well in St. Domingo. *The proprietors were in peaceable possession of their estates; cultivation was making a rapid progress; the Blacks were industrious, and beyond example happy.* He conjured him, therefore, in the name of humanity, not to reverse this beautiful state of things. But alas! his efforts were ineffectual. The die had been cast: and the only reward, which he received from Bonaparte for his manly and faithful representations, was banishment to the Isle of Elba.

Having carried my examination into the conduct of the Negroes after their liberation to 1802, or to the invasion of the island by Leclerc, I must now leave a blank for nearly two years, or till the year 1804. It cannot be expected during a war, in which every man was called to arms to defend his own personal liberty, and that of every individual of his family, that we should see plantations cultivated as quietly as before, or even cultivated at all. But this was not the fault of the *emancipated Negroes,* but of *their former masters.* It was owing to the prejudices of the latter, that this frightful invasion took place; prejudices, indeed, common to all planters, where slavery obtains, from the very nature of their situation, and upon which I have made my observations in a former place. Accustomed to the use of arbitrary power, they could no longer brook the loss of their whips. Accustomed again to look down upon the Negroes as an inferior race of beings, or as the reptiles of the earth, they could not bear, peaceably as these had conducted themselves, to come into that familiar contact with them, as *free laborers,* which the change of their situation required. They considered them, too, as property lost, but which was to be recovered. In an evil hour, they prevailed upon Bonaparte, by false representations and *promises of pecuniary support,* to restore things to their former state. The hellish expedition at length arrived upon the shores of St. Domingo:—a scene of blood and torture followed, *such as history had never before disclosed,* and compared with which, *though planned and executed by Whites* 12, all the barbarities said to have been perpetrated by the *insurgent Blacks* of the North, *amount comparatively to nothing.* In fine, the French were driven from the island. Till that time, the planters retained their property, and then it was, but not till then, that they lost their all; it cannot, therefore, be expected, as I have said before, that I should have any thing to say in favor of the industry or good order of the emancipated Negroes, *during such a convulsive period.*

In the year 1804, Dessalines was proclaimed emperor of this fine territory. Here I resume the thread of my history, (though it will be but for a moment,) in order that I may follow it to its end. In process of time, the black troops, containing the Negroes in question, were disbanded, except such as were retained for the peace-establishment of the army. They, who were disbanded, returned to cultivation. As they were free when they became soldiers, so they continued to be free when they became laborers again. From that time to this, there has been no want of subordination or industry among them. They or their descendants are the persons, by whom the plains and valleys of St. Domingo *are still cultivated*, and they are reported to follow their occupations still, and with *as fair a character* as other free laborers in any other quarter of the globe.

We have now seen, that the emancipated Negroes never abused their liberty, from the year 1793 (the era of their general emancipation) to the present day, a period of thirty years. An important question then seems to force itself upon us, "What were the measures taken after so frightful an event, as that of emancipation, to secure the tranquility and order which has been described, or to rescue the planters and the colony from ruin?" I am bound to answer this, if I can, were it only to gratify the curiosity of my readers; but more particularly when I consider, that if emancipation should ever be in contemplation in our own colonies, it will be desirable to have all the light possible upon that subject, and particularly of precedent or example. It appears then, that the two commissioners, Santhonax [Sonthonax] and Polverel, aware of the mischief which might attend their decrees, were obliged to take the best measures they could devise to prevent it. One of their first steps was to draw up a short code of rules to be observed upon the plantations. These rules were printed and made public. They were also ordered to be read aloud to all the Negroes upon every estate, for which purpose the latter were to be assembled at a particular hour once a week. The preamble to these regulations insisted upon *the necessity of working, without which everything would go to ruin.* Among the articles, the two the most worthy of our notice were, that the laborers were to be obliged to hire themselves to their masters for *not less than a year*, at the end of which (September) [the start of the year in the French

Republican Calendar], but not before, they might quit their service, and engage with others; and that they were to receive a *third part* of the produce of the estate, as a recompense for their labor. These two were *fundamental* articles. As to the minor, they were not alike upon every estate. This code of the commissioners subsisted for about three years.

Toussaint, when he came into power, reconsidered this subject, and adopted a code of rules of his own. His first object was to prevent oppression on the part of the master or employer, and yet to secure obedience on the part of the laborer. Conceiving that there could be no liberty where any one man had the power of punishing another at his discretion, he took away from every master the use of the whip, and of the chain, and of every other instrument of correction, either by himself or his own order: he took away, in fact, *all power of arbitrary punishment.* Every master offending against this regulation was to be summoned, on complaint by the laborer, before a magistrate or intendant of police, who was to examine into the case, and to act accordingly. Conceiving, on the other hand, that a just subordination ought to be kept up, and that, wherever delinquency occurred, punishment ought to follow, he ordained, that all laborers offending against the plantation laws, or not performing their contracts, should be brought before the same magistrate or intendant of police, who should examine them touching such delinquency, and decide as in the former case: thus he administered justice without respect of persons. It must be noticed, that all punishments were to be executed by a civil officer, a sort of public executioner, that they might be considered as punishments by the state. Thus he kept up discipline on the plantations, *without lessening authority* on the one hand, and *without invading the liberty of individuals* on the other.

Among his plantation offences was idleness on the part of the laborer. A man was not to receive wages from his master, and to do nothing. He was obliged to perform a reasonable quantity of work, or be punished. Another offence was absence without leave, which was considered as desertion.

Toussaint differed from the commissioners, as to the length of time for which laborers should engage themselves to masters.

He thought it unwise to allow the former, in the infancy of their liberty, to get notions of change and rambling at the end of every year. He ordained, therefore, that they should be attached to the plantations, and made, though free laborers, a sort of *adscripti glebae* [being tied to the soil/ a serf] for five years.

He differed again from the commissioners, as to the quantum of compensation for their labor. He thought one-third of the produce too much, seeing that the planter had another third to pay to the Government. He ordered, therefore, one-fourth to the laborer, but this was in the case only, where the laborer clothed and maintained himself: where he did not do this, he was entitled to a fourth only nominally, for out of this his master was to make a deduction for board and clothing.

The above is all I have been able to collect of the code of Toussaint, which, under his auspices, had the surprising effect of preserving tranquillity and order, and of keeping up a spirit of industry on the plantations of St. Domingo, at a time when only idleness and anarchy were to have been expected. It was in force when Leclerc arrived with his invading army, and it continued in force when the French army were beaten and Negro-liberty confirmed. From Toussaint it passed to Dessalines, and from Dessalines to Christophe and Petion, and from the two latter to Boyer; and it is the code therefore which regulates, and I believe with but very little variation, the relative situation of master and servant in husbandry at this present hour.

But it is time that I should now wind up the case before us. And, first, will any one say that this case is not analogous to that which we have in contemplation? Let us remember that the number of slaves liberated by the French decrees in St. Domingo was very little short of 500,000 persons, and that this was nearly equal to the number *of all the slaves* then in the British West Indian Islands when put together. But if there be a want of analogy, the difference lies on my side of the question. I maintain, that emancipation in *St. Domingo* was attended with *far more hazard* to persons and property, and with *far greater difficulties*, than it could possibly be, if attempted in *our own islands*. Can we forget that by the decree of Polverel, sanctioned afterwards by the Convention, all the slaves *were made free at once,* or *in a single day?* No notice was given of the event, and of course *no preparation* could be made for it. They were released *suddenly* from *all their former obligations and restraints.* They were let loose upon the Whites, their masters, with *all the vices of* slavery *upon them.* What was to have been expected but the dissolution of all civilized society, with the reign of barbarism and terror? Now all I ask for with respect to the slaves in our own islands is, that they should be emancipated by *degrees,* or that they should be made to pass through a certain course of discipline, *as through a preparatory school,* to fit them for the right use of their freedom. Again, can we forget the unfavorable circumstances, in which the slaves of St. Domingo were placed, for a year or two before their liberation, in another point of view? The island at this juncture was a prey to *political discord, civil war,* and *foreign invasion,* at the same time. Their masters were politically at variance with each other, as they were white or colored persons, or republicans or royalists. They were quarrelling and fighting with each other, and shedding each other's blood. The English, who were in possession of the strong maritime posts, were alarming the country by their incursions: they, the slaves, had been trained up to the same political animosities. They had been made to take the side of their respective masters, and to pass through scenes of violence and bloodshed. Now, whenever emancipation is to be proposed in our own colonies, I anticipate neither *political parties,* nor *civil wars,* nor *foreign invasion,* but a time of *tranquillity and peace.* Who then will be bold enough to say, after these remarks, that there could be any thing like the danger and difficulties in emancipating the slaves there, which existed when the slaves of St. Domingo were made free? But some objector may say, after all, "There is one point in which your analogy is deficient. While Toussaint was in power, the Government of St. Domingo was a *black* one, and the Blacks would be more willing to submit to the authority of a *black* (their own) Government, than of a *white one.* Hence there were less disorders after emancipation in St. Domingo, than would have probably occurred, had it been tried in our own islands." But to such an objector I should reply, that he knows nothing of the history of St. Domingo. The Government of that island was French, or white, from the very infancy of emancipation to the arrival of the expedition of Leclerc. The slaves were made free under the government of Santhonax and Polverel. When these retired, other white commissioners succeeded them. When Toussaint came into power, he was not supreme; Generals Hedouille, Vincent, and others, had a share in the government. Toussaint himself *received his commission from the French Directory*, and acted under it. He caused it every where to be made known, but particularly among his officers and troops, that he retained the island for the *French Government*, and that *France* was *the mother-country*.

AN 1863 ACCOUNT

William Wells Brown

This description of Toussaint Louverture comes from the 1863 book *The Black Man, His Antecedents, His Genius, and His Achievements* by Black abolitionist William Wells Brown. Brown (November 6, 1816 – November 6, 1884) was a prominent anti-slavery lecturer, novelist, playwright, and historian. Born into slavery near Lexington, Kentucky, Brown escaped to the North, where he worked for abolitionist causes and was a prolific writer.

W. Wells Brown.

At the commencement of the French revolution, in 1789, there were nine hundred thousand inhabitants on the Island of St. Domingo. Of these, seven hundred thousand were Africans, sixty thousand mixed blood, and the remainder were whites and Caribbeans. Like the involuntary servitude in our own Southern States, slavery in St. Domingo kept morality at a low stand. Owing to the amalgamation between masters and slaves, there arose the mulatto population, which eventually proved to be the worst enemies of their fathers.

Many of the planters sent their mulatto sons to France to be educated. When these young men returned to the island, they were greatly dissatisfied at the proscription which met them wherever they appeared. White enough to make them hopeful and aspiring, many of the mulattoes possessed wealth enough to make them influential. Aware, by their education, of the principles of freedom that were being advocated in Europe and the United States, they were ever on the watch to seize opportunities to better their social and political condition. In the French part of the island alone, twenty thousand whites lived in the midst of thirty thousand free mulattoes and five hundred thousand slaves. In the Spanish portion, the odds were still greater in favor of the slaves. Thus the advantage of numbers and physical strength was on the side of the oppressed. Right is the most dangerous of weapons--woe to him who leaves it to his enemies!

The efforts of Wilberforce, Sharp, Buxton, and Clarkson to abolish the African slave trade, and their advocacy of the equality of the races, were well understood by the men of color. They had also learned their own strength in the island, and that they had the sympathy of all Europe with them. The news of the oath of the Tennis Court [1] and the taking of the Bastile at Paris was received with the wildest enthusiasm by the people of St. Domingo.

The announcement of these events was hailed with delight by both the white planters and the mulattoes; the former, because they hoped that a revolution in the mother country would secure to them the independence of the colony; the latter, because they viewed it as a movement that would give them equal rights with the whites; and even the slaves regarded it as a precursor to their own emancipation. But the excitement which the outbreak at Paris had created amongst the free men of color and the slaves, at once convinced the planters that a separation from France would be the death-knell of slavery in St. Domingo.

Although emancipated by law from the dominion of individuals, the mulattoes had no rights: shut out from society by their color, deprived of religious and political privileges, they felt their degradation even more keenly than the bond slaves. The mulatto son was not allowed to dine at his father's table, kneel with him in his devotions, bear his name, inherit his property, nor even to lie in his father's graveyard. Laboring as they were under the sense of their personal social wrongs, the mulattoes tolerated, if they did not encourage, low and vindictive passions. They were haughty and disdainful to the blacks, whom they scorned, and jealous and turbulent to the whites, whom they hated and feared.

The mulattoes at once despatched one of their number to Paris, to lay before the Constitutional Assembly their claim to equal rights with the whites. Vincent Ogé, their deputy, was well received at Paris by Lafayette, Brissot, Barnave, and Gregoire, and was admitted to a seat in the Assembly, where he eloquently portrayed the wrongs of his race. In urging his claims, he said, if equality was withheld from the mulattoes, they would appeal to force. This was seconded by Lafayette and Barnave, who said, "Perish the colonies rather than a principle." of the men of color, and Ogé was made bearer of the news to his brethren. The planters armed themselves, met the young deputy on his return to the island, and a battle ensued. The free colored men rallied around Ogé, but they were defeated and taken, with their brave leader, were first tortured, and then broken alive on the wheel.

The prospect of freedom was put down for the time, but the blood of Ogé and his companions bubbled silently in the hearts of the African race; they swore to avenge them.

The announcement of the death of Ogé in the halls of the Assembly at Paris created considerable excitement, and became the topic of conversation in the clubs and on the Boulevards. Gregoire defended the course of the colored men, and said, "If Liberty was right in France, it was right in St. Domingo." He well knew that the crime for which Ogé had suffered in the West Indies, had constituted the glory of Mirabeau and Lafayette at Paris, and Washington and Hancock in the United States. The planters in the island trembled at their own oppressive acts, and terror urged them on to greater violence. The blood of Ogé and his accomplices had sown every where despair and conspiracy. The French sent an army to St. Domingo to enforce the laws.

The planters repelled with force the troops sent out by France, denying its prerogatives and refusing the civic oath. In the midst of these thickening troubles, the planters who resided in France were invited to return and assist in vindicating the civil independence of the island. Then was it that the mulattoes earnestly appealed to the slaves, and the result was appalling. The slaves awoke as from an ominous dream, and demanded their rights with sword in hand. Gaining immediate success, and finding that their liberty would not be granted by the planters, they rapidly increased in numbers; and in less than a week from its commencement, the storm had swept over the whole plain of the north, from east to west, and from the mountains to the sea. The splendid villas and rich factories yielded to the furies of the devouring flames; so that the mountains, covered with smoke and burning cinders, borne upwards by the wind, looked like volcanoes; and the atmosphere, as if on fire, resembled a furnace.

Such were the outraged feelings of a people whose ancestors had been ruthlessly torn from their native land, and sold in the shambles of St. Domingo. To terrify the blacks and convince them that they could could never be free, the planters were murdering them on every hand by thousands.

The struggle in St. Domingo was watched with intense interest by the friends of the blacks, both in Paris [2] and in London, and all appeared to look with hope to the rising up of a black chief, who should prove himself adequate to the emergency. Nor did they look in vain. In the midst of the disorders that threatened on all sides, the negro chief made his appearance in the person of a slave, named Toussaint. This man was the grandson of the King of Ardra, one of the most powerful and wealthy monarchs on the west coast of Africa. By his own energy and perseverance, Toussaint had learned to read and write, and was held in high consideration by the surrounding planters as well as their slaves.

His private virtues were many, and he had a deep and pervading sense of religion, and in the camp carried it even as far as Oliver Cromwell. Toussaint was born on the island, and was fifty years of age when called into the field. One of his chief characteristics was his humanity.

Before taking any part in the revolution, he aided his master's family to escape from the impending danger. After seeing them beyond the reach of the revolutionary movement, he entered the army as an inferior officer, but was soon made aid-de-camp to General Bissou [3]. Disorder and bloodshed reigned throughout the island, and every day brought fresh intelligence of depredations committed by whites, mulattoes, and blacks.

Such was the condition of affairs when a decree was passed by the Colonial Assembly giving equal rights to the mulattoes, and asking their aid in restoring order and reducing the slaves again to their chains. Overcome by this decree, and having gained all they wished, the free colored men joined the planters in a murderous crusade against the slaves. This union of the whites and mulattoes to prevent the bondman getting his freedom, created an ill feeling between the two proscribed classes which seventy years have not been able to efface. The French government sent a second army to St. Domingo, to enforce the laws giving freedom to the slaves; and Toussaint joined it on its arrival in the island, and fought bravely against the planters.

While the people of St. Domingo were thus fighting amongst themselves, the revolutionary movement in France had fallen into the hands of Robespierre and Danton, and the guillotine was beheading its thousands daily. When the news of the death of Louis XVI. reached St. Domingo, Toussaint and his companions left the French, and joined the Spanish army in the eastern part of the island, and fought for the king of Spain. Here Toussaint was made brigadier general, and appeared in the field as the most determined foe of the French planters.

The two armies met; a battle was fought in the streets, and many thousands were slain on both sides; the planters, however, were defeated. During the conflict the city was set on fire, and on every side presented shocking evidence of slaughter, conflagration, and pillage. The strifes of political and religious partisanship, which had raged in the clubs and streets of Paris, were transplanted to St. Domingo, where they raged with all the heat of a tropical clime and the animosities of a civil war. Truly did the flames of the French revolution at Paris, and the ignorance and self-will of the planters, set the island of St. Domingo on fire. The commissioners, with their retinue, retired from the burning city into the neighboring highlands, where a camp was formed to protect the ruined town from the opposing party. Having no confidence in the planters, and fearing a reaction, the commissioners proclaimed a general emancipation to the slave population, and invited the blacks who had joined the Spaniards to return. Toussaint and his followers accepted the invitation, returned, and were enrolled in the army under the commissioners. Fresh troops arrived from France, who were no sooner in the island than they separated-- some siding with the planters, and others with the commissioners. The white republicans of the mother country arrayed themselves against the white republicans of St. Domingo, whom they were sent out to assist; the blacks and the mulattoes were at war with each other; old and young, of both sexes and of all colors, were put to the sword, while the fury of the flames swept from plantation to plantation and from town to town.

During these sad commotions, Toussaint, by his superior knowledge of the character of his race, his humanity, generosity, and courage, had gained the confidence of all whom he had under his command. The rapidity with which he travelled from post to post astonished every one. By his genius and surpassing activity, Toussaint levied fresh forces, raised the reputation of the army, and drove the English and Spanish from the island.

With the termination of this struggle every vestige of slavery and all obstacles to freedom disappeared. Toussaint exerted every nerve to make Hayti what it had formerly been. He did every thing in his power to promote agriculture; and in this he succeeded beyond the most sanguine expectations of the friends of freedom, both in England and France. Even the planters who had remained on the island acknowledged the prosperity of Hayti under the governorship of the man whose best days had been spent in slavery.

The peace of Amiens left Bonaparte without a rival on the continent, and with a large and experienced army, which he feared to keep idle; and he determined to send a part of it to St. Domingo.

The army for the expedition to St. Domingo was fitted out, and no pains or expense spared to make it an imposing one. Fifty-six ships of war, with twenty-five thousand men, left France for Hayti. It was, indeed, the most valiant fleet that had

ever sailed from the French dominions. The Alps, the Nile, the Rhine, and all Italy, had resounded with the exploits of the men who were now leaving their country for the purpose of placing the chains again on the limbs of the heroic people of St. Domingo. There were men in that army that had followed Bonaparte from the siege of Toulon to the battle under the shades of the pyramids of Egypt--men who had grown gray in the camp.

News of the intended invasion reached St. Domingo some days before the squadron had sailed from Brest; and therefore the blacks had time to prepare to meet their enemies. Toussaint had concentrated his forces at such points as he expected would be first attacked. Christophe was sent to defend Cape City, and Port-au-Prince was left in the hands of Dessalines.

With no navy, and but little means of defence, the Haytians determined to destroy their towns rather than they should fall into the hands of the enemy. Late in the evening the French ships were seen to change their position, and Christophe, satisfied that they were about to effect a landing, set fire to his own house, which was the signal for the burning of the town. The French general wept as he beheld the ocean of flames rising from the tops of the houses in the finest city in St. Domingo.

Another part of the fleet landed in Samana, where Toussaint, with an experienced wing of the army, was ready to meet them. On seeing the ships enter the harbor, the heroic chief said, *"Here come the enslavers of our race. All France is coming to St. Domingo, to try again to put the fetters upon our limbs; but not France, with all her troops of the Rhine, the Alps, the Nile, the Tiber, nor all Europe to help her, can extinguish the soul of Africa. That soul, when once the soul of a man, and no longer that of a slave, can overthrow the pyramids and the Alps themselves, sooner than again be crushed down into slavery."* The French, however, effected a landing, but they found nothing but smouldering ruins, where once stood splendid cities. Toussaint and his generals at once abandoned the towns, and betook themselves to the mountains, those citadels of freedom in St. Domingo, where the blacks have always proved too much for the whites.

Toussaint put forth a proclamation[4] to the colored people, in which he said, "You are now to meet and fight enemies who have neither faith, law, nor religion. Lot us resolve that these French troops shall never leave our shores alive." The war commenced, and the blacks were victorious in nearly all the battles. Where the French gained a victory, they put their prisoners to the most excruciating tortures; in many instances burning them in pits, and throwing them into boiling caldrons. This example of cruelty set by the whites was followed by the

blacks. Then it was that Dessalines, the ferocious chief, satisfied his long pent-up revenge against the white planters and French soldiers that he made prisoners. The French general saw that he could gain nothing from the blacks on the field of battle, and he determined upon a stratagem, in which he succeeded too well.

A correspondence was opened with Toussaint, in which the captain-general promised to acknowledge the liberty of the blacks and the equality of all, if he would yield. Overcome by the persuasions of his generals and the blacks who surrounded him, and who were sick and tired of the shedding of blood, Toussaint gave in his adhesion to the French authorities. This was the great error of his life.

Vincent, in his "*Reflections on the Present State of the Colony of St. Domingo*," says, "Toussaint, at the head of his army, is the most active and indefatigable man of whom we can form an idea; we may say, with truth, that he is found wherever instructions or danger render his presence necessary. The particular care which he employs in his march, of always deceiving the men of whom he has need, and who think they enjoy a confidence he gives to none, has such an effect that he is daily expected in all the chief places of the colony. His great sobriety, the faculty, which none but he possesses, of never reposing, the facility with which he resumes the affairs of the cabinet after the most tiresome excursions, of answering daily a hundred letters, and of habitually tiring five secretaries, render him so superior to all those around him, that their respect and submission are in most individuals carried even to fanaticism. It is certain that no man, in the present times, has possessed such an influence over a mass of people as General Toussaint possesses over his brethren in St. Domingo."

The above is the opinion of an enemy--one who regarded the negro chief as a dangerous man to his interest.

Invited by the captain-general of the island to attend a council, the black hero was treacherously seized and sent on board the ship of war Hero, which set sail at once for France. On the arrival of the illustrious prisoner at Brest, he was taken in a close carriage and transferred to the castle of Joux, in the Lower Pyrenees. The gelid atmosphere of the mountain region, the cold, damp dungeon in which he was placed, with the water dripping upon the floor day and night, did not hasten the death of Toussaint fast enough. By Napoleon's directions the prisoner's servant was taken from him, sufficient clothing and bedding to keep him warm were denied, his food curtailed, and his keeper, after an absence of four days, returned and found the hero of St. Domingo dead in his cell [April 7, 1803]. Thus terminated the career of a self-made man.

Toussaint was of prepossessing appearance, of middle stature, and possessed an iron frame. His dignified, calm, and unaffected features, and broad and well-developed forehead, would cause him to be selected, in any company of men, as one born for a leader. Endowed by nature with high qualities of mind, he owed his elevation to his own energies and his devotion to the welfare and freedom of his race. His habits were thoughtful; and like most men of energetic temperaments, he crowded much into what he said. So profound and original were his opinions, that they have been successively drawn upon by all the chiefs of St. Domingo since his era, and still without loss of adaptation to the circumstances of the country. The policy of his successors has been but a repetition of his plans, and his maxims are still the guidance of the rulers of Hayti. His thoughts were copious and full of vigor, and what he could express well in his native patois he found tame and unsatisfactory in the French language, which he was obliged to employ in the details of his official business. He would never sign what he did not fully understand, obliging two or three secretaries to re-word the document, until they had succeeded in furnishing the particular phrase expressive of his meaning. While at the height of his power, and when all around him were furnished with every comfort, and his officers living in splendor, Toussaint himself lived with an austere sobriety which bordered on abstemiousness. He was entirely master of his own passions and appetites. It was his custom to set off in his carriage with the professed object of going to some particular point of the island, and when he had passed over several miles of the journey, to quit the carriage, which continued its route under the same escort of guards, while Toussaint, mounted on horseback and followed by his officers, made rapid excursions across the country, to places where he was least expected. It was upon one of these occasions that he owed his life to his singular mode of traveling. He had just left his carriage when an ambuscade of mulattoes, concealed in the thickets of Boucassin, fired upon the guard, and several balls pierced the carriage, and one of them killed an old domestic who occupied the seat of his master. No person knew better than he the art of governing the people under his jurisdiction. The greater part of the population loved him to idolatry. Veneration for Toussaint was not confined to the boundaries of St. Domingo; it ran through Europe; and in France his name was frequently pronounced in the senate with the eulogy of polished eloquence. No one can look back upon his career without feeling that Toussaint was a remarkable man. Without being bred to the science of arms, he became a valiant soldier, and baffled the skill of the most experienced generals that had followed Napoleon.

Without military knowledge he fought like one born in the camp. Without means he carried on the war. He beat his enemies in battle, and turned their own weapons against them. He laid the foundation for the emancipation of his race and the independence of the island. From ignorance he became educated by his own exertions. From a slave he rose to be a soldier, a general, and a governor, and might have been king of St. Domingo. He possessed splendid traits of genius, which was developed in the private circle, in the council chamber, and on the field of battle. His very name became a tower of strength to his friends and a terror to his foes. Toussaint's career as a Christian, a statesman, and a general, will lose nothing by a comparison with that of Washington. Each was the leader of an oppressed and outraged people, each had a powerful enemy to contend with, and each succeeded in founding a government in the new world. Toussaint's government made liberty its watchword, incorporated it in its constitution, abolished the slave trade, and made freedom universal amongst the people. Washington's government incorporated slavery and the slave trade, and enacted laws by which chains were fastened upon the limbs of millions of people. Toussaint liberated his countrymen; Washington enslaved a portion of his. When impartial history shall do justice to the St. Domingo revolution, the name of Toussaint L'Ouverture will be placed high upon the roll of fame.

APPENDIX

WHY TELL? THE BETRAYAL OF AMERICAN SLAVE REVOLTS

A complete understanding of the issue of slave insurrections is incomplete without addressing the foremost cause of their failure: an inside element which betrays the rebellion itself in allegiance to the forces the revolt seeks to overthrow. In Herbert Aptheker's monumental *American Negro Slave Revolts*, he documents a prolonged and constant trend of resistance to slavery that often manifested itself as full-fledged violent uprising. Though these occurrences were exceptional, they were not as isolated or few as many historians have suggested. Slave resistance took place daily in myriad ways, most of them passive-aggressive or covert, such as the outwitting of the slaveholder, acts of theft, and even poisoning and arson. These latter tactics demanded less planning and conspirators, though highly effective in attaining their goals, that is, killing master (or destroying his property) and thus freeing themselves.

A slave rebellion, on the other hand, demanded a great degree of planning in order to ensure its expected success, and the agreed participation of as many of the enslaved as possible. It is herein that lay the dilemma: with the inclusion of certain slaves into knowledge of the conspiracy arose the possibility of detection. Rare instances occasioned an enslaved Black inadvertently revealing the plans for revolt, due to either intoxication or simplemindedness (though this has occurred often enough to give it notice), though more often it is enslaved Blacks who, by their own will, voluntarily inform slaveholding whites of the plot so as to suppress it.

One of the most famous insurrection conspiracies in American history is that of Denmark Vesey in 1822, where one report claims that the plans had been in formulation for nine years. His conviction that all slaves would want their freedom (an idea shared by many whites which kept them in constant fear of such rebellion) is well documented. The leader is reported to have said "Let us assemble a sufficient number to commence the work with spirit, and we'll not want men; they'll fall in behind us fast enough." When one of Vesey's co-conspirators, William Paul was captured, he testified first against two individuals he claimed to be taking part in raising an insurrection, Mingo Harth and Peter Poyas. These two were released, but as according to the proceedings published in 1822, Black spies were sent amongst them to further monitor their dealings from thereon. (The role of Black spies in the defeat of slave rebellions is also a recurring trend in the study of this topic.) Things remained stagnant awhile afterwards until William Paul, this time fearing he would soon be led to the scaffold (after having been in solitary confinement since his arrest) for execution, gave a lengthier confession which detailed that the plot was "very extensive" and thus prompted sixteen-hundred rounds of ball cartridge ammunition to be distributed amongst numbers of sentinels and patrols put on duty with loaded arms. According to Governor Thomas Bennett, "Extensive and efficient preparations had been made for the safety and the protection of our city." Indeed, Vesey expected a turnout in the thousands for his revolt, from various territories reaching as far as San Domingo; Mingo Harth himself had organized an army of four-thousand men from James Island to be deployed on the South Bay.

However three or four days would pass with no confirmation of Paul's disclosure, until one of the Governor's slaves, Ned Bennett (who was himself involved) "came voluntarily to the intendant" and "indignantly offered himself for examination" which, according to Joseph Cephas Carroll in his *Slave Insurrections in the United States*, puzzled and bewildered the authorities who, nonetheless, kept all goings-on secret until further arrests could be made. The *Account of the Late Intended Insurrection among a Portion of the Blacks of this City*, published in Charleston shortly after these events, records:

> On the night, however, of Friday the 14th, the information of William was amply confirmed, and details infinitely more abundant and interestingly afforded. At 8 o'clock this evening, the Intendant received a visit from a gentleman, who is advantageously known in this community for his worth and respectability.
> This gentleman...stated to the Intendant, that, having the most unbounded confidence in a faithful slave belonging to his family, who was distinguished alike for his uncommon

intelligence and integrity, he was induced to inform him, that rumors were abroad of an intended insurrection of the blacks... On being strongly enjoined to conceal nothing, he, the next day, Friday the 14th, came to his master, and informed him, that the fact was really so, that a public disturbance was contemplated by the blacks, and not a moment should be lost in informing the constituted authorities, as the succeeding Sunday, the 16th, at 12 o'clock, at night, was the period fixed for the rising, which, if not prevented, would inevitably occur at that hour. This slave, it appears, was in no degree connected with the plot, but he had an intimate friend, A---- (one of his class) who had been trusted by the conspirators with this secret, and...it would seem that it was a subject of great regret and contrition with him, that he had ever appeared to lend his approbation to a scheme so wicked and atrocious, and that he sought to make atonement, by divulging the plot, which on the 14th he did, to the slave of the gentleman in question, his class leader.

On June 18th, ten slaves were arrested (among them Mingo Harth and Peter Poyas), Vesey discovered, and the insurrection foiled.

Another of the notable slave insurrections never to materialize due to the same circumstances was that of Gabriel Prosser in 1800. According to Prosser and his company's plans:

> One thousand men were to be recruited from Richmond, six hundred from Ground Squirrel Bridge, four hundred from Goochland, and six thousand from Caroline County, besides others in different places.

According to Prosser's own testimony, he had about ten thousand men. Plans were formulated, as was in Vesey's plot, to secure arms and eliminate whites. Prosser furthermore sought to establish a government, having already allocated positions for presidents, princes, governors, and counselors, once he was crowned as the King of Virginia. If the plan failed, there remained the option for retreat into the mountains. The plans seemed to many foolproof, and would have been carried out as such, until on August 30th, two slaves, Tom and Pharaoh Sheppard "entered their master's office, closed the door behind them, and related to him the well-planned insurrection of General Gabriel, which was to have taken place than night." Governor Monroe was "so impressed with the magnitude of the danger" that he stationed troops in Manchester, turned the

Capitol in Richmond "into a training camp," and hired for himself three aides de camp. Meanwhile, the two main ringleaders, General Gabriel and Jack Bowler, alias Jack Ditcher, had escaped. The Governor offered a reward of three-hundred dollars and a pardon to any one of their confederates who would turn them in. A Black man named Peter Smith convinced Jack Bowler to surrender upon learning of the reward, but "since Smith was a Negro, fifty dollars were paid him instead of three hundred." The General suffered a similar fate; Carroll writes:

> Gabriel had seen the futility of any further attempt, and had fled from the scene. Four miles below Richmond, he went aboard the Schooner Mary, and might had made good his escape but for two Negroes...

These two immediately reported him, and he was soon thereafter executed.

The question arises upon observing this recurring phenomenon, i.e. that of the slave betrayer: What would cause a man, as equally enslaved and afflicted by the torments and rigor of the same oppressor, choose not to resist and revolt against his oppressor, but instead to ally with the oppressor in putting down the resistance and revolt of those with whom he shares an equal condition and fate?

During Nat Turner's famous rebellion (which is perhaps exceptional in regards to this topic as it is one of the insurrections that, while relevant to the issue, actually materialized, and was not aborted by outside forces in its planning stages), there is one encounter that stands out most. It was first made known by Styron in his somewhat fictionalized and altogether unrealistic portrayal of Turner, and thus attacked by critics, but more recently, has garnered credibility through publication of Higginson's chapters on "Black Rebellion" in *Travellers and Outlaws*, first published in 1889. According to Higginson, the one encounter that broke up Nat Turner's group so that it would never reunite occurred upon their reaching a Dr. Blunt's house. When they came to fire upon it, Blunt's slaves fired back upon them, causing them to scatter. Styron's detractors labeled his account of this happening as "false" and "impossible," assuming, as historian James M. McPherson has suggested, "that all slaves seethed with rebellious hatred against the white oppressors..." This appears to be an incorrect assumption, as the evidence continues to bear out. However, the question remains as to what causes this phenomenon. Didn't these enslaved Blacks want to be free? Or did they desire to remain slaves?

Josiah Henson was a slave so loyal and dedicated to his master that he was trusted to transport all the other slaves over a thousand miles to Kentucky. Though Henson alone was left to do the task, and did not only travel through a number of free territories, but was repeatedly offered freedom by free Blacks, should he chose to accept it there and, in doing so, provide it for the other slaves he was to be transporting. Henson recalled:

> I had never dreamed of running away. I had a sentiment of honor on the subject. The duties of the slave to his master as appointed over him in the Lord, I had ever heard urged by ministers and religious men. It seemed like outright stealing...I had undertaken a great thing; my vanity had been flattered all along the road by hearing myself praised; I thought it would be a feather in my cap to carry it through thoroughly, and had often painted the scene in my imagination of the final surrender to Master Amos, and the immense admiration and respect with which he would regard me.

And so Henson continued with his task, undaunted. The above example hints at two sources for Henson's otherwise unreasonable actions, and those two are the influence of religion and the vain hopes of attaining privilege in master's care through unquestioning allegiance. This allegiance, which develops together with an identification and internalization of attitude with the master, as will be demonstrated further on, is still carried on without the physical presence of the master, once it has been substantially internalized. The influence of religion will be a later topic as well. Returning to the issue at hand, which is allegiance and identification with the master, we find it most common among those closest to the master and mistress.

Peter Poyas, identified in the Vesey case, harbored a distrust for house-servants which validated itself in an incident on May 25th, which would be the catalyst leading to the arrest of William Paul and then ultimately to Vesey himself. Devany, confidential house slave of Colonel Prioleau, was sent on errands which ended him up at the Wharf, where he met William Paul. After exchanging small-talk for a short time, Paul questioned Devany as to whether he had any knowledge of "something about to happen." Devany replied that he know of nothing more important than the upcoming family dinner. William Paul outlined to him their plans to "shake off their bondage," and gave him instructions on what he could do to join the movement. According to Carroll:

> He said that he was satisfied with his condition as a slave, found excuse for breaking away from his interlocutor, and went at once to a free colored man, named Pensil or Pencell, with whom he shared the startling news and whose advice he sought. Mr Pencell's advice was that he should inform his mistress and young master immediately of was he had heard. This, Devany lost no time in doing, and five days later when Colonel Prioleau returned from the country the secret was revealed to him.

Former slave Henry Bibb expressed a popular view among slaves that the preferential treatment of house slaves weakened the slave class:

> ...that the domestic slaves are often found to be traitors to their own people, for the purpose of gaining favor with their masters; and they are encouraged and trained up by them to report every plot they know of being formed about stealing anything, or running away, or any thing of the kind; and for which they are paid. This is one of the principal causes of the slaves being divided among themselves, and without which they could not be held in bondage one year, and perhaps not half that time.

An anonymous slave first quoted by Bontemps-Hughes and cited by Julius Lester, in his *To Be a Slave*, narrates:

> They taught us to be against one another and no matter where you would go you would always find one that would tattle and have the white folks pecking on you. They would be trying to make it soft for themselves.

Austin Steward also wrote at length about this type of slave, and claimed that a domestic slave "will for the sake of his master and mistress, frequently betray his fellow-slave...hence it is insurrections and stampedes are so generally detected. Such slaves are always treated with more affability that others, for the slaveholder is well aware that he stands over a volcano." A Mrs. Martha L. Nelson of Mecklenburg County, Virginia wrote, during a period of Black unrest, to Governor Henry Wise, asking a pardon of her domestic slave Coleman. She claimed his devotion to her, adding that he would "inform on the negroes, as soon as any white person would, if he knew or suspected anything wrong was planning among them...such a servant out not to be sent away particularly in these perilous times of insurrection."

William Hayden, famous for his slave narrative, wrote of how he became aware of slave mutiny that was abroad, while sleeping in a room adjacent to the quarters wherein the other slaves were held ironed and fettered. He learned that he too was included to be murdered along with all the whites on board (due to, as he relates, the "attention" paid him). He states:

> They had even provided themselves with a file from the lot of blacksmith tools on board, and that many were at that moment free from their chains. This information I carried to my master; and after ascertaining the truth of my statement, he had them again bound more firmly than ever.

In *The Peculiar Institution*, Kenneth Stampp describes the domestic slaves as:

> ...devoted to the master and his family and alienated from the other slaves. "They are just the same as white folks," said a former slave in disgust, "Some of them will betray another to curry favor with the master." In this way, observed a visitor in Virginia, the master destroyed "the sympathy that unites...the victims of the same oppression...He has but to arm the human passions against each other."

This alienation from the rest of the slaves was not common to all domestic slaves, but it did occur more frequently among them than among any other class of slaves. The issue of class lines in slavery is also important, and will be discussed later as well. House slaves inevitably and, most times, unconsciously traded their affections and loyalties for privileges and preferential treatment. Though the brutality of slavery loomed over their heads as well as any other's, their close proximity to the oppressor was a first a physical nearness, which eventually garnered an emotional nearness, that ultimately led to a firm emotional nearness through a process of constant conditioning.

A study on obedience, conducted by Milgram at Yale University, demonstrated that, while 65 percent of people were willing to punish individuals with an electric shock of 450 volts for making errors, they were less likely to comply with the task and resist the leader when given the orders by phone, or when the individual whom they were to shock was visible or touchable. Closeness to the master, and distance from the other slaves produced results that coincide completely with the conclusions reached by this experiment. Made to feel different from the rest of the slaves, they identified instead with the master, and in many cases, came to love him unconditionally. This process of identification with the aggressor is not so much a natural reaction as it is a mechanism for defense. Anna Freud delved into the topic of such identification in her *The Ego and the Mechanisms of Defense*. Before addressing this issue more fully, the simple boundaries of house slave and field slave must first be disregarded in light of the fact that field slaves faced this predicament as well. Among slaves as a whole, the adoption of "samboism," or an expression of complete servility, was a common form of subordination.

Samboism produced slaves who displayed "an insensitivity to others, and a dangerous selfishness. The untroubled sambos served masters and themselves, sowing suspicion in the quarters and thus adding to the troubles of all." Hussein Abdilani Bulhan, in his *Frantz Fanon and the Psychology of Oppression*, explains:

> The processes of internalization and objectification that Kojeve [in his interpretation of the master-slave relationship in the Introduction to the Reading of Hegel] explained so well are relevant to the psychology of oppression. For in prolonged oppression, the oppressed group [will] internalize the oppressor without. They adopt his guidelines and prohibitions, they assimilate his image and his social behaviors, and they become agents of their own oppression. The oppressor without becomes an intropressor - an oppressor within. The well-known inferiority complex of the oppressed originates in this process of internalization.... Intropression refers to something more specific than Freud's superego. It is an ensemble of internalized aspects of oppression that prompts a betrayal of self and loved ones and plots of resistance.

Albert Memmi, in his important work *Dominated Man: Notes*

Toward a Portrait, proposed that, "in every dominated man, there is a certain degree of self-rejection, born mostly of his downcast condition and exclusion... When the objective conditions are so weighty and corrosive, how could we imagine that they will not result in some destruction, that they will not warp the soul, the behavior and even the physiognomy of the oppressed man?"

The incidences of betrayal in slave rebellions are by no means isolated, nor are they exceptions to the rule. In fact, the data is more inclined to suggest that they are the rule, and that insurrections such as the one in Surinam, where there was upheld a code of honor disallowing betrayal of any kind, were the rare exceptions. The dichotomy between house slave and field slave is apparent, but applies only to a degree, as the lines of betrayal were not clearly drawn there. To be sure, one of the major difficulties Vesey encountered in organizing his rebellion was a dichotomy that also existed between enslaved Blacks and the free Black elite. Here too, the motives and aspirations were clearly divided, as were loyalties. Larry Koger documents this in his book *Black Slaveowners*, in a chapter titled "The Denmark Vesey Conspiracy: Brown Masters vs. Black Slaves".

It is evident that the Black community was divided along a number of lines, including those between free and slave, Black and Brown (mulatto), house slave and field slave, and any number of others, though these are the most influential in the issue of insurrection. These class lines, created ultimately by the master, provided him a position of relative security and stability in the slavery superstructure as he was neither affected nor judged by these standards, and was thus the only one free from their divisiveness and the combative inferiority and superiority complexes associated with them. Superiority in the slavemaster's mind was something absolute on account of his white manhood; in comparison, superiority in the enslaved Black's mind was something relative to the master's ultimate superiority. So the mulatto house slave was superior to the dark field slaves, but still had no amount of power in regards to the white master they all answered to.

Inferiority and superiority played a pivotal role in the self-image of Blacks, creating roles of submissiveness, servility and docility to whites, as well as creating rifts disunity between the enslaved through each side of each class line having a negative image of the opposing side. One of the major tools used to implant such ideas both consciously and subconsciously was slave religion.

Aptheker writes, "The words of man were reinforced by those of God, the latter carefully selected, interpreted and censored." The cases of Vesey, Prosser, and Turner are important to note here because, in each of them, religion played a significant role, but not through the slavemaster's interpretation. In each of their campaigns, the Bible was used as a tool in itself, the interpretations being arrived at and administered personally, while in institutional slavery on a broad scale, the conditions were not the same. Thus, slaves were given what is called "slave religion," and as Aptheker notes, "The aim of this instruction was to inculcate meekness and docility." Stampp repeats the same idea, and further notes that through religious instruction, "the bondsmen learned that slavery had divine sanction, that insolence was as much an offence against God as against the temporal master...and they heard of the punishments awaiting the disobedient slave in the hereafter." This hereafter promised of, would be a fundamental point in not only instilling fear of rebellion against whites, who were being made out to be the closest thing to God, if not the voice of God himself. It was taught that:

> ...the moral virtue of a non-resistant spirit was a favorite theme of southern ministers, when they preached to slaves. [William] Parker [a freed man] recalls: "The preachers of a slave-trading gospel frequently told us, in their sermons, that we should be 'good boys' and not break into master's henroost, nor steal his bacon..."

Frederick Douglass, in his autobiography, elucidates this dilemma further: "Trained from the cradle up to think and feel their masters were superior and invested with a sort of sacredness, there were few who could rise above the control which that sentiment exercised." Indeed, in the world of the enslaved, the term Lord had not only a dual meaning in that it was applied to both the white master and God alike, but the dividing line between those two no doubt blurred at some points and the identification of the Supreme was more and more readily identified with the white slaveowner as the conditioning took root. Christian religion played a dual purpose as well in retarding the development of resistance to slavery as well as in producing the elements that destroyed any that arose. While it planted the fear of a vengeful God who demanded submission of a slave to his or her master, it also pacified and contented the slave with the promise of a better life after death. Stampp informs us, "They heard, too, that eternal salvation would be their reward for faithful service... Their Christian preceptors, Fanny Kemble noted, 'jump[ed] the present life' and went on 'to furnish them with all the requisite conveniences for the next."

In summation, there are likely as many reasons for betraying a slave revolt as there are slaves who have done so, however for the sake of simplicity and furthering our own understanding, most of these reasons can be neatly categorized among any of the following four phenomena:

First, the most natural to man, and the most easily explained by human nature - Fear. The fear of death so often outweighed the slave's inherent desire for freedom that he chose not to risk his life and instead humbly submit himself to his condition. The betrayal of a rebellion is rare due to such circumstances, but occurs in the cases where fear prompts one who has knowledge of a conspiracy to withdraw. If this man or woman should later be questioned, he or she will undoubtedly also confess fully out of fear for his or her own life. This mindset also requires a certain degree of disregard for the slave's fellow slaves, as he or she is only seeking to preserve his or her own life. This may demand a Sambo personality, or the alienation from other Blacks and allegiance to whites (in some cases).

Second, a belief system which fosters not only the acceptance of the miserable conditions of slavery, in obedience to the oppressor's God, but a resilient submissiveness in vain hope of a heaven in the hereafter. This belief system is always accompanied by identification of the oppressor with the oppressor's God, as the two share similar status and the same demands.

Third, the internalization of the attitudes of the oppressor, and the identification of the oppressed with the oppressor, owing to total allegiance and unswaying loyalty to the oppressor. This is the most prevalent of the four in the study of the betrayal of slave rebellions, and is possible the foremost issue at hand in understanding this topic.

Fourth, the promise of slightly better treatment at the hands of the oppressor. This reward system earns the oppressor a positive image in the eyes of the oppressed and allows for the existence of a paternalistic dichotomy within the slave system. This paternalism produced the personality of the passive, childlike enslaved Black who viewed the slave master as a father, and therefore owed total allegiance to him.

RESISTANCE TO SLAVERY AMONG AFRICAN LEADERS

Leopold Senghor, first president of Senegal, said the slave trade "ravaged Black Africa like a brush fire, wiping out images and values in one vast carnage." The majority of the human destruction occurred in West Africa, where civilization on the continent had reached its highest point outside of Egypt. The removal of the best of the population deprived the continent of its most valuable resource: young men and women. To make matters worse, not only did Europeans provoke and intensify conflicts between African groups, they supplied the rivals with deadly guns and explosives to take the destruction to previously unseen levels.

Africa was culturally on equal footing with Europe and Asia at the beginning of the fifteenth century, not counting the European tradition of exploiting people economically, which wasn't a part of socialist African culture. But by the time the damage of the slave trade had really set in, and Europeans had begun taking over, Africa was in terrible shape. Several questions arise from examinations of this historical narrative. First, weren't African leaders aware of what was happening? Why didn't they do something to prevent it? Were they equally committed to the profitability of the slave trade? In regard to these questions, historians often portray African leaders as willing participants in the process, anxious to make personal gains by selling off prisoners of war and debtors into lifetimes of servitude in unknown lands.

The historical record suggests that this portrayal is skewed and incomplete at best. Not only are there many documented cases of early resistance to the slave trade among African leaders, but it also appears that many leaders only did so under intense external pressure. For example, at the beginning of the 16th century, the king of Kongo asked the Portuguese envoys for masons, physicians, and people who could offer technical expertise. Instead, he was overwhelmed by slave ships.

Early European slave raids were oftenmet with local resistance, but the African militaries fared no match for the advanced firepower of the Europeans. In some cases, groups of

Africans relocated their communities deeper into the wilderness to avoid slaving, while others built fortifications to keep slave raiders out. One example is in the present-day Gwolu Area, in the Sisala West District of Ghana, describes the fortifications constructed to protect the people against the slave raiders. According to current Paramount Chief Koro Liman IV:

In ancient times when slavery was rampant, our great great ancestor King Tanja Musa built the wall to ward away slave raiders and slave traders from coming into Gwolu to enslave our people. The reason we have the inner and outer wall is that between the two walls we had ponds and farms, so that the inhabitants would be protected from being kidnapped by slave raiders. First, there was only the inner wall. Then they realised that people who went to farm, find firewood and fetch water were kidnapped by slave raiders. The king found it necessary to construct a second wall and that is why it is a two-walled city. And I know that in the whole of Ghana there are only two such walls.

Some leaders, familiar with their own communities' ancient system of indentured servitude and unfamiliar with the inhumane European system of chattel slavery, engaged in the slave trade early on. The king of Benin (now part of Nigeria, not to be confused with the present-day Republic of Benin) began trading slaves with Europeans as soon as they'd entered the country and proposed it. Yet by 1530 the king could see this was draining the kingdom of male manpower and he banned the sale of slaves. By 1550, there was almost no slave trade in Benin. Trade in pepper and elephant tusks thrived temporarily, but local leaders soon found themselves outarmed by increasingly hostile neighboring states, who now engaged in war using growing caches of European firearms.

One example, the kingdom of Dahomey (now known as Republic of Benin), also resisted the slave trade initially, but eventually became one of the biggest slave states in West Africa, earning itself the name "the Slave Coast," along with untold wealth and the ire of their African neighbors. Historian Walter Rodney, in his How Europe Underdeveloped Africa estimates that by 1770, the king of Dahomey was earning an estimated £250,000 a year (the equivalent of nearly £348 million today) by selling captive Africans to European slave traders. He spent most of the money on British-made firearms (of poor quality) and industrial-grade alcohol. As late as the 1840s, King Gezo of Dahomey said, "The slave trade is the ruling principle of my people. It is the source and the glory of their wealth...the mother lulls the child to sleep with notes of triumph over an enemy reduced to slavery." However, the slave trade profited the people little, as all land and wealth in Dahomey was considered the property of the king, who exercised a monopoly on all trade.

Obviously, attitudes towards European slavery were not monolithic in Africa. While some leaders obviously sacrificed the well-being of others in furtherance of their own interests, it is academically irresponsible to ignore the many who wanted desperate to avoid or eliminate slavery. Even those leaders who eventually participated in the slave trade often had strong reservations, but found themselves unable to do anything about the situation. Afonso I, king of the Congo, like others, observed the slave trade rapidly grow out of control to the detriment of his authority and the well-being of his kingdom. In an October 1526 letter to the king of Portugal Joao III, quoted in Hugh Thomas' The Slave Trade, Afonso I laments, "There are many traders in all parts of the country. They bring ruin...Every day people are kidnapped and enslaved, even members of the King's family."

In the 1670's Muslim leader Nasr al-Din engaged in a campaign throughout Senegal, calling for puritanical reforms among rulers and denouncing them pillaging and enslaving their subjects. Al-Din effectively banned the sale of slaves to Europeans, undermining the French trade in slaves. The French, fearing the formation of a Muslim state resistant to slavery and able to dictate the terms of trade, supported a coup led by local warriors. By 1673, Nasr al-Din had been killed, and the traditional rulers had resumed their rulership, and the slave trade along with it.

In Angola, the state of Matamba was founded in 1630 in direct response to the threat of the Portuguese. Queen Nzinga, acting as its head, attempted to garner widespread support in resisting the Portuguese efforts in Angola. So by 1648, Portugal had not only blocked Queen Nzinga's efforts to assemble a coalition against them, but had effectively isolated the state of Matamba from its Angolan neighbors. As long as Matamba stood in opposition to trade with the Europeans, it suffered hostility from the neighboring African states that had already succumbed to the pressures of being involved with the slave trade. Backed into a corner with no allies, Nzinga was forced to resume business with the Portuguese. Intensified tribal and political divisions among neighboring Africans made such coalition attempts nearly impossible. In what is now Guinea, the Baga people were once organized in small states. In 1720, Toomba, one of their leaders, wanted to build an alliance to stop the slave traffic in the region. Toomba, too, was crushed by a mix of local white traders, slave trading Africans, and "proud mulattos."

As a final note, it is appropriate that we return to Dahomey. In the 1730s, the kingdom of Dahomey stood firm against the European slave traders. As a result, Dahomey was denied European imports. By this time, African societies were dependent on goods from Europe. Dahomey's king, Agaja Trudo, realized that the slave trade was detrimental to Dahomey's development. From 1724 to 1726, Trudo worked tirelessly to destroy the business, looting and burning European forts and slave camps, and blocking the paths into the country, where slaves were obtained. Within two years, he had reduced the slave trade in his region to "a mere trickle." The Europeans were enraged. At first, they attempted to sponsor African collaborators against Trudo, but couldn't unseat him or crush his state. However, Trudo was also unable to steer the other African leaders to develop new means of economic productivity. For example, with the profitable slave trade in place, few leaders wanted to return to growing crops. Also, the growing threat of his now unfriendly neighbors created a need for European firearms in Dahomey. In 1730, Agaja Trudo agreed to resume participation in the slave trade in exchange for European guns and goods. Trudo likely believed he was doing what was best in the interests of his people. Yet within a few decades, Trudo's difficult decision had led to Dahomey becoming one of the biggest slave states in Africa, resulting in millions of Africans being forced into the Atlantic slave trade (of whom nearly 50% died during captivity or transport), and rampant depopulation of the region. But by the height of this trade, many leaders were motivated solely by financial interests. In 1807, when the British Parliament abolished the trading of slaves, the King of Bonny (now in Nigeria) was horrified at the conclusion of the practice, protesting, "We think this trade must go on. That is the verdict of our oracle and the priests. They say that your country, however great, can never stop a trade ordained by God himself." While it may be accurate to say some African leaders were motivated by self-interest, it is irresponsible to simultaneously omit the many accounts of leaders who actively resisted and protested the trade, or to ignore the historical events leading to such developments when they occurred.

THE CULTURE OF REBELLION: SLAVE SONGS

On September 9, 1739, an enslaved Angolan named Cato led 20 enslaved Africans in what became known as the Stono Rebellion. His band gathered by Stono River near Charleston, South Carolina and marched to a local store. There they armed themselves, killing the two white shopkeepers. They then marched from house to house, killing slaveowners and their families, only skipping one man because he was said to have been "kind to his slaves." As they continued down their path, beating a drum and singing songs as they marched, their numbers swelled to 100 marchers. The rhythm of the procession was something familiar to many of the Africans, resembling traditional African marches to war.

The drumming also garnered attention from local whites. Before long, there was a large mob of whites trailing close behind them. Thirty rebel slaves were killed in the ensuing battle, and another 30 that escaped were caught and executed within a month. As a result of the Stono Rebellion, the Negro Act was passed, restricting Blacks from assembling in groups and reading, among other things.

But most significantly, the events of the Stono Rebellion and other events like it led to an eventual 1838 ban against drums on plantations. It was clear that the drums served as far more than a source of entertainment. In fact, not only were the drums used as a call to war, but they were also being used as a form of secret communication between slaves on distant plantations. Through the music of the drums, and the songs that often accompanied, the message of uprising had spread far and wide.

Yet although music was a dependable means of conveying feelings and ideas in the slave community, few documented songs sang by slaves expressed the intent of outright rebellion. Far more often, slave songs attempted to bring light and leisure to otherwise inhumane circumstances. Some of these songs expressed veiled sentiments of protest (eg, "All the Pretty Horses") or poked fun at slave masters, while others expressed desires for a flight to freedom (eg, "Canaan," "Run Nigger Run," "Steal Away" or "Let my People Go"). Still others contained coded instructions, disguised as spiritual songs. Two examples are "Wade in the Water" and "Follow the Drinking Gourd," which gave listeners clues to escaping for the North. Such coding was often intricate and ingenious. For example, we can decode the first two stanzas of "Follow the Drinking Gourd":

> When the sun comes up and the first quail calls
> Follow the drinking gourd
> For the old man is a-waiting to carry you to freedom
> If you follow the drinking gourd

With the beginning of winter on Dec. 21, the sun starts climbing higher in the sky each day. And in winter, the call of migratory quail echoes across southern fields. Thus this song, attributed to a character known only as "Peg Leg Joe," advised slaves to escape in long nights of winter and head north by following the Big Dipper, called the drinking gourd. According to the song, a guide will be waiting at the end of the line. The next stanza goes as follows:

> The riverbank makes a very good road
> The dead trees show you the way
> Left foot, peg foot, traveling on
> Follow the drinking gourd

This verse directs fugitives to the Tombigbee River, where special "Peg Leg" markings on fallen trees will show they're on the correct northerly course. Traveling under cover of darkness, slaves could find their way along the left bank of the river even on nights too overcast for the Big Dipper's stars to shine through.

Other songs may have encouraged covert forms of resistance, such as the ballads celebrating the tenacity and destructiveness of the boll weevil. Dorothy Scarborough, in her *On the Trail of Negro Folk Songs* wrote:

> The boll weevil is a promising subject for balladry, since he furnishes many romantic motifs. He is an outlaw, hunted in every field. He has apparently superhuman powers of resistance to hardship, exposure, and attacks from man, the individual, and from organized society. He has an extraordinary cunning and trickery, can outwit and flout man, and go his way despite all human efforts to stop him. He is coming to be a beloved rascal like Bre'r Rabbit, his exploits and cunning joyed in even by those he defies; a picaresque hero

with an international reputation for evil; a Robin Hood of the cotton-patch, admired while he is hunted down...Some of the versions of the ballad now in existence are said to have the mythical "hundred stanzas," so that already contemporary legendry is playing with this tiny, powerful villain. One correspondent writes, "I wish you could see the Negroes' faces light up when I mention The Boll Weevil, and they all say they could think of many stanzas if they had time."

Based on such examples, we can speculate there other such songs (which unfortunately have not been as well-preserved), and that other songs were used to communicate plans for revolt. One of the few examples we can document, although it is a secondhand account, is the song allegedly sung by the conspirators of the 1813 slave revolt plot on the Sea Islands off of South Carolina's coast. The lyrics of the song are as follows:

> Hail! all hail! ye Afric clan!
> Hail! ye oppressed, ye Afric band!
> Who toil and sweat in slavery bound (repeat)

> And when your health and strength are gone,
> Are left to hunger and to mourn.
> Let Independence be your aim,
> Ever mindful what 'tis worth;
> Pledge your bodies for the prize,
> Pile them even to the skies!

> Firm, united let us be,
> Resolved on death or liberty!
> As a band of patriots joined,
> Peace and plenty we shall find.
> Look to heaven with manly trust,
> And swear by Him that's always just,
> That no white foe, with impious hands (repeat)

> Shall slave your wives and daughters no more,
> Or rob them of their virtue dear!
> Be armed with valour firm and true,
> Their hopes are fixed on Heaven and you,
> That Truth and Justice will prevail.

> Firm, united, etc.
> Arise! arise! shake off your chains!
> Your cause is just, so Heaven ordains;
> To you shall freedom be proclaimed! (repeat)

Raise your arms and bare your breasts,
Almighty God will do the rest.
Blow the clarion's warlike blast;
Call every negro from his task;
Wrest the scourge from Buckra's hand,
And drive each tyrant from the land!

Another example can be found in the work of Martin Delaney, who reinvented many popular slave ballads with themes of resistance and rebellion. In chapter 11 of his 1859 novel *Blake, or the Huts of America*, the following song is sung:

Insurrection shall be my theme!
My watchword 'Freedom or the grave!'
Until from Rappahannock's stream,
To where the Cuato waters lave,
One simultaneous war cry
Shall burst upon the midnight air!
And rouse the tyrant but to sigh
Mid sadness, wailing and despair

Delaney's novel was written in response to Harriet Beecher Stowe's *Uncle Tom's Cabin*, which Delaney and other Black abolitionists felt portrayed slaves as passively resigned to their fate. *Blake* expresses a militant response to the slave system, advocating violent insurrection as a method of radical abolition, with a rebel slave, Blake, as its protagonist. In the search for insurrectionist themes in antebellum Black literature, works like Blake were rare in their militancy, but not alone. Frederick Douglass' only work of fiction, an 1852 novella titled *The Heroic Slave*, also promoted violent rebellion, a notion that appears counterintuitive to most followers of Douglass' work. But *The Heroic Slave* was, like *Blake*, written in response to the passive portrayals of *Uncle Tom's Cabin*, and was probably also influenced by the work of another radical abolitionist, David Walker. David Walker's 1829 *Appeal to the Coloured Citizens of the World*, possibly the most incendiary piece of anti-slavery literature written at the time, did not merely argue the merits of rebellion; it demanded it. Ironically, it was the responses of critics like Delaney, Douglass, and Garrison that led Harriet Beecher Stowe to write a follow up novel for *Uncle Tom's Cabin*. This novel, titled *Dred: Tales from a Dismal Swamp* paints a grimmer picture of the slave epidemic, and features a rebel slave, Dred, as its hero. Stowe appears to have lost some faith in the prospect of a peaceful end to slavery, and *Dred* appears to promote a more revolutionary approach than her previous work. While *Dred* was, in its time, far more popular than *Uncle Tom's Cabin*, it has been, like *Blake* and *The Heroic Slave*, mostly ignored by historians using literature and popular culture to paint depictions of abolitionist thought. Yet it is in these works that radical abolitionism finds its voice, in narrative, rhetorical argument, and even song. Chapter 42 of *Blake* features the following song:

> Were I a slave I would be free!
> I would not live to live a slave;
> But rise and strike for liberty,
> For Freedom, or a martyr's grave!
> One look upon the bloody scourge,
> Would rouse my soul to brave the fight,
> And all that's human in me urge
> To battle for my innate right!
> One look upon the tyrant's chains,
> Would draw my sabre from its sheath,
> And drive the hot blood through my veins
> To rush for liberty or death!
> One look upon my tortured wife,
> Shrieking beneath the driver's blows,
> Would nerve me on to desp'rate strife,
> Nor would I spare her dastard foes!
> Arm'd with the vindicating brand,
> For once the tyrant's heart should feel,
> No milk sop plea should stay my hand,
> The slave's great wrong would drive the steel!
> Away the unavailing plea!
> Of peace, the tyrant's blood to spare,
> If you would set the captive free,
> Teach him for freedom bold to dare!
> To throw his galling fetters by,
> To wing the cry on every breath,
> Determined manhood's conquering cry,
> For Justice, Liberty, or death!

While these songs were Delany's invention, it is possible that Delaney intended for these songs to become known in the slave community, and sow the seeds of real insurrection. One clear example of this approach was to be found in William Lloyd Garrison's abolitionist paper *The Liberator*. On July 1831, Garrison printed a song meant to be sung by slaves in insurrection. The editor even went so far as to preface it by requesting, "Will Southern Nullifiers do us the favor to read it to their slaves!" The song begins:

> See tyrants, see your empire shakes
> Your flaming roofs the wild winds fan
> Stung to the soul the negro wakes

The song ends with the following lines:

> Up Africa, the land is free
> Our battle cry is Liberty
> Oh, strike for God and vengeance now
> Fly tyrants fly
> Or stay to die

A month after the song's publication, Nat Turner led his revolt in Southampton, Virginia. Traditions of militant abolitionism existed in nearly every mode of human culture during slavery's oppressive reign. Music too, it appears, was employed widely as a medium to communicate such calls for revolution. Concluding with another tradition, we can turn to Black poetry for other examples of protest and rebellion. One salient example from the era is "To the White People of America" by Joshua McCarter Simpson (1820 – 1876). Sung to the tune of "Massa's in the Cold, Cold Ground," Simpson's work is one of the few surviving examples of such overt defiance:

> O'er this wide extended country,
> Hear the solemn echoes roll,
> For a long and weary century,
> Those cries have gone from pole to pole;
> See the white man sway his sceptre,
> In one hand he holds the rod –
> In the other hand the Scripture,
> And says that he's a man of God.
>
> *Hear ye that mourning?*
> *'Tis your brothers' cry!*
> *O! ye wicked men take warning,*
> *The day will come when you must die.*
>
> Lo! Ten thousand steeples shining
> Through this mighty Christian land
> While four millions slaves all pining
> And dying 'neath the Tyrant's hand.

See the "blood-stained" Christian banner
Followed by a host of saints
While they loudly sing Hosannah
We hear the dying slave's complaints:

Hear ye that mourning?
Anglo-sons of God
O! ye Hypocrites take warning
And shun your sable brothers blood

In our Legislative members
Few there are with humane souls
Though they speak in tones of thunder
'Gainst sins which they cannot control
Women's rights and annexation
Is the topic by the way
While poor Africa's sable nation
For mercy, cry both by night and day.

Hear ye that mourning?
'Tis a solemn sound,
O! ye wicked men take warning
For God will send his judgment down

Tell us not of distant Island –
Never will we colonize:
Send us not to British Highlands
For this is neither just nor wise
Give us equal rights and chances
All the rights of citizens –
And as light and truth advances
We'll show you that we all are men.
Hear ye that mourning?
'Tis your brothers sigh
O! ye wicked men take warning
The judgment day will come by and by.

Though the documentary record is sparse, it is clear that traditions of militant abolitionism existed in nearly every mode of human culture during slavery's oppressive reign. Music too, it appears, was employed widely as a medium to communicate such calls for revolution.

BLACK REBELLION TIMELINE

1441   Start of European slave trading in Africa. The Portuguese captains Antão Gonçalves and Nuno Tristão capture 12 Africans in Cabo Branco (modern Mauritania) and take them to Portugal as slaves. The Africans work as servants but are also used to supply strategic information about Africa.

1442   Slavery and Christianity. Church authorities frames the edict called *Illius qui*, which promised all those who would join the slave raiding parties spiritual reward and eternal salvation.

1444   Lançarote de Freitas, a Portuguese tax-collector, forms a company to trade with Africa. He acquires 235 kidnapped and enslaved Africans in Lagos, the first large group of African slaves brought to Europe.

1452   When the Portuguese seek confirmation that they can enslave infidels seized in the crusade, the Pope responds with *Dum Diversus*, which allows them to conquer and reduce to "perpetual slavery" all "Saracens and pagans and other infidels and enemies of Christ," in West Africa.

1454   Pope Nicholas V issues *Romanus Pontifex*, a Papal bull granting the Portuguese a perpetual monopoly in trade with Africa. Nevertheless, Spanish traders also begin to bring slaves from Africa to Spain.

1476   Carlos de Valera of Castille in Spain brings back 400 slaves from Africa. Despite Papal opposition, Spanish merchants begin to trade in large numbers of slaves in the 1470s.

1492   Christopher Columbus becomes the first European since the Viking era to discover the New World, setting foot on an unidentified island he named San Salvador (modern Bahamas).

1493   On his second voyage, Columbus again reaches the New World (modern Dominica). On this voyage he initiates the first transatlantic slave voyage, a shipment of several hundred Taino people sent from Hispaniola to Spain.

1496   Columbus returns from his second voyage, carrying around 30 Native American slaves.

1499   More than 200 slaves taken from the northern coast of South America by Amerigo Vespucci and Alonso de Hojeda are sold, apparently without legal problems, in Cádiz, Spain.

1502   African slaves in the New World. Juan de Córdoba of Seville becomes the first merchant we can identify to send an African slave to the New World.

1504   A small group of Africans - probably slaves captured from a Portuguese vessel - are brought to the court of King James IV of Scotland.

1509   Columbus's son, Diego Cólon, becomes governor of the new Spanish empire in the Caribbean, ruling from Santo Domingo in Hispaniola, which now comprises Haiti and the Dominican

Republic. He soon complains that Native American slaves do not work hard enough.

1510   The start of systematic transportation of African slaves to the New World: King Ferdinand of Spain authorizes a shipment of 50 African slaves to be sent to Santo Domingo.

1516   The governor of Cuba, Diego Velázquez, authorizes slave-raiding expeditions to Central America. One group of slaves aboard a Spanish caravel rebel and kill the Spanish crew before sailing home - the first successful slave rebellion recorded in the New World.

1522   Slave revolt. The first large-scale slave uprising in the Western Hemisphere takes place on the plantation of Christopher Columbus' son Diego.

1526   The first slaves used by Europeans in the present-day United States are among Lucas Vásquez de Ayllón's colonization attempt of present-day South Carolina. The attempt is a failure, lasting only one year; the slaves revolted and fled into the wilderness to live among the Cofitachiqui people.

1530   Juan de la Barrera, a Seville merchant, begins transporting slaves directly from Africa to the New World (before this, slaves had normally passed through Europe first). His lead is quickly followed by other slave traders.

1552   Bayano's slave revolt in Panama. The Mandinka Bayano leads the biggest of the slave revolts of 16th century Panama. Different tales tell of the revolt beginning either on the ship en route, or after landing in Panama. After the revolt, the rebel slaves, known as cimarrones, set up strongholds known as palenques, many of which successfully fend off Spanish control for centuries using guerrilla warfare and alliances with indigenous nations who are in similar circumstances.

1562   Britain Joins slave Trade. John Hawkins, the first Englishman we know about to take part in the slave trade, makes a huge profit obtaining 300 African slaves and selling them in the West Indies.

1570   Gaspar Yanga's revolt, near the Mexican city of Veracruz. The group then escapes to the highlands and built a free colony.

1581   Slaves in Florida. Spanish residents in St. Augustine, the first permanent settlement in Florida, import African slaves.

1600   King Philip III of Spain outlaws the use of Native American slaves in Spanish colonies.

1612   Slave revolt conspiracy in Mexico. 33 slaves (29 males and 4 women) are tortured and executed for their involvement. Their heads are cut off and displayed in the main square of Mexico City for a long time as an example.

1619   Slaves in Virginia. Africans brought to Jamestown are the first slaves imported into Britain's North American colonies. Like white indentured servants, they were probably freed after a fixed period of service.

1624   The Dutch, who had entered the slave trade in 1621 with the formation of the Dutch West Indies Co., import blacks to serve on Hudson Valley farms. According to Dutch law, the children of freed slaves are bound to slavery.

1625   Ten slaves are listed in the first census of Jamestown, Virginia.

1638   The first public slave auction of 23 individuals is held in Jamestown square.

1640   Whipping and branding, borrowed from Roman practice via the Iberian-American colonies, appears early and with vicious audacity. One Virginian slave, named Emanuel, is convicted of trying to escape and is sentenced to thirty lashes, with the letter "R" for "runaway" branded on his cheek and "work in a shackle one year or more as his master shall see cause."

1641   Massachusetts colony legalizes slavery.

1644   Barbados is the first British possession to enact restrictive legislation governing slaves. Other colonies soon follow suit.

1649   Slave rebellion in Barbados.

1661   Virginia authorities noted that indentured servants are planning a rebellion. After 1691, freed black slaves were banished from Virginia.

1662   Hereditary slavery. Virginia law decrees that children of Black mothers "shall be bond or free according to the condition of the mother."

1663   Maryland officials face a possible strike in slave labor.

1663   Slave revolt in Gloucester County, Virginia. White servants and black slaves conspire to revolt, but are betrayed by a fellow servant.

1664   Maryland passes a law making lifelong servitude for black slaves mandatory to prevent them from taking advantage of legal precedents established in England which grant freedom under certain conditions, such as conversion to Christianity. Similar laws are later passed in New York, New Jersey, the Carolinas and Virginia.

1669   The colonial Virginia Assembly declares that, if a Negro slave died at the hands of a master who used "extremity of correction" to overcome the slave's "obstinacy," it was not murder. In "An act about the casuall killing of slaves," lawmakers reasoned that no man would deliberately destroy his own property.

1671   A Virginia law is enacted providing for a bounty on the heads of "Maroons," black fugitives who form communities in the mountains, swamps, and forests of southern colonies. Many Maroon communities attack towns and plantations.

1672   After several colonies legalize slavery, the slave population in North America begins to grow from the low hundreds. The king of England charters the Royal African Company to bring the shiploads of slaves into trading centers like Jamestown, Hampton, and Yorktown.

1673   Slave revolt in St. Ann's Parish, Jamaica, resulting in 200 slaves becoming the Leeward Maroons. These Maroons unite with a group of Madagascars who had survived the shipwreck of a slave ship and formed their own maroon community in St. George's parish.

1675   Slave rebellion in Barbados.

1676   Bacon's Rebellion leads planters to worry about the prospective dangers of creating a large class of restless, landless, and relatively poor white men (most of them former indentured servants). Wealthy Virginia and Maryland planters begin to buy African slaves in preference to white indentured servants, and poorer planters soon follow suit.

1676   Haitian slave rebellion. Padre Jean leads a slave rebellion near Port de Paix, in the north of Saint-Domingue. He organizes 25 slaves and begins killing slave holders before retreating into the mountains nearby. He is tracked down by pirates and killed 3 years later.

1676-   Quilombo dos Palmares Maroon War in Alagoas, Brazil, led by
1694   Zumbi.

1692   Slave rebellion in Barbados.

1698   Parliament opens the slave trade to British merchants, who will carry on a triangular trade from New England to Africa to the Caribbean islands to New England. The merchant vessels will carry New England rum to African slavers, African slaves on "the middle passage" to the West Indies, and West Indian sugar and molasses to New England for the rum distilleries.

1705   Slaves as Property. Describing slaves as real estate, Virginia lawmakers allow owners to bequeath their slaves. The same law allowed masters to "kill and destroy" rebels and runaways.

1710   Slave revolt conspiracy discovered in Surry County, Virginia.

1712   Slave revolt in New York City. 20-30 Blacks and a few Native Americans set fire to a building and ambushed several whites that came to put out the flames. After several whites had been either killed or wounded, a general alarm was sounded and soldiers were brought in to stop the rebellion. 20 slaves were executed for their participation in the revolt. As a result of the revolt, New York passed the 1712 slave Act to suppress insurrections, Massachusetts enacted a law against further importation of slaves into that colony, and Pennsylvania instituted high taxes to restrain African importations.

1718   Slave revolt conspiracy discovered in New Orleans, Louisiana.

1720   Slave revolt in South Carolina results in the death of three whites.

1721   Mutiny on the slave ship Henry of London. Eight enslaved Africans manage to free themselves of their irons and attempt to subdue the ship and its 50-man crew. After being driven back by cut lances and firearms, they jump overboard.

1722   Slave revolt conspiracy discovered near Rappahannock River in Virginia. About 200 slaves allegedly arm themselves with the intention of killing all the whites while they attend church.

1723   Several fires break out in Boston, purportedly started by rebel slaves.

1728   Attempted insurrection in Savannah, Georgia.

1729   Slave revolt conspiracy in Antigua.

1730   Slave revolt conspiracy in Charleston, South Carolina.

1730   Slave revolt conspiracy discovered in Norfolk and Princess Anne counties, Virginia.

1730   Mutiny on slave ship Little George of Captain George Scott, sailing from the Guinea Coast en route to Rhode Island with a cargo of some 96 enslaved Africans. Several days into the voyage, several Africans slip out of their irons and kill the three watchmen who were on deck. The captain and his crew are forced into their cabins, where the Africans imprison them. For several days, the Africans control the ship and manage to sail it back to the Sierra Leone River. Finally, the Captain and the enslaved Africans make a deal and agree to grant each other their freedom.

1731   Mutiny on the Massachusetts schooner, William, off the coast of Africa.

1732   Slave mutiny on a ship of Capt. John Major of New Hampshire.

1733   St. John slave revolt. Occurring on St. John in the Virgin Islands, it is considered the first successful slave rebellion in the Western Hemisphere.

1734   Slave insurrection in Burlington, Pennsylvania.

1735   Slave ship mutiny. Africans on the ship Dolphin of London, upon having their mutiny suppressed, retreat into the powder room, and intentionally blow themselves up with the crew.

1739   Stono slave rebellion. In September, approximately 12 slaves revolt in Stono, South Carolina. Led by a recently arrived Kongolese slave named Cato, the group kills two white men guarding a warehouse, takes weapons found inside and march southward to escape to freedom in what was then St. Augustine, Spanish Florida. During their march, other Blacks hear the marchers drumming and join the group, eventually bringing the total to over 75. The group is discovered 10 miles from Stono and attacked by an armed militia. The resulting battle claims the lives of 25 whites and 55 Blacks. The Stono rebellion leads to a temporary decline in the importation of Africans to South Carolina, and a ban on the use of drums among slaves.

1739   Slave revolt in St. Paul's Parish, South Carolina.

1739   Slave revolt in St. Johns, South Carolina.

1740   Slave revolt in South Carolina.

1741   New York slave insurrection. A series of suspicious fires and reports of slave conspiracy leads to general hysteria in New York City, March and April. New Yorkers charge a "Negro conspiracy," and four whites and 18 blacks are hanged and 13 blacks are burned at the stake.

1742   Mutiny. While taking on slaves in the Sierra Leone River, a vessel named the Jolly Batchelor is attacked and captured by enslaved captives on board and African men on shore. The Africans strip the vessel of its rigging and sails, free the other Africans in the hold, and then abandon the ship.

1747   Mutiny on the slave ship of Capt. Beers off Cape Coast in West Africa.

1755   Georgia slave code, adopted from South Carolina, stipulates that seven Blacks "being out together constituted a mob."

1757   Mackandal's conspiracy. In Haiti, a slave named Mackandal, having traditional African knowledgeable of poisons, organizes a widespread plot to poison the masters, their water supplies and animals. The movement spreads great terror among slave owners and hundreds die. After 12 years of meticulous planning and preparation, Mackandal was on the verge of a massive rebellion. But as he prepared to carry out a mass poisoning of whites to set the stage for his coup, he was betrayed by a tortured female slave and captured.

1759   Slave revolt conspiracy in Charleston, South Carolina.

1760   Tacky's War in Jamaica. In what may be the most significant slave rebellion in the Caribbean until the Haitian Revolution, Tacky, a former African chief, led a group of rebels who took over plantations and killed the white owners. Their plan was to overthrow British rule and establish an African kingdom in Jamaica. As is typical, a slave in one of the liberated plantations informed white authorities. A planter militia, military troops and a Maroon force allied to the British, regain control. Tacky and a few others fought on, but when Tacky was killed by a Maroon sharpshooter, the last fighters killed themselves before capture.

1761   Mutiny on the Boston slave ship, Thomas, commanded by Thomas Day.

1762   Insurrection conspiracy in Bermuda.

1763   Cuffy's slave revolt in Guyana. Cuffy, or Kofi, is an Akan sold into slavery to work in the plantations of the Dutch colony of Berbice. He leads a revolt of more than 2,500 slaves against the colony regime.

1764   Mutiny on the slave ship Adventure, based in Rhode Island or New London. The ship is overthrown by Africans while trading for slaves at Sierra Leone on the West Coast of Africa.

1765   Mutiny. Captive Africans aboard a slave ship recently arrived in Barbados rise up in rebellion. In the fighting, 13 African jump overboard, one is killed and several more are wounded before the rebellion is put down.

1765   Mutiny on British slave-trading ship, Three Friends.

1765-   Maroon war in Surinam.
1793

1767   Slave revolt in Grenada.

1775   American Revolution Begins. Battles at the Massachusetts towns of Lexington and Concord spark the war for American independence from Britain.

1776   Declaration of Independence. The Continental Congress asserts "that these United Colonies are, and of Right ought to be Free and Independent States". "How is it," asks Samuel Johnson, "that we hear the loudest yelps for liberty among the drivers of Negroes?" The British author is only one of many Europeans who thought it strange that a nation run by slave owners should be so noisily demanding its own freedom.

1783   American Revolution Ends. Britain and the infant United States sign the Peace of Paris treaty.

1785   A slave-trading ship belonging to the firm of Seymour and Company of Grenada, is found adrift upon the high seas by an English ship. Her sails are gone, and fifteen emaciated Africans "in a very wretched condition, having been long at sea," are found on its deck. The Africans had risen up and slain the captain and his crew, and then attempted to steer the ship back to Africa.

1790   According to the first United States Census, nearly 700,000 slaves live and toil in a nation of 3.9 million people.

1790   Slave revolt in British Virgin Islands.

1791   Mutiny on the ship of Captain William Wignall of New England.

1791   In Louisiana, twenty-three slaves are hanged and three white sympathizers deported, following suppression of a black revolt.

1791 - The Haitian Revolution. This is the only slave rebellion to
1804   liberate an entire slave population. Inspired by the French Revolution, slaves in St. Dominique succeed in overthrowing the white planter class, repelling the French Army, and defeating the Spanish and British forces. The revolution's success is attributed to leader General Toussaint L'Ouverture, who outwits all three European forces before being betrayed and captured. However the seeds of the revolution can be traced back to a slave named Boukman who initiated the conspiracy in 1791.

1793   Fugitive slave Act. The United States outlaws any efforts to impede the capture of runaway slaves.

1794   Cotton Gin. Eli Whitney patents his device for pulling seeds from cotton. The invention turns cotton into the cash crop of the American South, and creates a huge demand for slave labor.

1795   Cuban slave rebellion.

1795   Louisiana slave uprisings. The uprisings are suppressed with some 50 blacks killed and executed.

1795   Tula's slave rebellion in Curacao.

1795   Pointe Coupée conspiracy in Louisiana.

1795   First Demerara rebellion in Guyana.

1795   José Leonardo Chirino's insurrection in Venezuela.

1798   Cuban slave rebellion.

1800   Prosser's rebellion. 24 year old Gabriel Prosser organizes a slave revolt in Richmond, Virginia. On the eve of the battle against 600 troops, a bridge washes out and Prosser's army of 1,000 scatters. It is later learned that two slaves had told their masters of Prosser's plan.

1802   Cuban slave rebellion

1802   Slave boatmen plot rebellion along Roanoke River in Virginia.

1803   New York Uprising. Blacks of New York burn parts of the city and destroy several homes.

1803   Slave rebellion in Montevideo, Uraguay. Twenty slave and free African men fled and founded a maroon colony on the Yi River, which was later defeated.

1805   Chatham Manor rebellion on the Rappahannock River in Virginia.

1805   Cuban slave rebellion.

1807   Slave revolt planned in Brazil. This revolt is to take place during the Corpus Christi celebrations. Six days before the revolt would take place, the conspirators are betrayed by a slave loyal to his master.

1807   Passing of the Insurrection Act of 1807, a set of laws governing the US President's ability to deploy troops within the United States to put down insurrection and rebellion. The general aim is to limit Presidential power and rely on state and local governments for initial response in the event of insurrection. Coupled with the Posse Comitatus Act, Presidential powers for law enforcement are limited and delayed. The original wording of the Act required the conditions for deployment to be met as the result of "insurrection, domestic violence, unlawful combination, or conspiracy" In 2007, following Hurricane Katrina, the Act was amended, adding that those conditions could also be a result of "natural disaster, epidemic, or other serious public health emergency, terrorist attack or incident, or other condition" and only if "domestic violence has occurred to such an extent that the constituted authorities of the State or possession are incapable of maintaining public order." In 2008, the changes were repealed, reverting to the previous wording of the Insurrection Act of 1807.

1808	United States bans slave trade. Importing African slaves is outlawed, but smuggling continues.
1811	German Coast uprising. 400-500 slaves led by Charles Dislondes revolt on a plantation near New Orleans. They march from plantation to plantation, sending whites fleeing. They are finally stopped by militiamen and army soldiers. Many are killed, but many escaped. Those that are captured are beheaded and their heads displayed on pikes on the levees and roads around New Orleans, as a message to other would-be rebel slaves.
1812	Aponte revolt in Cuba.
1812	Marines escorting a convoy of supply wagons are ambushed by an irregular force of Native Americans and Blacks in Twelve Mile Swamp near St. John's, East Florida. Two marines are killed and seven are wounded.
1812	Planned slave revolt in Henry County, Virginia.
1813	Slave revolt conspiracy in Sea Islands off South Carolina's coast.
1814	Slave revolt in Brazil. Four of the captured slaves are hanged in public and 12 are deported to Portuguese colonies in Africa.
1815	Boxley rebellion. A slave rebellion led by George Boxley, a white man, fails in Virginia.
1816	Ambush of Navy personnel on Apalachicola River, Spanish Florida, during reconnaissance of fort and settlement occupied by free Blacks and escaped slaves. Four Navy are killed.
1816	300 fugitive slaves and about 20 Indian allies hold Fort Blount on Apalachicola Bay, Florida, for several days before it is attacked by U.S. Troops.
1816	Bussa's Insurrection in Barbados, also known as the Easter Rebellion. Between 500 and 1000 slaves are killed in the fighting; more than 140 slaves are executed; and 123 are forcibly removed from the colony. Frightened by the uprising and hoping to avoid future insurrections, officials in London insist that the colonists implement reforms to ease the burdens of slavery.
1820	Missouri Compromise. Missouri is admitted to the Union as a slave state, Maine as a free state. slavery is forbidden in any subsequent territories north of latitude 36°30'
1822	Denmark Vesey conspiracy. Vesey, a freed slave, constructs a plan to overthrow Charleston, South Carolina. Loyal slaves reveal the plans to white planters and he and his conspirators are arrested and hanged.
1822-1830	Bahia rebellion in Brazil.
1823	Second Demerara rebellion in Guyana.
1823	Slave revolt in the British Virgin Islands.
1825	Cuban slave rebellion.

1827   Cuban slave rebellion.

1829   Cuban slave rebellion.

1829   *Walker's Appeal.* David Walker, a black abolitionist, publishes his pamphlet *David Walker's Appeal to the Colored Citizens of the World*. In it, Walker denounces the American institution of slavery as the most oppressive in world history and calls on people of African descent to resist slavery and racism by any means. The book terrifies southern slave owners, who place a sizable bounty on his head. Banned in several states, *Walker's Appeal* argues, among other things, for the necessity of insurrection. His work is instrumental in initiating slave escapes and insurrections.

1830   Slave revolt in British Virgin Islands.

1831   Nat Turner's slave revolt. Slave preacher Nat Turner leads a two-day uprising against whites, killing about 60 whites in Southampton, Virginia, making it the most lethal slave revolt in North America. The revolt is eventually stopped by hundreds of white vigilantes and militia. Militiamen crush the revolt and then spend months searching for Turner, who is eventually caught, tried and hanged. Enraged Southerners impose harsher restrictions on their slaves.

1831-   Baptist War in Jamaica, led by Baptist slave preacher, Samuel
1832   Sharpe.

1832   In the wake of the Nat Turner's insurrection in Virginia, Georgetown strengthens its Black code, punishing with particular severity any person of color possessing abolitionist literature.

1833   Cuban slave rebellion.

1834   Cuban slave rebellion.

1835   Malé revolt (also known as The Great revolt). This is perhaps the most significant slave rebellion in Brazil. On a Sunday during Ramadan, in the city of Salvador da Bahia, a group of Black slaves and freedmen, inspired by their Muslim teachers, rise up against the government.

1835   Cuban slave rebellion.

1835   Mexicans incite slave revolt in Texas.

1835   Censorship. Southern states expel abolitionists and forbid the mailing of antislavery propaganda.

1835-   Black Seminole slave rebellion in Florida. 385 Seminoles and
1838   Blacks massacre a 103-man U.S. Army force under Major Francis L. Dade in Florida.

1838   Cuban slave rebellion.

1839   Amistad ship rebellion. About 50 Africans who, against international law, had been captured and shipped to Havana, Cuba, seize the schooner Amistad, which was taking them to a plantation. Two crewmen are killed in the fight, and the rest of the crew are put ashore. The Africans, led by "Joseph" Cinque, order the owners to sail the ship back to Africa. However, the Amistad is seized by a U.S. brig and the Africans are imprisoned in Connecticut. The court decides in favor of the Africans and 32 of them are returned to their homeland of Sierra Leone.

1839-1843   Cuban slave rebellion.

1841   Creole ship rebellion. Slave revolt on slave trader 'Creole' which was en route from Hampton, Virginia to New Orleans, Louisiana. The captives overpower the crew and sail the vessel to Bahamas where they are granted asylum and freedom.

1844   La Escalera revolt in Cuba.

1846-1848   Mexican-American War. Defeated, Mexico yields an enormous amount of territory to the United States. Americans then wrestle with the topic of whether slavery is permitted in the new lands.

1850   Compromise of 1850. In exchange for California's entering the Union as a free state, northern congressmen accept a harsher Fugitive Slave Act.

1851   In separate incidents, Black abolitionists crash into courtrooms in Boston and Syracuse, New York, and rescue fugitive slaves.

1851   Blacks disperse a group of slave catchers in Christiana, Pennsylvania conflict. One white man is killed, another wounded.

1852   Uncle Tom's Cabin published. Harriet Beecher Stowe's novel about the horrors of slavery sells 300,000 copies within a year of publication. However, critics argue that the novel makes Blacks appear too passively resigned to their fate.

1852   Black abolitionist Frederick Douglass's first and only work of fiction, The Heroic Slave, is published. Unlike the work he is commonly associated with, this story, featuring the leader of a slave ship mutiny, promotes resistance and revolt among the enslaved. Douglass appears to be responding to the submissive portrayal presented in Uncle Tom's Cabin.

1854   Kansas-Nebraska Act. Setting aside the Missouri Compromise of 1820, Congress allows these two new territories to choose whether to allow slavery. Violent clashes erupt.

1856   Slave revolt conspiracies in Lafayette, Kentucky and Clarksville, Tennessee

1856   Mexicans incite slave revolt in Texas.

1856   Harriet Beecher Stowe's next novel, Dred: Tales from a Dismal Swamp, appears to be a response to the criticism she received for her first novel. In this book, Stowe features the story of a rebel slave named Dred, plotting revolution. Though this book outsells Uncle Tom's Cabin, it is rarely discussed.

1857   Dred Scott Decision. The United States Supreme Court decides, seven to two, that blacks can never be citizens and that

Congress has no authority to outlaw slavery in any territory.

1858   Mutiny on the French slave ship Regina Coeli. In perhaps the most successful revolt yet documented, 270 insurgents kill most of the French crew and escape into the wilderness of Liberia.

1859   John Brown's Raid on Harpers Ferry.

1859   Martin Delaney, a Black abolitionist who would later go on to play an implemental role in the Civil War, begins publishing *Blake, Or the Huts of America*. *Blake*, the first novel published in America by a Black man, features as its protagonist a free Black man who travels through the South sowing the seeds of violent uprising against slavery. Delaney also appears to be responding to *Uncle Tom's Cabin*.

1859   The last slave ship arrives. During this year, the last ship to bring slaves to the United States, the Clothilde, arrives in Mobile Bay, Alabama.

1860   Abraham Lincoln elected. Abraham Lincoln of Illinois becomes the first Republican to win the United States Presidency.

1860   Southern Secession. South Carolina secedes in December. More states follow the next year.

1861-   United States Civil War. Four years of brutal conflict claim
1865   623,000 lives. As a strategic decision, President Abraham Lincoln issues the Emancipation Proclamation, decreeing that all slaves in Rebel territory are free on January 1, 1863. Because the Confederacy no longer observes Lincoln's presidency, there is little effect. Meanwhile, slavery remains in effect and enforced by law elsewhere.

1865   Slavery Abolished. Following the end of the Civil War and reconsolidation of the Union, the 13th Amendment to the United States Constitution outlaws slavery throughout the U.S. The amendment abolishes involuntary servitude, with an exception for those convicted and imprisoned: "Neither slavery nor involuntary servitude, except as a punishment for crime whereof the party shall have been duly convicted, shall exist within the United States, or any place subject to their jurisdiction."

REFERENCES

Anstey, Roger T. *The Atlantic Slave Trade and British Abolition, 1760-1810*. Atlantic Highlands, N. J.: Humanities Press, 1975.

Aptheker, Herbert. *American Negro Slave Revolts*, 6th ed., New York : International Publ., 1993.

Berlin, Ira. *Many Thousands Gone: The First Two Centuries of Slavery in North America*. Cambridge, Mass.: Belknap Press of Harvard University Press, 1998.

Blassingame, John. *The Slave Community, Plantation Life in the Antebellum South*. New York, 1974.

Campbell, Edward D. C. and Kim York. *Before Freedom Came: African American Life in the Antebellum South*. Richmond: The Museum; 1991. Charlottesville: University Press of Virginia, 1991.

Campbell, Mavis C. *The Maroons of Jamaica 1655-1796: A History of Resistance, Collaboration and Betrayal*. Trenton: African World Press, 1990.

Cheek, William F. *Black Resistance Before the Civil War*. Beverly Hills: Glencoe Press, 1970.

Childs, Matt D. *The 1812 Aponte Rebellion in Cuba and the Struggle Against African Slavery*. Chapel Hill: University of North Carolina Press, 2006.

Clarke, John Henrik. *Slave Trade and Slavery*. New York, NY: Holt, Rinehart and Winston, 1970.

Conniff, Michael. *Africans in the Americas: A History of the Black Diaspora*. New York: St. Martin's Press, 1994.

Coughtry, Jay. *The Notorious Triangle: Rhode Island and the African Slave Trade, 1700-1807*. Philadelphia: Temple University Press, 1981.

Davidson, Basil. *The African Slave Trade*. Boston: Back Bay Books, 1980.

Donnan, Elizabeth, ed. *Documents Illustrative of the History of the Slave Trade*. 2 vols. New York: Octagon, 1965.

Dow, George Francis. *Slave Ships and Slavings*. Salem, Mass.: Marine Research Society, 1927.

Egerton, Douglas R. *Gabriel's Rebellion: The Virginia Slave Conspiracies of 1800 and 1802*. Chapel Hill, NC: University of North Carolina Press, 1993.

Egerton, Douglas R. *He Shall Go Out Free: The Lives of Denmark Vesey*. Madison, Wis.: Madison House, 1999.

Eltis, David. *The Rise of African Slavery in the Americas*. Cambridge, UK: Cambridge University Press, 2000.

Finkelman, Paul. *Defending Slavery: Proslavery Thought in the Old South: A Brief History with Documents*. Boston: Bedford/St. Martin's, 2003.

Fogel, Robert William. *The Slavery Debates, 1952-1990: A Retrospective*. Baton Rouge: Louisiana State University Press, 2003.

Franklin, John Hope and Loren Schweninger. *Runaway Slaves: Rebels on the Plantation*. New York: Oxford University Press, 1999.

Geggus, David P., ed. *The Impact of the Haitian Revolution in the Atlantic World*. Columbia: University of South Carolina Press, 2001.

Genovese, Eugene D. *From Rebellion to Revolution: Afro-American Slave Revolts in the Making of the Modern World*. Baton Rouge: Louisiana State University Press, 1979.

Greenberg, Kenneth S. *The Confession of Nat Turner and Related Documents*. Boston: Bedford Books of St. Martin's Press, 1996.

Gutman, Herbert. *The Black Family in Slavery and Freedom, 1750-1825*. New York: Pantheon Books, 1976.

Harding, Vincent. *There Is a River: The Black Struggle for Freedom in America*. New York: Harcourt Brace, 1981.

James, C. L. R. *The Black Jacobins: Toussaint L'Ouverture and the San Domingo Revolution*. New York, NY: Vintage Books, 1963.

Jordan, Winthrop. *White Over Black: American Attitudes Toward the Negro, 1550-1812.* Chapel Hill, NC., 1968.

Katz, Johnathan. *Resistance at Christiana: The Fugitive Slave Rebellion, Christiana, Pennsylvania.* New York, NY: Thomas Y. Crowell, 1974.

Katz, William Loren. *Breaking the Chains: African American Slave Resistance.* New York, NY: Macmillian, 1990.

Kolchin, Peter. *American Slavery, 1619-1877.* New York: Hill and Wang, 2003.

Litwack, Leon, ed. and August Meier, ed. *Black Leaders of the Nineteenth Century.* Urbana, Illinois: University of Illinois Press, 1988.

Lowance, Jr, Mason. *A House Divided: The Antebellum Slavery Debates in America, 1776-1865.* Princeton, NJ: Princeton University Press, 2003.

Mellon, James. Bullwhip Days: *The Slave Remembers, an Oral History.* New York, NY: Avon Books, 1990.

Miller, Joseph. *Way of Death: Merchant Capitalism and the Angolan Slave Trade, 1730-1830.* Madison: University of Wisconsin Press, 1988.

Mullin, Michael. *Africa in America: Slave Acculturation and Resistance in the American South and the Caribbean, 1736-1831.* Urbana: University of Illinois Press, 1992

Price, Richard. *Maroon Societies: Rebel Slave Communities in the Americas.* Baltimore, MD: Johns Hopkins University, 1979.

Rawly, James A. *The Transatlantic Slave Trade: A History.* New York: W. W. Norton, 1981.

Reis, Joao Jose. *Slave Rebellion in Brazil: The Muslim Uprising of 1835 in Bahia.* (Johns Hopkins Studies in Atlantic History and Culture), Johns Hopkins Univ. Press, 1993.

Rodriguez, Junius P., ed. *Encyclopedia of Slave Resistance and Rebellion.* Westport, CT: Greenwood, 2007.

Rodriguez, Junius P., ed. *Slavery in the United States: A Social, Political, and Historical Encyclopedia.* Santa Barbara, CA: ABC-

CLIO, 2007.

Stampp, Kenneth M. *The Peculiar Institution: Slavery in the Ante-Bellum South.* New York, NY: Vintage Books, 1955.

Thomas, Hugh. *The Slave Trade: The Story of the Atlantic Slave Trade: 1440-1870.* New York: Simon & Shuster, 1997.

Thompson, Vincent B. *The Making of the African Diaspora in the Americas, 1441-1900.* New York: Longman, 1987.

Thompson, Vincent Bakpetu. *The Making of the African Diaspora in the Americas, 1441-1900.* New York: Longman, 1987.

Thornton, John. *Africa and Africans in the Making of the Atlantic World, 1400-1680.* Cambridge, UK: Cambridge University Press, 1992.

Walker, David. *David Walker's Appeal in Four Articles: Together with a Preamble, to the Coloured Citizens of the World, But in Particular, and Very Expressly, to Those of the United States of America.* New York, NY: Hill and Wang, 1965.

ALSO FROM OUR COMPANY

How to Hustle and Win, Part 1: A Survival Guide for the Ghetto

By Supreme Understanding
Foreword by the Real Rick Ross

This is the book that started it all. Now an international bestseller, this book has revolutionized the way people think of "urban literature." It offers a street-based analysis of social problems, plus practical solutions that anyone can put to use.

CLASS	PAGES	RETAIL	RELEASE
I-1	336	$14.95	Jun. 2008

ISBN: 978-0-9816170-0-8

How to Hustle and Win, Part 2: Rap, Race, and Revolution

By Supreme Understanding
Foreword by Stic.man of Dead Prez

Seen here in its original green cover, the controversial follow-up to *How to Hustle and Win* digs even deeper into the problems we face, and how we can solve them. Part One focused on personal change, and Part Two explores the bigger picture of changing the entire hood.

CLASS	PAGES	RETAIL	RELEASE
I-1	384	$14.95	Apr. 2009

ISBN: 978-0-9816170-9-1

Knowledge of Self: A Collection of Wisdom on the Science of Everything in Life

Edited by Supreme Understanding, C'BS Alife Allah, and Sunez Allah, Foreword by Lord Jamar of Brand Nubian

Who are the Five Percent? Why are they here? In this book, over 50 Five Percenters from around the world speak for themselves, providing a comprehensive introduction to the esoteric teachings of the Nation of Gods and Earths.

CLASS	PAGES	RETAIL	RELEASE
I-2	256	$14.95	Jul. 2009

ISBN: 978-0-9816170-2-2

The Hood Health Handbook, Volume One (Physical Health)

Edited by Supreme Understanding and C'BS Alife Allah, Foreword by Dick Gregory

Want to know why Black and brown people are so sick? This book covers the many "unnatural causes" behind our poor health, and offers hundreds of affordable and easy-to-implement solutions.

CLASS	PAGES	RETAIL	RELEASE
PH-1	480	$19.95	Nov. 2010

ISBN: 978-1-935721-32-1

The Hood Health Handbook, Volume Two (Mental Health)

Edited by Supreme Understanding and C'BS Alife Allah

This volume covers mental health, how to keep a healthy home, raising healthy children, environmental issues, and dozens of other issues, all from the same down-to-earth perspective as Volume One.

CLASS	PAGES	RETAIL	RELEASE
MH-1	480_	$19.95	Nov. 2010

ISBN: 978-1-935721-33-8

A Taste of Life: 1,000 Vegetarian Recipes from Around the World

Edited by Supreme Understanding and Patra Afrika

This cookbook makes it easy to become vegetarian. In addition to over 1,000 recipes from everywhere you can think of, plus over 100 drink and smoothie recipes, this book also teaches how to transition your diet, what to shop for, how to cook, as well as a guide to nutrients and vitamins.

CLASS	PAGES	RETAIL	RELEASE
W-1	400	$19.95	Jun. 2011

ISBN: 978-1-935721-10-9

La Brega: Como Sobrevivir En El Barrio

By Supreme Understanding

Thanks to strong demand coming from Spanish-speaking countries, we translated our groundbreaking How to Hustle and Win into Spanish, and added new content specific to Latin America. Because this book's language is easy to follow, it can also be used to brush up on your Spanish.

CLASS	PAGES	RETAIL	RELEASE
0-1	336	$14.95	Jul. 2009

ISBN: 978-0981617-08-4

Locked Up but Not Locked Down: A Guide to Surviving the American Prison System

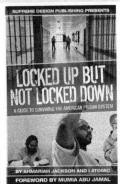

By Ahmariah Jackson and IAtomic Allah
Foreword by Mumia Abu Jamal

This book covers what it's like on the inside, how to make the most of your time, what to do once you're out, and how to stay out. Features contributions from over 50 insiders, covering city jails, state and federal prisons, women's prisons, juvenile detention, and international prisons.

CLASS	PAGES	RETAIL	RELEASE
J-1	288	$14.95	Jul. 2012

ISBN: 978-1935721-00-0

The Science of Self: Man, God, and the Mathematical Language of Nature

By Supreme Understanding and C'BS Alife Allah

How did the universe begin? Is there a pattern to everything that happens? What's the meaning of life? What does science tell us about the depths of our SELF? Who and what is God? This may be one of the deepest books you can read.

CLASS	PAGES	RETAIL	RELEASE
I-4	360	$19.95	Jun. 2012

ISBN: 978-1935721-67-3

The Science of Self: Man, God, and the Mathematical Language of Nature (Hardcover Edition)

By Supreme Understanding

A beautiful hardcover edition of the bestselling work, *The Science of Self*. Under the full-color dust jacket is an embossed clothbound hard cover. Autographed and numbered as part of a special limited edition series, this book also includes the 16 full-color inserts found in the paperback edition.

CLASS	PAGES	RETAIL	RELEASE
I-4	360	$34.95	Jun. 2012

Only available direct from publisher.

365 Days of Real Black History Calendar (2012 Edition)

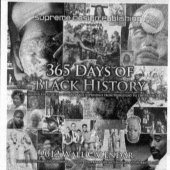

By Supreme Understanding and Robert Bailey

A calendar that'll never be out-dated! Over 365 important facts and quotes covering little-known, but important, moments in Black history. Written in brief chunks and easy language for all audiences.

CLASS	PGS	PRICE	RELEASE
I-2	26	$2.95	2011

Only available direct from publisher.

365 Days of Real Black History Calendar (2013 Edition)

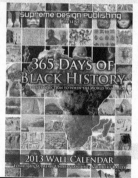

By Supreme Understanding

Our 2013 calendar and planner was also designed to be timeless, as it's a beautifully-designed companion to *When the World was Black*. You'll find dozens of striking full-color images that help tell the stories of global Black history.

CLASS	PAGES	PRICE	RELEASE
I-2	26	$4.95	2012

Only available direct from publisher.

When the World was Black, Part One: Prehistoric Cultures

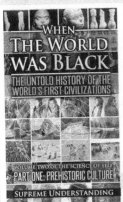

By Supreme Understanding
Foreword by Runoko Rashid

When does Black history begin? Certainly not with slavery. In two volumes, historian Supreme Understanding explores over 200,000 years of Black history from every corner of the globe. Part One covers the first Black communities to settle the world, establishing its first cultures and traditions. Their stories are remarkable.

CLASS	PAGES	RETAIL	RELEASE
I-3	400	$19.95	Feb. 2013

ISBN: 978-1-935721-04-8

When the World Was Black, Part Two: Ancient Civilizations

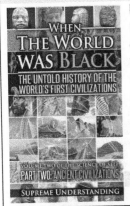

By Supreme Understanding

Part Two covers the ancient Black civilizations that gave birth to the modern world. Black people built the first urban civilizations in Africa, Asia, Europe, and the Americas. And every claim in these books is thoroughly documented with reputable sources. Do you want to know the story of your ancestors? You should. We study the past to see what the future will bring.

CLASS	PAGES	RETAIL	RELEASE
I-3	400	$19.95	Feb. 2013

ISBN: 978-1-935721-05-5

When the World was Black, Parts One and Two (Hardcover)

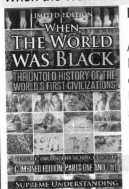

By Supreme Understanding

An incredible limited edition that combines Part One and Part Two into a single book, cased in an embossed clothbound hardcover and dust jacket. Autographed and numbered, this collector's item also includes both sets of full-color inserts.

CLASS	PAGES	RETAIL	RELEASE
I-3	800	$19.95	Dec. 2013

Only available direct from publisher.

Black Rebellion: Eyewitness Accounts of Major Slave Revolts

Edited by Dr. Sujan Dass

Who will tell the stories of those who refused to be slaves? What about those who fought so effectively that they forced their slavers to give up? Black Rebellion is a collection of historical "eyewitness" accounts of dozens of major revolts and uprisings, from the U.S. to the Caribbean, as well as a history of slavery and revolt.

CLASS	PAGES	RETAIL	RELEASE
P-3	272	$14.95	May 2010

ISBN: 978-0-981617-04-6

The Heroic Slave

By Frederick Douglass

Most people don't know that Douglass wrote a novel...or that, in this short novel, he promoted the idea of violent revolt. By this time in his life, the renowned abolitionist was seeing things differently. This important piece of history comes with *David Walker's Appeal*, all in one book.

CLASS	PAGES	RETAIL	RELEASE
P-3	160	$14.95	Apr. 2011

ISBN: 978-1-935721-27-7

David Walker's Appeal

By David Walker

This is one of the most important, and radical, works ever published against slavery. Rather than call for an end by peaceful means, Walker called for outright revolution. His calls may have led to over 100 revolts, including those described in *Black Rebellion*. This important piece of history comes with Douglass' *The Heroic Slave*, which it may have helped inspire.

CLASS	PAGES	RETAIL	RELEASE
P-3	160	$14.95	Apr. 2011

ISBN: 978-1-935721-27-7

Darkwater: Voices from Within the Veil, Annotated Edition

By W.E.B. Du Bois

This book makes Du Bois' previous work, like *Souls of Black Folk*, seem tame by comparison. *Darkwater* is revolutionary, uncompromising, and unconventional in both its content and style, addressing the plight of Black women, the rise of a Black Messiah, a critical analysis of white folks, and the need for outright revolution.

CLASS	PAGES	RETAIL	RELEASE
I-4	240	$14.95	Jun. 2011

ISBN: 978-0-981617-07-7

The African Abroad: The Black Man's Evolution in Western Civilization, Volume One

By William Henry Ferris

Who would think a book written in 1911 could cover so much? Ferris, chairman of the UNIA, speaks up for the Black man's role in Western civilization. He discusses a wealth of history, as well as some revolutionary Black theology, exploring the idea of man as God and God as man.

CLASS	PAGES	RETAIL	RELEASE
I-5	570	$29.95	Oct. 2012

ISBN: 978-1935721-66-6

The African Abroad: Volume Two

By William Henry Ferris

The second volume of Ferris' epic covers important Black biographies of great leaders, ancient and modern. He tells the stories of forty "Black Immortals." He also identifies the African origins of many of the world's civilizations, including ancient Egypt, Akkad, Sumer, India, and Europe.

CLASS	PAGES	RETAIL	RELEASE
I-5	330	$19.95	Oct. 2012

ISBN: 978-1-935721-69-7

From Poverty to Power: The Realization of Prosperity and Peace

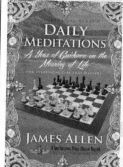

By James Allen

Want to transform your life? James Allen, the author of the classic *As a Man Thinketh,* explores how we can turn struggle and adversity into power and prosperity. This inspirational text teaches readers about their innate strength and the immense power of the conscious mind.

CLASS	PAGES	RETAIL	RELEASE
I-3	144	$14.95	May 2010

ISBN: 978-0-981617-05-3

Daily Meditations: A Year of Guidance on the Meaning of Life

By James Allen

Need a guidebook to a productive and healthy year? This is it. James Allen delivers another great work in this book, this time offering 365 days of inspiration and guidance on life's greatest challenges. This book includes sections for daily notes.

CLASS	PAGES	RETAIL	RELEASE
C-3	208	$14.95	Apr. 2013

ISBN: 978-1-935721-08-6

The Kybalion: The Seven Ancient Egyptian Laws _

By the Three Initiates

Thousands of years ago, the ancients figured out a set of principles that govern the universe. In *The Kybalion,* these laws are explored and explained. This edition includes research into the authorship of the book, and where the laws came from.

CLASS	PAGES	RETAIL	RELEASE
C-4	130	$14.95	Oct. 2012

ISBN: 978-1-935721-25-3

Real Life is No Fairy Tale (w/ Companion CD)

By Sujan Dass and Lord Williams

Looking for a children's book that teaches about struggle? Written for school age children, this full-color hardcover book is composed entirely in rhyme, and the images are as real as they get. Includes a CD with an audio book, animated video, review questions, and printable worksheets and activities.

CLASS	PGS	RETAIL	RELEASE
CD-4	36+	$16.95	Jun. 2010

ISBN: 978-0-9816170-2-2

Aesop's Fables: 101 Classic Tales and Timeless Lessons

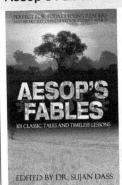

Edited by Dr. Sujan Dass

What's better to teach our children than life lessons? This easy-to-read collection of classic tales told by an African storyteller uses animals to teach valuable moral lessons. This edition includes dozens of black-and-white images to accompany the timeless fables. Color them in!

CLASS	PAGES	RETAIL	RELEASE
CD-3	112	$14.95	Feb. 2013

ISBN: 978-1-935721-07-9

Heritage Playing Cards (w/ Companion Booklet)

Designed by Sujan Dass

No more European royalty! This beautiful deck of playing cards features 54 full-color characters from around the world and a 16-page educational booklet on international card games and the ethnic backgrounds of the people on the cards.

CLASS	PGS	RETAIL	RELEASE
CD-2	16+	$6.95	May 2010

UPC: 05105-38587

Black God: An Introduction to the World's Religions and their Black Gods

By Supreme Understanding

Have you ever heard that Christ was Black? What about the Buddha? They weren't alone. This book explores the many Black gods of the ancient world, from Africa to Europe, Asia, and Australia, all the way to the Americas. Who were they? Why were they worshipped? And what does this mean for us today?

CLASS	PAGES	RETAIL	RELEASE
C-3	200	$19.95	Jan. 2014

ISBN: 978-1-935721-12-3

Black People Invented Everything

By Supreme Understanding

In *The Science of Self* we began exploring the origins of everything that modern civilization depends on today. In this book, we get into specifics, showing how Black people invented everything from agriculture to zoology, with dozens of pictures and references to prove it!

CLASS	PAGES	RETAIL	RELEASE
I-3	180	$14.95	Feb. 2014

NOT YET PUBLISHED

The Yogi Science of Breath: A Complete Manual of the Ancient Philosophy of the East

By Yogi Ramacharaka

A classic text on the science of breathing, one of the most ignored, yet important, aspects of our physical and emotional health. This book has been used by both martial arts experts and legendary jazz musicians. This edition explores the "secret science" of breath, and where its mysterious author learned such teachings.

CLASS	PAGES	RETAIL	RELEASE
PH-4	112	$14.95	Apr. 2012

ISBN: 978-1-935721-34-5

How to Get Our Books

To better serve our readers, we've streamlined the way we handle book orders. Here are some of the ways you can find our books.

In Stores

You can find our books in just about any Black bookstore or independent bookseller. If you don't find our titles on the shelves, just request them by name and publisher. Most bookstores can order our titles directly from us (via our site) or from the distributors listed below. We also provide a listing of retailers who carry our books at www.bestblackbooks.com

Online (Wholesale)

Now, you can visit our sites (like www.supremeunderstanding.com or www.bestblackbooks.com) to order wholesale quantities direct from us, the publisher. From our site, we ship heavily discounted case quantities to distributors, wholesalers, retailers, and local independent resellers (like yourself – just try it!). The discounts are so deep, you can afford to GIVE books away if you're not into making money.

Online (Retail)

If you're interested in single "retail" copies, you can now find them online at Amazon.com, or you can order them via mail order by contacting one of the mail order distributors listed below. You can also find many of our titles as eBooks in the Amazon Kindle, Nook, or Apple iBooks systems. You may also find full-length videobook or audiobook files available, but nothing beats the pass-around potential of a real book!

By Mail Order

Please contact any of the following Black-owned distributors to order our books! For others, visit our site.

Afrikan World Books
2217 Pennsylvania Ave.
Baltimore, MD 21217
(410) 383-2006

Lushena Books
607 Country Club Dr
Bensenville, IL 60106
(800) 785-1545

Special Needs X-Press
3128 Villa Ave
Bronx, NY 10468
(718) 220-3786

About the Publishers

Two Horizons Press is an imprint of Supreme Design, LLC. **Two Horizons Press** is a publisher of educational content that may go back more than 100 years. By republishing classic works that have gone ignored for political reasons, THP brings timeless information back to the public eye.

Supreme Design is the parent company for Supreme Design Publishing, Two Horizons Press, and Proven Publishing. Supreme Design was founded as a media firm in 2006 to improve society and eliminate oppression through transformative content and targeted delivery.

As an independent publisher of cutting-edge educational materials for urban families, **Supreme Design Publishing** engages difficult issues like racial justice and capitalism in the language of modern hiphop culture. Visit www.supremedesignonline.com to learn more!

Proven Publishing, another subsidiary of Supreme Design, offers our low-cost and high-quality publishing services to authors looking for greater control of their content. Proven Publishing provides the "proven" body of best practices that bring books from both Supreme Design Publishing and Two Horizons Press to life.

Visit www.provenpublishing.com to learn more!

These independent, family-run, community-based businesses are built and run according to the principles of honor and ethics of the **#360Movement**. For explanations of this cultural change campaign and its many manifestations, visit www.the360movement.com

NOTES